T0139071

Innovations in Intelligent Internet of Everything (IoE)
Series Editor: Fadi Al-Turjman, Near East University, Nicosia, Cyprus

Computational Intelligence in Healthcare: Applications, Challenges, and Management
Meenu Gupta, Shakeel Ahmed, Rakesh Kumar, and Chadi Altrjman

Advances in SIoT (Social Internet of Things)
Gururaj H L, Pramod H B, and Gowtham M

For more information about this series, please visit: https://www.routledge.com/
Innovations-in-Intelligent-Internet-of-Everything-IoE/book-series/IOE

Advances in SIoT (Social Internet of Things)

Edited by
Gururaj H L
Pramod H B
Gowtham M

CRC Press
Taylor & Francis Group
Boca Raton London New York

CRC Press is an imprint of the
Taylor & Francis Group, an **informa** business

First edition published 2023
by CRC Press
6000 Broken Sound Parkway NW, Suite 300, Boca Raton, FL 33487-2742

and by CRC Press
4 Park Square, Milton Park, Abingdon, Oxon, OX14 4RN

CRC Press is an imprint of Taylor & Francis Group, LLC

ISBN: 978-1-032-25404-3 (hbk)
ISBN: 978-1-032-25405-0 (pbk)
ISBN: 978-1-003-28299-0 (ebk)

DOI: 10.1201/9781003282990

Typeset in Times
by MPS Limited, Dehradun

Contents

Preface

This book is a descriptive summary of challenges and methods using Social IoT with various case studies from diverse authors across the globe. The authors of Chapters 1 and 2 present the game-changer technology and smartphone android application.

In Chapter 3, recent advancements in networking, intelligent network management, battery management, remote sensing, sensors, and other related technologies convinced users and designers to adopt IoT; large-scale applications are explained. Trust management, architecture, and components with emerging domains in SIOT are elaborated on in Chapter 4. The main aim behind SIoT is to allow things to build social relationships on their own that could make network navigation and information and service discovery easier.

Chapters 5 and 6 use the expansion of the Internet of Things (IoT) that meets with person-to-person communication ideas to make informal organizations of interconnected smart objects. In Chapter 7, the next-generation cellular networks need to be designed to explore the benefits of device-to-device (D2D) communications with reference to the social and industrial IoT. As the requirements of high-speed data communications are increasing at a rapid speed, current technologies are focusing on short-range communications for better energy and spectral efficiency.

Chapter 8 delivers a case study. The COVID-19 pandemic is causing a worldwide prosperity crisis, so the hit-affirmation procedure is to wear a facial covering in open regions, as demonstrated through the field wellness endeavor (WHO).

Chapter 9 fine points the smart environment for SIoT security architecture, the framework designed to function easily with a variety of IoT applications, the aids in the separation of security and practical privacy disputes, and talk over how to isolate modules that offer functionality for each layer (for example, internet, interface, and IoT device).

Chapters 10 and 11 deliberate the efficient data transmissions is calculated using signal-to-noise ratio. Furthermore, at the time of data communication, security is provided with the help of an encryption technique. Two important case studies use IoT-enabled smart parking to reduce vehicle flooding, as depicted in Chapter 12. The proposed parking system provides real-time slot information and also helps in booking the slot in advance, thus saving the drivers' time and also helps in decreasing traffic congestion. Another case study IoT device discovery technique based on semantic ontology is exemplified in Chapter 13. In this proposed system, NLP is used to annotate the vendor specification of the devices. The annotated documents serve as the semantically enabled documents and help in the retrieval of the appropriate devices for the user request in identifying the resources of their interest.

In Chapter 14, a proposed work is being carried out to provide technology-based protection for women who will facilitate adult special care. Chapter 15 discusses several algorithms for machine learning that are used for predicting air quality.

In Chapter 16, a model has been proposed to capture the movement of the green-tipped pen as a video using OpenCV, detect it in each frame, track its movement, identify the characters being drawn and display the same as the output on the screen. In Chapter 17, the performance of various machine-learning algorithms and tools, such as decision tree (DT), Naive Bayes (NB), K-Nearest neighbors (KNN), artificial neural network (ANN), etc., in discovering the vulnerabilities and threats in SIoT are discussed here.

Gururaj H L
Pramod H B
Gowtham M

Acknowledgements

We would like to thank all of the contributors to this book and all the people involved in the organization of this book.

Editors

Gururaj H L, PhD, is currently working as Associate Professor, Department of Information Technology, Manipal Institute of Technology, Bengaluru, India. He earned a PhD in computer science and engineering at Visvesvaraya Technological University, Belagavi, India, in 2019. He is a professional member of ACM and working as ACM Distinguish Speaker since 2018. He is the founder of Wireless Internetworking Group (WiNG). He is a senior member of IEEE and lifetime member of ISTE and CSI. Dr. Gururaj received the young scientist award from SERB, DST, and the Government of India in December 2016. He has 9 years of teaching experience at both undergraduate and graduate levels. His research interests include blockchain technology, cybersecurity, wireless sensor networks, ad-hoc networks, IoT, data mining, cloud computing, and machine learning. He is an editorial board member of the International Journal of Blockchains and Cryptocurrencies (Inderscience Publishers) and Special Editor of EAI Publishers. He has published more than 75 research papers, including 2 SCI publications, in various international journals such in IEEE Access, Springer book chapters, WoS, Scopus, and UGC referred journals. He has presented 30 papers at various international conferences. He has authored a book on network simulators. He worked as reviewer for various journals and conferences. He also received best paper awards at various national and international conferences. He was honored as Chief Guest, Resource Person, Session Chair, Keynote Speaker, TPC member, advisory committee member at national and international seminars, workshops and conferences.

Pramod H B, PhD, is currently working as Associate Professor, Department of Computer Science and Engineering, Rajeev Institute of Technology, Hassan, India. He earned a PhD in computer science and engineering at SVU, India. He has 10 years of teaching experience at both the undergraduate and graduate levels. His research interests include machine learning, wireless sensor networks, IoT, and Social IoT. He was published more than 15 research papers, including SCI publications in various international journals, Taylor & Francis and Wiley book chapters, WoS, Scopus, and UGC referred journals. He has published a Government of India patent. He worked as a reviewer for *IEEE Transactions on Network Science and Engineering* and various conferences.

Gowtham M is currently working as Assistant Professor, Department of Computer Science and Engineering, NIE Institute of Technology, Mysuru, India. He is a PhD candidate in computer science and engineering at Visvesvaraya Technological University. He has 6.5 years of teaching experience at both the undergraduate and graduate levels. His research interests include network security, wireless sensor network, ad-hoc networks, IoT and cloud computing. He has published more than 30 research papers, including SCI publications in various international journals, IEEE Transactions, and Springer, Elsevier, Taylor & Francis and Wiley book chapters.

Contributors

T Ananthapadmanabha
Mysuru University School of
  Engineering
Manasagangotri Campus
Mysuru, Karnataka, India

Anija Starry B
Department of Computer Science
Christ University
Bangalore, India

Pramod H B
Department of Computer Science and
  Engineering
Rajeev Institute of Technology
Hassan, Karnataka, India

Vishwas D B
Department of Computer Science and
  Engineering
NIE Institute of Technology
Mysuru, Karnataka, India

Pradip Kumar Barik
Department of Information and
  Communication Technology
Pandit Deendayal Energy
  University
Gandhinagar, Gujarat, India

Sharon Christa
Department of Computer Science and
  Engineering
Graphic Era Deemed to be
  University
Dehradun, India

Rajeshwari D
Department of Information Science and
  Engineering
The National Institute of Engineering
Mysuru, Karnataka, India

Raja Datta
Department of Electronics and Electrical
  Communication Engineering
IIT Kharagpur
West Bengal, India

Putul Gorai
Department of Electronics and
  Communication Engineering
NIT Durgapur
West Bengal, India

Pallavi K J
Department of Computer Science and
  Engineering
RV Institute of Technology and
  Management
Bangalore, India

Prasanna Kumar M J
Department of Computer Science and
  Engineering
BGS Institute of Technology
Adichunchanagiri University
B.G. Nagara, Mandya, India

R Jayavadivel
Department of Computer Science and
  Engineering
School of Engineering
Presidency University
Bangalore, Karnataka, India

Raghavendra K
Department of Computer Science and
    Engineering
The National Institute of Engineering
Mysuru, Karnataka, India

Mohammed Hussam Khatib
Department of Computer Science and
    Engineering
Vidyavardhaka College of Engineering
Mysuru, Karnataka, India

Gururaj H L
Department of Information Technology
Manipal Institute of Technology
Bengaluru, India

Gowtham M
Department of Computer Science and
    Engineering
The National Institute of Engineering
Mysuru, Karnataka, India

Manu Y M
Department of Computer Science and
    Engineering
BGS Institute of Technology
Adichunchanagiri University
B.G. Nagara, Mandya, India

Nayan Kanti Majumdar
Department of Computer Science and
    Engineering
Graphic Era Deemed to be University
Dehradun, India

Asha S Manek
Department of Computer Science and
    Engineering
RV Institute of Technology and
    Management
Bangalore, India

Nimesh Mohanakrishnan
Department of Computer Science and
    Engineering
Vidyavardhaka College of Engineering
Mysuru, Karnataka, India

Arulkumar N
Department of Computer Science
Christ Deemed to be University
Bangalore, India

Nalini N
Department of Computer Science and
    Engineering
Nitte Meenakshi Institute of Technology
Yelahanka, Karnataka, India

Nishkala I N
Department of Computer Science and
    Engineering
Vidyavardhaka College of Engineering
Mysuru, Karnataka, India

Megha Annappa Naik
Department of Computer Science and
    Engineering
Vidyavardhaka College of Engineering
Mysuru, Karnataka, India

Deepak P
Department of Computer Science and
    Engineering
The National Institute of Engineering
Mysuru, Karnataka, India

Puneeth S P
Department of Information Science and
    Engineering
Bapuji Institute of Engineering and
    Technology
Davanagere, Karnataka, India

Andu Pujitha
Department of Computer Science and
    Engineering
Vidyavardhaka College of Engineering
Mysuru, Karnataka, India

Meghana R
Department of Computer Science and
    Engineering
RV Institute of Technology and
    Management
Bangalore, India

Nismon Rio R
Department of Computer Science
Christ University
Bangalore, India

Parivarthana S R
Department of Computer Science and
    Engineering
Vidyavardhaka College of Engineering
Mysuru, Karnataka, India

Raghu Nandan R
Department of Computer Science and
    Engineering
Navkis College of Engineering
Hassan, Karnataka, India

Srinidhi H R
Department of Computer Science and
    Engineering
The National Institute of Engineering
Mysuru, Karnataka, India

Tejaswini P R
Department of Computer Science and
    Engineering
Vidyavardhaka College of Engineering
Mysuru, Karnataka, India

N Rajkumar
Department of Computer Science and
    Engineering
School of Engineering
Presidency University
Bangalore, Karnataka, India

Senthil Ramadoss
Engineering Department
University of Technology and Applied
    Sciences-Shinas
Sultanate of Oman

Venkadeshan Ramalingam
Information Technology Department
University of Technology and Applied
    Sciences-Shinas
Sultanate of Oman

Aditi S
Department of Computer Science and
    Engineering
RV Institute of Technology and
    Management
Bangalore, India

Anusha K S
Department of Computer Science and
    Engineering
Vidyavardhaka College of Engineering
Mysuru, Karnataka, India

Mohan Kumar K S
Department of Electronics and
    Communication Engineering
BGS Institute of Technology
Adichunchanagiri University
B.G. Nagara, Mandya, India

Mohammed Saqlain
Department of Computer Science and
   Engineering
Vidyavardhaka College of Engineering
Mysuru, Karnataka, India

B Prabhu Shankar
Department of Computer Science and
   Engineering
School of Engineering
Presidency University
Bangalore, Karnataka

Venkatesh Shankar
Department of Computer Science
   and Engineering
KLS Vishwanathrao Institute of
   Technology
Haliyak, Karnataka, India

Shrinivas A Sirdeshpande
Department of Computer Science
   and Engineering
KLS Vishwanathrao Institute of
   Technology
Haliyak, Karnataka, India

J Mary Stella
Department of Computer Science
   and Engineering
HKBK College of Engineering
Bangalore, Karnataka, India

Nashra Tanseer
Department of Computer Science
   and Engineering
Vidyavardhaka College
   of Engineering
Mysuru, Karnataka, India

Ajay A V
Visvesvaraya Technological
   University
Department of Computer Science and
   Engineering
Rajeev Institute of Technology
Hassan, Karnataka, India
and
Department of Computer Science and
   Engineering
The National Institute of Engineering
Mysuru, Karnataka, India

E Vetrimani
Department of Computer Science
   and Engineering
School of Engineering
Presidency University
Bangalore, Karnataka, India

C Viji
Department of Computer
   Science and Engineering
HKBK College of
   Engineering
Bangalore, Karnataka, India

Internet of Lights

1

A Way to Energy-Efficient Lighting System

Sharon Christa[1], Asha S Manek[2], and Nayan Kanti Majumdar[1]

[1]*Computer Science and Engineering, Graphic Era Deemed to be University, Dehradun, India*
[2]*Computer Science and Engineering, RV Institute of Technology and Management, Bangalore, India*

Contents

DOI: 10.1201/9781003282990-1

1.1 INTRODUCTION

Inter-connecting physical devices via the internet is the basic definition for the Internet of Things (IoT). The same is enabled by the emergence of cheaper hardware and the ubiquity of wireless networks [1]. These physical objects are integrated with sensors, or software systems that enable data collection and sharing. A basic example is a light bulb embedded with sensors; if its functioning can be controlled by a mobile application, then it is an IoT device [1]. IoT broadens internet protocol (IP) articulation into the physical environment to billions of commodity terminals ('things'), such as programmable lamps and detectors. Things are usually connected using commodity access networks that use minimal, lossless, decreased asymmetrical channels and restricted group articulation primitives [2]. IoT links universally recognizable devices to 'normal' online services and speed connections as a network. Data on the things can be collected and analysed, and their status altered from everywhere, at any time, by anyone. IoT provides full connection, situational solutions, and information sharing across objects. It is causing major shifts in various sectors by drawing together a diverse set of market sectors. The illumination sector is one among them. As simple as it seems, the market size of light manufacturing is $1 billion in 2019 [3]. The lockdown in 2020 and 2021 impacted the sector, but the sector is having steady growth with the integration of solid-state lighting (SSL). The source of illumination in SSL includes light-emitting diodes (LED), organic LED, etc. [4,5]. In 2020, global LED market value hit an all-time high of $6.7 billion. "The same is driven by the adequate power generation and high power consumption rate" [4]. This in turn converts to an increase in the demand for energy-efficient electric products including LED illumination products. LED-based lighting systems can optimise controls (e.g., swapping and dimmer), as well as profit analysis and carbon emissions. IOT in light sources opens up new possibilities and customer value. The IoT is now mature enough that connecting each illumination to the internet is cost-effective [6,7].

As a result, now is a great time to start building the Internet of Lights (IoL), which is a sophisticated light source with IoT at its core. There are several advantages to making the switch to IoT:

- It allows the energy systems to be controlled and powered using the property's data centres rather than a devoted lamp connection.
- Having internet protocol integration to all luminous points offers greater flexibility and interconnectivity with other technologies, such as distributed generation and cloud computing.
- It empowers the transformation from functional home automation to provider smart lighting, allowing for the introduction of a wide range of new service providers, the creation of new eco-systems, the stimulation of investors and inventions, and the usage of global procedure and tool advancements.

Sharing tenancy information collected by light insulation with a building-automation system for air conditioners or the cloud for big data, for example, allows for greater flexibility and help [8]. Overall, it can improve occupant comfort and well-being, which leads to better building utilisation, and it can even aid enable accreditations by increasing the building's energy efficiency [9]. This chapter therefore presents smart and intelligent SSSL systems, implementation details, and architectures and discusses how specialised systems may be designed using these lighting systems. The standards and criteria that can be used as a benchmark to identify the most suitable architecture. Further, the chapter will present the plethora of capabilities of IoL.

1.2 OVERVIEW ON IOT

As presented in the introduction, "Internet of Things (IoT) encapsulates a vision of a world in which objects that have embedded intelligence, communication systems, sensing and actuation capabilities will connect over IP (Internet Protocol) networks" [10]. In the IoT, "I" stands for "internet," which maps to enabling interconnectivity over the internet protocol. "T" stands for "things," and it is nothing but cyber-physical systems, sensors, devices one uses in day-to-day life, like smart watches, communication devices, etc. [10]. These IoT entities, which are connected to the communication network, use protocol stacks suitable for communication [11].

However, new business models are required to encourage the change, and they are frequently difficult to deliver with the current locked and copyrighted roof. That is where the significance of open environments comes into picture. Integrated architecture in the context of the intreoperable platforms with open environments provides more flexibility [11]. Mostafa et al. identified the existing paradigms and pointed out where IoT can grow further; in their words, "power management, trust and privacy, fog computing, and resource management are the leading open issues which need to be focused further" [12]. Efficient power management with environment-sensed lighting is the primary focal point of the "IoT" of Lights [13].

1.3 WHAT IS SMART LIGHTING?

The current lighting system in its primitive form was introduced in the 19th century and is currently undergoing a transition with the introduction of semiconductor-based light sources. Smart lighting focuses on "digital enabled and controlled lighting interfaces and systems, allowing lighting functions to become more dynamic, controllable and interactive, and adaptive depending on external and internal variables, leading to more intelligent lighting solutions" [14]. What are the internal and external variables? They are precise light installations that lead to efficient light coverage, automatic light control with respect to the number of people in a room, controlling the light brightness depending on the physical parameters, achieving maximum energy efficiency and responsible usage. The energy (W) spent in illuminating the interior of a building is equal to:

$$W = P_N * t \ [kWh] \tag{1.1}$$

where P_N is the total installed lightning power measured in kW and t is the total operating time measured in hours. To reduce the energy spent, the focus should be on efficiency that can be achieved by adopting semiconductor-based lighting solutions. The second focus point is effectiveness, which can be achieved if there is a means to control the lighting systems based on the actual use of the building spaces [15]. Smart lighting aims to achieve lighting controls like dimming, daylighting, zoning, etc., with integrated circuits and sensors. The lighting system will work in real time, depending on the presence of activity, energy impact, etc. [15].

Smart refers to autonomous and efficient systems and the existing conventional systems like setting up lamp ON/OFF duration, using advanced lamp technology, etc., can be costly at the implementation level, and also it may not result in the energy consumption as intended [16,17]. Smart lighting systems, on the other hand, integrate sensors like fog sensors, light sensors, motion sensors, etc., along with the lamp units that are controlled via a local and central management system through communication protocols [16]. Figure 1.1 depicts a general smart lighting solution [18].

1.4 THE CONNECTION BETWEEN SMART LIGHTING AND IOT

The smartwatch industry is having rapid growth, currently projected to be 364.1%. It enables one to monitor and measure various physical aspects and activities of the user via different applications and even through text messages. The smart home industry is also seeing similar growth. Gadgets like nest thermostats are integrated with artificial intelligence components that will adjust the room temperature according to the user

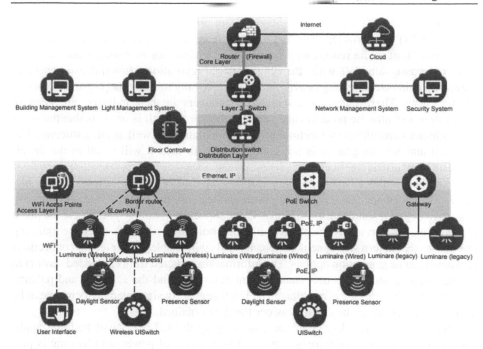

FIGURE 1.1 General smart lighting system.

preference in different rooms at different times per the family's schedule. Further, the same can be controlled remotely. Sensors are the key elements that enable the proper working of the system. Sensors send notification to the devices to perform tasks like abnormal rises in the heartbeat, increases in the room temperature, etc. Even though the use of this equipment is entirely different, a common feature is the way it is interconnected. Both the gadgets have sensors. Both are data driven and respond according to the environment changes. In one way or the other, these gadgets are enhancing the user's quality of life.

Sensors have a wide range of applications. Sensors like passive infrared (PIR) sensors can be used in a larger commercial real estate setup to detect motion. Data provided by the sensor will give details of the used and unused data spaces. This data will enable effective space management. A similar application is its use in lamp management. Sensors like PIR will collect, organize, and transfer data on the present room conditions, like occupancy, to the data-processing system. Based on the data, the software will light up or switch off the smart light network and adjust the brightness. Heating, ventilation, and air conditioning, generally called the HVAC system, can be controlled in a similar way. With the help of internet connectivity and the integration of intelligent software systems, data notifications can be communicated to the HVAC system, thereby controlling it effectively and efficiently. The primary focus of almost all smart building applications is saving energy and associated features. But the IoT is allowing for more benefits. "… the Internet of Things (IoT) is already having a substantial impact on the Commercial Real Estate (CRE) business, enabling companies to move beyond a cost reduction emphasis," according to Deloitte.

The IoT is still in its infancy. Researchers are yet to uncover the potential use cases that IoT can provide. The IoT, in fact, can revolutionize the way things are connected. That is the reason why futurists and visionaries in research and development have associated IoT with "the next industrial revolution." Enterprises in vast and varied domains are investing heavily in the same to stay relevant, hoping to stay ahead of the curve. These enterprises, which are pioneers in their industry, are keen in integrating IoT into the products and services they provide. It is obvious that the same will enhance capabilities and technology implementation, as well as infrastructure. The research and IoT integration is not going to stop; in fact, it will result in the development of futuristic applications.

Another, indirect benefit IoT applications have to offer has various aspects like economic, social societal, etc. IoT applications decrease the power usage and improve the efficiency of resource utilization, etc. These aspects will indirectly increase the profit margins of the service provider. An efficient building will have effective building operations that in turn will benefit the tenants. This will enable greater tenant connections and new income generation options. The information gathered from embedded sensors in 'things' can be utilized to understand tenant behaviour and the schedule and patterns associated with the usage of building. The intelligent software system associated can be used for incorporating the changes as per the data obtained.

Smart lighting is a key component in bringing the IoT and smart building applications to life. Every luminaire is connected to a source of power, and lighting is pervasive throughout all structures. It's the ideal way to get information on what's going on in the building at any given moment. Each light point is a data node on the network thanks to sensors installed in the luminaire.

What motivates people to use intelligent, interconnected lamp technology?

a. *Energy and operational savings:* As per the research presented by IBM, the cost of running a building every day accounts for more than 70% of its overall cost over its lifetime. In commercial buildings, the immediate consequence of IoT is lower operating expenses. Cutting down upto 60% of the energy consumption is one such aspect.

b. *Building Efficiencies:* The insights obtained from the data can provide better insights on the activities that are happening in the building. Building management decisions pertaining to the day-to-day operations of the building like internal and external operations, security, lighting, HVAC, inhabitants activities, etc., can be taken based on the digital version of the building, which is nothing but the collected data. The granularity of data from different sensors inside a lighting system enables the better evaluation of the system, which in turn will provide precise data. The upside of the same is better facility management with improved efficiency.

c. *Occupant Health and Well-Being:* "In recent years, there has been a rising trend toward occupant health and well-being as a driver in commercial buildings," according to Navigant Research. Within this overarching purpose, lighting has been a leader of building technology, providing for enhanced controllability.

1.5 WHY IOL?

1.5.1 Actual Lighting Specification

BACnet, KNX, LonWorks, and DALI are just a few of the lighting and proof-of-concept protocols that have been developed throughout the years. Some are more specialised, such as DALI, which is used to control lights, while others, such as LonWorks, BACnet, and KNX, are more general and may be used to control the entire structure. Such a combination is possible because of servers that convert data interchange, file formats, and semantics. BACnet, KNX, and LonWorks, on the other hand, are difficult to integrate, leading to incompatibility and compatibility issues. The following is a closer look at the most extensively used energy management and smart building standards.

1.5.1.1 Building automation controls network (BACnet)

BACnet is a facility access control standard for industrial control. ARCNET, moment, professional, Ethernet, BACnet/IP, LonTalk, and ZigBee are all data connectivity levels defined by the BACnet protocol. Due to its complexity and high potential per light point, it is commonly utilized by industries that provide environment and temperature-controlling services, but not for lighting controls.

1.5.1.2 KNX

KNX is a more prevalent building services management technology in Europe. The most popular physical messaging service is coaxial cable. Powerline, radio frequency, and the ethernet (also known as KNXnet/IP) are some of the other transmission methods. However, this leaves KNX vulnerable to a number of security issues.

1.5.1.3 The LonTalk data transmission

Through twisted pairs, powerlines, fibre optics, and RF, the LonTalk data transmission is ideal for low-bandwidth process control applications as well as data centres. The information structure and content that has to be delivered is defined by LonWorks. Its marketability was impeded by its exclusivity and lack of adaptability. The move to an open standard may not be enough to compete with other operators at that level.

1.5.1.4 The digital addressable lighting interface (DALI)

The digital addressable lighting interface is a data format and delivery technique for electricity control. A DALI system contains controlling equipment, controllers, and bus power sources. On the other side, DALI has no defined security. Expanding existing lighting rules to include such benefits is a possible option, given the benefits of moving toward IoT. Despite the fact that they are standardised, accreditation is required for the finer points, such as application compatibility. Because of their restricted design, limiting APIs, and lack of an authentication system, the norms are infeasible for IoL. As a result, a new lighting event has been planned to naturally handle limited deviants.

1.5.2 Objective of the Internet of Lights Specification

1.5.2.1 Client

Using a generic technology like IP, a method is feasible. Several distinct types of programmes may share the same connection at the same time. IP allows the use of many sensors. IP's edge module enables basic compatibility, allowing components to function without the need for specification interpretation or data sharing across many systems. A wide range of techniques and hardware, such as inspections and authoring processes, are now available, and the IP system may benefit from worldwide public progress. IP also offers a considerably more effective programme.

1.5.2.2 Open and refillable

Because closed standards would create concerns among prospective owners regarding accessibility, cost, and flexibility of use, having open standards is preferred for getting wider support within the lighting and structure control groups. Inclusiveness fosters capital and third-party innovation, resulting in a thriving ecosystem of integrations and integration suppliers. Furthermore, it is desirable to reuse as many blocks as possible rather than constructing each one from scratch. This will add value to the standardization efforts as well as the time and cost involved.

1.5.2.3 Composable

The standard would be designed to disintegrate and adapt fast in response to new market concerns and advances. It should be possible to switch to or upgrade to the latest cellular networks, add new systems and sensors to an existing structure with ease, fix issues and improve capabilities, and so on.

1.5.2.4 Compatibility

Various systems can communicate with one another through to a compatibility protocol. A collaborative decision, data and report exchange, or the establishment of logical groupings across systems could all be examples. Lighting institutions are projected to connect with other devices, particularly BAS, as a result of the new IoL protocol, and benefit from each other's capabilities.

1.5.2.5 Internal risk

IoL systems could benefit from national IT security methods and improvements. It's an added bonus to be able to improve them with the support of a worldwide community. Authorized dealers' convenience, matter security, and solidity must all be maintained.

1.5.2.6 Performance

Changing from an illumination network to an IT connection with cloud-based IoT connectivity presents a number of challenges. The most difficult problem to overcome is ensuring the dependability and proper operation of specialised lighting systems in a web-based fluorescent-tube environment.

1.5.2.7 Privacy

IoT-enabled data collection and analysis can be beneficial. However, personal customer data like as constitution adoption, mobility traces, and user profiles may raise privacy concerns. The platform must enable security criteria, including privacy protection and the freedom to remove data. While allowing data interchange, security safeguards must be implemented.

1.5.2.8 Energy

Switching to SSL lighting saves a lot of money compared to older neon or halogen lighting. In modern LED lighting, the command logic, electric potential logic, and interaction logic all require more power.

1.6 SMART LIGHTING AND IOT

A smart lamp unit in the smart lighting system will have a weather sensors, communication devices, and highly efficient LED lighting, as well as a local control device, a video camera, and a computing unit for video processing [19]. The communication of individual elements with the central control system and between each other is very important. Figure 1.2 depicts a typical smart street lighting solution with its communication requirements [19]. The system requires long-range and short-range communication depending on the requirements.

This is where IoT-enabled communication protocols come into picture. The basic requirements in choosing and adopting a protocol is its ability to interlink a large number of lighting units, low-cost, data rate, and complexity, and most importantly, support long battery life [16,20]. The protocols can be wired and wireless. The IEEE 802.15.4 based wireless protocols that are adopted by different researchers for smart lighting are depicted in Figure 1.3 [21–23].

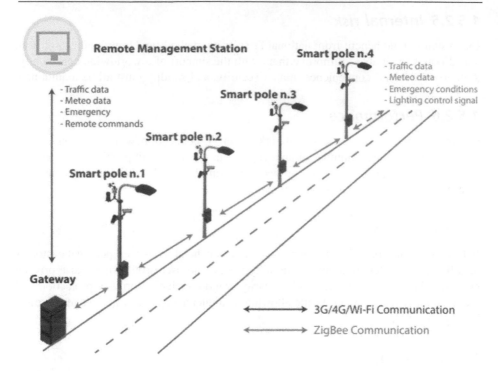

FIGURE 1.2   Smart street lighting concept.

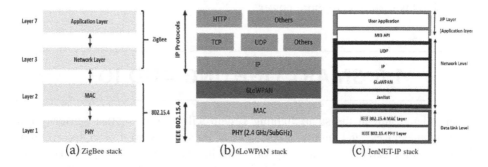

FIGURE 1.3   IEEE 802.15.4-based wireless protocols.

1.7 SCOPE OF IOL

The lighting sector is seeing a plethora of new products. Examples of customised IP-based artificial lighting include Daintree Networks' ZigBee PRO wireless network, Enlighted Inc.'s IEEE 802.15.4 devices, Gooee (a full-stack IoT solution), Zumtobel's

TELECOM light management system, Philips Connected Office Lighting, and others. DALI can be extended wirelessly in some devices. There were also numerous initiatives involving lighting and building automated systems. EnLight was an EU project that used the publish-subscribe design pattern to create an architectural and decentralised lighting control system with scaling and an infrastructure eventing system. Greener Buildings was an EU Seventh Framework Programme (FP7) project that used smart objects and cloud technologies to produce an energy-aware adaptation of public facilities for enhanced sturdiness and failure resistance. Self-organising, cooperative, and robust building automation was a European Union FP7 project that developed a unique systematic engineering methodology using an integrated design toolchain and an online connectivity and control framework to solve the difficulties of the splintered BAS market [24,25].

Researchers have presented the integration of the IoL integration in the context of smart cities [14,16,26]. The International Initiative for a Sustainable Built Environment proposed standards for environmental assessment methods for buildings in which energy management was the issue presented with the highest weightage [27]. The same can be achieved only by adapting smart lighting systems [28]. Various researchers have presented lighting solutions like adaptive street lighting systems, smart home lighting systems, and smart lighting in warehouses [19,29,30]. Along with the technology transition, IoL is aided with price reduction of SSL backed by government policies [31].

1.8 SMART LIGHTING SYSTEM IMPLEMENTATION IN REAL TIME

As per the research presented by Neida and her colleagues [32], smart lighting systems can provide energy saving up to 17% to 60% more than the traditional lighting system. It is no doubt that industrial applications and research in horticulture, architecture, building management, light quality control, and human physiology will benefit from smart lighting systems [33]. But how can it be implemented in real time? The development of lighting solutions can be classified under commercial and energy-saving light control systems. The lighting systems that can be purchased off-the-shelf are the commercial system. As the name says, energy-saving systems have an integrated energy-saving control system. It can include one or more of the following features, occupancy sensing, day-light linked control system, etc.

As mentioned in Section 1.7, interconnection of the various components, its communication is crucial for effective working of the system. The devices connected to the system include light devices as well as controller devices. The same are interconnected via gateway devices and the signals are transmitted via various communication protocols. The data is loaded to data centres, and real-time monitoring is performed by various software systems. According to real-time analytics, lighting decisions are made by the software system and are communicated to the controller system, which will act according to the instruction received. Figure 1.4 depicts the connections and components [33].

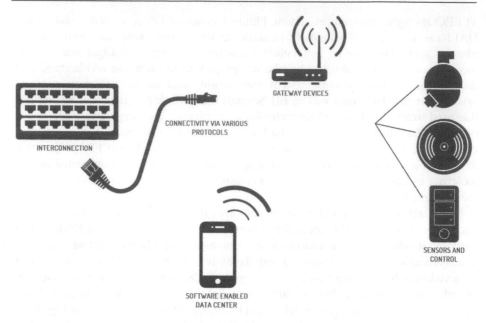

FIGURE 1.4   Real-time smart lighting system implementation.

1.9 IMPLEMENTATION STANDARDS

KNX is an open standard that is derived from the European home systems protocol. The same can be used to automate various functionalities like lighting, security systems, energy management, display systems of commercial and domestic buildings [34]. Architecture of the same is presented in Figure 1.5. Evolving and existing automation protocols have adopted various modes and internetworking concepts from KNX as per their requirements.

Open AIS is a European Union project, and the same is developed specifically for the designing and deployment of IoT-based smart lighting systems. Open AIS standards rely on standardized open APIs, enable interoperability, thereby enabling easy-to-install systems and components from different vendors. The overall impact in turn will be a drastic reduction in the carbon footprint.

Reference architecture of OpenAIS mainly has logical, physical, deployment, networking, and security views where the logical view is segregated into the application layer and infrastructural layer depending on the functionality. Figure 1.6 presents the functional decomposition of Open AIS architecture [8].

The functional decomposition aids in implementing domain-specific functionality of the lamp units, which includes the sensors, control system, light source, etc., which comes under the application layer. The infrastructure layer is software enabled; it supports the security features and handles the communication system.

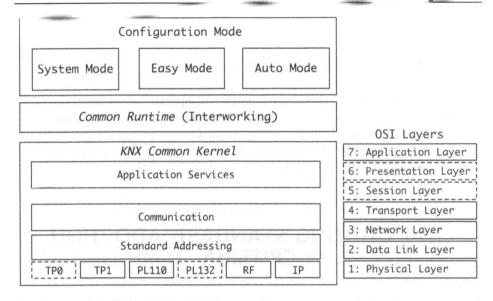

FIGURE 1.5 Open KNX architecture.

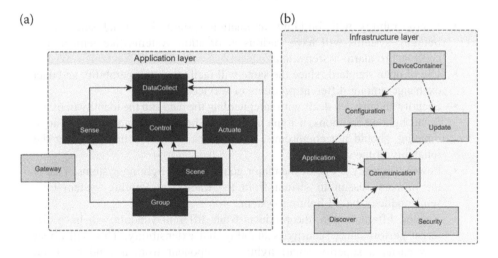

FIGURE 1.6 Functional decomposition of the Open AIS lighting system.

When designing a real-time, smart lighting system based on Open AIS architecture, the life cycle to be followed is depicted in Figure 1.7. The five phases of designing will deal with the interoperability, installations of hardware, customization of hardware and software systems, diagnostics and deployment. Further, it also considers the maintenance aspects like extendibility and security parameters [8].

Other notable open smart lighting implementation standards are BACnet, LonWorks, DALI (digital addressable lighting interface), as explained in Section 1.5.

FIGURE 1.7 Lifecycle of an Open AIS lighting system.

"Daintree Networks based on ZigBee PRO, Enlighted Inc. wireless network based on IEEE 802.15.4, Gooee (a full-stack IoT solution), the LITECOM lighting management system from Zumtobel, Philips Connected Office Lighting, etc., are examples of proprietary IP-based lighting systems and are some of the smart lighting solutions that are available in the market" [8].

1.10 LIGHTING STANDARD ADOPTION CRITERIA

There are various smart lighting standards, and to compare and identify the best-suited standard will require decision-making criteria. The following are some of the decision-making criteria that can be considered in such scenarios.

- Interoperability with building automation systems is crucial since smart building systems will have various automation systems like temperature control, fire alarm systems, etc.
- Use of open standards since the same will facilitate interoperability and data exchange among different products or services.
- Security and privacy deals with safeguarding the data and the identity of users. Smart lighting solutions, if implemented in a home environment or sensitive building, should not compromise the same since it will in turn affect the reliability of the system.
- Power efficiency is one of the major goals of smart lighting systems. That is the primary reason to switch from the traditional lighting system to a semiconductor-based lighting system.
- Vendor differentiation, the products from different vendors will have different performance, security, scalability and extensibility. This will affect how easily a superior smart lighting component from a vendor can be integrated to the already existing lighting system matters.
- Performance sensitive operations like time to light, start-up time, etc., and other time-sensitive operations should meet the deadline. Performance of smart lighting systems measures the same.
- Scalability will measure the working of the system when more and more resources are added to the system, and in this context, the lamp units and sensors.
- Extensibility is nothing but how easily the functionality, network size, and coverage can be extended.

Why these criteria are presented is because each criteria presented here is crucial to the proper working of an interconnected lighting system. The components can be from different vendors, more and more components may be added to the system in future, the smart lighting system may need to interoperate with other components like cctv, temperature control system, etc.

1.11 CAPABILITIES OF SMART LIGHTING SYSTEMS

The smart lighting system enables the user to control one or multiple lamp units at a time. The system can be automated with a timer that will ON/OFF the lighting units automatically. Apart from these basic functionalities, occupancy sensors and motion sensors can be integrated into the lighting system that will work as per the movement. The lighting levels can be changed as per the requirements, which in turn can save energy. These systems can be remotely controlled; to a larger extent, they save electricity. They also offer a plethora of customization features. The system is not confined to smart homes, but the same can be integrated in multiple scenarios like office buildings, street lighting, warehouse lighting, outdoor lighting, etc. User experience can be customised depending on the type of infrastructure, user requirements, etc.

1.12 APPLICATIONS OF IOL

Emerging mobile and sensor network technologies are opening up new ways to improve indoor health and safety while saving energy. The "light bulb" is being used as an opportunistic carrier of new sensors and control in the smart lighting center. We're looking for ways to improve people's and society's quality of life.

- *Monitoring older people's activities at home:* Elderly individuals should be able to live in their own houses without assistance. In-home activities can now be measured using new technology to determine senior well-being and quantify long-term changes that may require intervention. In circumstances of unexpected inaction, a quick response can be offered.
- *Using blue-spectrum light to improve sleep quality:* Human circadian rhythm research suggests that the blue spectrum of visible light is responsible for cortisol/melotonin cycles, which influence sleep. Sleep quality can be affected by increasing or decreasing the presence of this blue spectrum. Blue-filter glasses or LED luminaires can reduce the amount of blue light in the room, increasing sleep quality.
- *Using need-based lighting management in homes and offices to save energy:* We can optimise the required light output for each onsite luminaire both day

and night by collecting and detecting real-time data regarding occupants, incident sunlight, and light-field sensors. The predicted energy savings from maximising light utilisation in the appropriate settings are 40%–70% higher than simply switching to CFL or LED lightbulbs.

- *Computer networking with optical transceivers for localised, high-performance computing:* The high density of existing WiFi connection points in apartment or condo buildings causes interference. The use of light to carry data could free up wireless bandwidth and increase network availability.
- *Indoor navigation:* In high-traffic buildings, indoor navigation can make it easier to find your way around and provide better information. Hospitals, doctors' offices, retail malls, and museums are among the buildings that can benefit from light-sensitive navigation.

Smart lighting technology provides the following features:

- Recognition and analysis of gestures
- Sensing and monitoring of colour intensity
- Smart grid management
- Monitoring and analysing activity
- Controlling the entire spectrum of lighting
- Navigation within (indoor GPS)

1.13 CONCLUSION

The lighting industry itself can reduce the carbon footprint by adopting smart lighting solutions. Smart lighting solutions have various components like sensors, controllers, image-capturing systems along with the semiconductor-based light source. The data centres at remote locations will be equipped with software systems that can perform real-time data analytics based on the data obtained from sensors, controllers, etc., and can control the lighting system accordingly. The IoT enters the picture in the data transmission and communication part. Various communication protocols that are developed for IoT-based systems can be adopted for the design and deployment of the IoL. Implementation standards aid in identifying the strengths, weakness, opportunities, and threats of each that can make or break the lightning system that is under design.

REFERENCES

[1] WebLink "https://www.zdnet.com/article/what-is-the-internet-of-things-everything-you-need-to-know-about-the-iot-right-now/" (accessed on 19 January 2022).

[2] Ahmad, Nulm, and Rashid Mehmood. *"Enterprise systems for networked smart cities."* In Smart Infrastructure and Applications, pp. 1–33. Springer, Cham, 2020.

[3] WebLink "https://www.ibisworld.com/united-states/market-research-reports/lighting-bulb-manufacturing-industry/" (accessed on 19 January 2022).

[4] Zissis, Georges, Paolo Bertoldi, and Tiago Serrenho. *"Update on the Status of LED-Lighting World Market since 2018."* Publications Office of the European Union, Luxembourg, 2021.

[5] Teshome, Bezawit, and Getachew Bekele. *"Energy Conserving Electrical System Design and Performance Analysis for Commercial Buildings in Addis Ababa",* Master of Science in Electrical Engineering Thesis, Addis Ababa University Addis Ababa Institute of Technology, Electrical & Computer Engineering Department, June (2013), Weblink: "http://etd.aau.edu.et/bitstream/handle/123456789/6689/Bezawit %20Teshome.pdf?isAllowed=y&sequence=1" (accessed on 20 February 2022).

[6] Abinaya, B., S. Gurupriya, and M. Pooja. *"Iot based smart and adaptive lighting in street lights."* In 2017 2nd International Conference on Computing and Communications Technologies (ICCCT), pp. 195–198. IEEE, 2017.

[7] Phan, Cao Tho, Duy Duong Pham, Hoang Vu Tran, Trung Viet Tran, and Phat Nguyen Huu. *"Applying the IoT platform and green wave theory to control intelligent traffic lights system for urban areas in Vietnam."* KSII Transactions on Internet and Information Systems (TIIS) 13, no. 1 (2019): 34–52.

[8] Mathews, Emi, Salih Serdar Guclu, Qingzhi Liu, Tanir Ozcelebi, and Johan J. Lukkien. *"The internet of lights: An open reference architecture and implementation for intelligent solid state lighting systems."* Energies 10, no. 8 (2017): 1187.

[9] WebLink https://www.mdpi.com/ (accessed on 19 January 2022).

[10] Cirani, Simone, Gianluigi Ferrari, Marco Picone, and Luca Veltri. *"Internet of Things: Architectures, Protocols and Standards",* John Wiley & Sons, United States, 2018.

[11] Singh, Saurabh, ASM Sanwar Hosen, and Byungun Yoon. *"Blockchain security attacks, challenges, and solutions for the future distributed iot network."* IEEE Access 9 (2021): 13938–13959.

[12] Kashani, Mostafa Haghi, Mona Madanipour, Mohammad Nikravan, Parvaneh Asghari, and Ebrahim Mahdipour. *"A systematic review of IoT in healthcare: Applications, techniques, and trends."* Journal of Network and Computer Applications 192 (2021): 103164.

[13] Minerva, R., A. Biru, and D. Rotondi. *"Towards a Definition of the Internet of Things (IoT)".* IEEE Internet Things 2015. Available online: http://iot.ieee.org/images/files/pdf/IEEE_ IoT_Towards_Definition_Internet_of_Things_Revision1_27MAY15.pdf (accessed on 9 August 2017).

[14] Castro, Miguel, Antonio J. Jara, and Antonio F.G. Skarmeta. *"Smart lighting solutions for smart cities."* In 2013 27th International Conference on Advanced Information Networking and Applications Workshops, pp. 1374–1379. IEEE, 2013.

[15] Martirano, Luigi. *"A smart lighting control to save energy."* In Proceedings of the 6th IEEE International Conference on Intelligent Data Acquisition and Advanced Computing Systems, vol. 1, pp. 132–138. IEEE, 2011.

[16] Sikder, Amit Kumar, Abbas Acar, Hidayet Aksu, A. Selcuk Uluagac, Kemal Akkaya, and Mauro Conti. *"IoT-enabled smart lighting systems for smart cities."* In 2018 IEEE 8th Annual Computing and Communication Workshop and Conference (CCWC), pp. 639–645. IEEE, 2018.

[17] Sevincer, Abdullah, Aashish Bhattarai, Mehmet Bilgi, Murat Yuksel, and Nezih Pala. *"LIGHTNETs: Smart LIGHTing and mobile optical wireless NETworks—A survey."* IEEE Communications Surveys & Tutorials 15, no. 4 (2013): 1620–1641.

[18] Mathews, Emi, and Gerrit Muller. *"Transition from closed system to Internet of Things: A study in standardizing building lighting systems."* In 2016 11th System of Systems Engineering Conference (SoSE), pp. 1–6. IEEE, 2016.

[19] Gagliardi, Gianfranco, Marco Lupia, Gianni Cario, Francesco Tedesco, Francesco Cicchello Gaccio, Fabrizio Lo Scudo, and Alessandro Casavola. *"Advanced adaptive street lighting systems for smart cities."* Smart Cities 3, no. 4 (2020): 1495–1512.

[20] Gowda, V. Dankan, Arudra Annepu, M. Ramesha, K. Prashantha Kumar, and Pallavi Singh. *"IoT enabled smart lighting system for smart cities."* In Journal of Physics: Conference Series 2089, no. 1 (2021): 012037. IOP Publishing.

[21] Leccese, Fabio. *"Remote-control system of high efficiency and intelligent street lighting using a ZigBee network of devices and sensors."* IEEE Transactions on Power Delivery 28, no. 1 (2012): 21–28.

[22] Mulligan, Geoff. *"The 6LoWPAN architecture."* In Proceedings of the 4th Workshop on Embedded Networked Sensors, pp. 78–82. 2007.

[23] Lavric, A., and V. Popa. *"Performance evaluation of large-scale wireless sensor networks communication protocols that can be integrated in a smart city."* International Journal of Advanced Research in Electrical, Electronics and Instrumentation Engineering 4, no. 5 (2015).

[24] BACnet. *"A Data Communication Protocol for Building Automation and Control Networks (ANSI Approved)"*, ASHRAE, New York, 2012.

[25] Newman, M. *"BACnet: The Global Standard for Building Automation and Control Networks"*, Momentum Press, New York, 2013.

[26] De Paz, Juan F., Javier Bajo, Sara Rodríguez, Gabriel Villarrubia, and Juan M. Corchado. *"Intelligent system for lighting control in smart cities."* Information Sciences 372 (2016): 241–255.

[27] Saunders, Thomas. *"A discussion document comparing international environmental assessment methods for buildings."* BRE, March (2008).

[28] International Electrotechnical Commission. *"Digital Addressable Lighting Interface"*, International Electrotechnical Commission, Geneva, Switzerland, 2014.

[29] Tang, Samuel, Vineetha Kalavally, Kok Yew Ng, and Jussi Parkkinen. *"Development of a prototype smart home intelligent lighting control architecture using sensors onboard a mobile computing system."* Energy and Buildings 138 (2017): 368–376.

[30] Füchtenhans, Marc, Eric H. Grosse, and Christoph H. Glock. *"Smart lighting systems: State-of-the-art and potential applications in warehouse order picking."* International Journal of Production Research 59, no. 12 (2021): 3817–3839.

[31] Baumgartner, T., F. Wunderlich, A. Jaunich, T. Sato, G. Bundy, N. Grießmann, and J. Hanebrink. *"Lighting the Way: Perspectives on the Global Lighting Market; Technical Report"*, McKinsey, New York, 2012.

[32] Von Neida, Bill, Dorene Maniccia, and Allan Tweed. *"An analysis of the energy and cost savings potential of occupancy sensors for commercial lighting systems."* Journal of the Illuminating Engineering Society 30, no. 2 (2001): 111–125.

[33] Chew, Ivan, Dilukshan Karunatilaka, Chee Pin Tan, and Vineetha Kalavally. *"Smart lighting: The way forward? Reviewing the past to shape the future."* Energy and Buildings 149 (2017): 180–191.

[34] *KNX System Specification—Architecture.* Available online: www.knx.org (accessed on 30 June 2017).

A Prototype of a Smart Phone-Controlled Lawn Mower Using Android App

2

Rajeshwari D[1] and T Ananthapadmanabha[2]

[1]*Department of Information Science and Engineering, The National Institute of Engineering, Mysuru, Karnataka, India*
[2]*Mysuru University School of Engineering, Manasagangotri Campus, Mysuru, Karnataka, India*

Contents

DOI: 10.1201/9781003282990-2

2.1 INTRODUCTION

Grass grows almost anywhere there is enough room and humidity. Lawnmowers are inconvenient and inaccurate. As a result, we must manage the landscape of grass growth while improving the appearance and beauty of our gardens or yards. Thanks to technological advancements and ingenuity, we can now use remotely operated robots to solve complicated challenges.

The planned system is depicted in Figure 2.1. The objective of this system was to create a lawnmower that a smartphone could operate via Bluetooth [3]. This concept enables us to handle existing issues. It actively displays the capability of wearable technologies like Arduino, IoT [1], and robotics technology in constructing a robust robotic or mobile application-controlled lawnmower. As a result, it is critical to find a solution that automates the process using new technologies such as mobile–controlled lawnmowers to prevent the risk and cost of a manual lawnmower [4]. The Agile software-development process [5] was used to create a prototype that an Android mobile application can control [6]. According to the review, many frameworks use a battery and a solar-powered charger as a power source for the robot's head Electric lawn cutters, like engine-powered grass shapers, are dangerous and unsuitable for everyone. As a result, it is beneficial to use a solar-powered grass shaper that is energy-efficient and consumes less power [7]. The first item will be charged by the sun

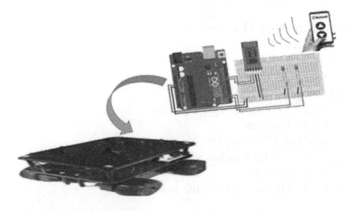

FIGURE 2.1   Lawnmower controlled via a smartphone.

through solar-powered chargers direct current (DC) engine, a battery-powered battery, a sunlight-based charger, a treated steel edge, and a control switch will be included in sun-oriented cool horticulture gear (for example, grass shaper) [8]. The user will manage the grass cutter's pace and direction using the remote [9,10]. Designing and controlling an autonomous vehicle-like robot that can travel in the desired direction and record photographs and videos of the appropriate place is also part of the research. The MIT App Creator was used [2]. This research aims to use an Android phone's Bluetooth device.

The advantages are:

- Cost-effectiveness
- User-friendliness
- High efficiency
- Time saving
- Extreme accuracy

2.2 TOOLS AND TECHNOLOGY OVERVIEW

1. **Eclipse:** Eclipse is primarily written in Java. Based on Java client applications, IDEs and other tools can be created.
2. **Android Studio** is the official IDE of Google. It is constructed on JetBrains' IntelliJ IDEA software for Android programming. In 2020, it is accessible as a free download and a subscription-based service for Windows, MacOS, and Linux.
3. **SQLyog Ultimate** is a sophisticated application that combines a graphic management solution that is quick, simple, and small.
4. **MySQL:** MySQL is a free and open-source relational database management system (RDBMS). It is used to manage user access while creating, modifying, and retrieving relational databases. One or more tables are used to organise data in RDBMS and allowing data to be managed by its data types. MySQL is one such relational database management system works with an operating system, which allows creation of a relational database in a computer's storage system, manages user creation, permits network access, and simplifies database integrity testing and backup generation. Linux, Apache, MySQL, Perl/PHP/Python (LAMP) is an acronym that stands for Linux, Apache, MySQL, Perl/PHP/Python. MySQL is part of the LAMP (and other) web application software stack. MySQL is used by many database-driven internet technologies, including Drupal, Joomla, phpBB, and WordPress. MySQL is used by several popular websites, including Facebook, Flickr, MediaWiki, Twitter, and YouTube.
5. **XML:** XML is extensible language. Simplicity, universality, and cross-platform usability are all critical design goals for XML. It's a Unicode-compatible textual data format for various human languages. Arbitrary data

structures are often encoded using extensible markup language (XML). [10], further it is also used in internet services, despite its design focusing on texts.

6. **Java:** Java is object-oriented language with minimal implementation requirements. Compiling Java programs to byte code is useful in Java virtual machine (JVM) and to run on any platform without being recompiled.

7. **Apache Tomcat:** Tomcat is a cross-platform application that is straightforward to set up if Java is installed. We can utilize the Tomcat web program manager GUI to deploy the program to a running Tomcat server if we want to deploy it on the fly. Go to the official website, download the desired version, and then unpack it on your computer's file system. A startup script can be used to test Tomcat's installation by launching the server from the $CATALINA BASE/bin folder. Open your browser after the server is up and running and navigate to http://localhost:8080 (if the default configuration is used). The application is simple to deploy to the server. Using Tomcat's startup deployment feature, you can copy compressed (.WAR) or uncompressed (exploded web application) files to the correct directory, $CATALINA BASE/web apps/. All of the deployed apps can be managed through Tomcat's Manager App.

2.3 SYSTEM ARCHITECTURE

As shown in Figure 2.2, the system architecture examines a system as a collection of many diverse components and how they interact to generate the intended result.

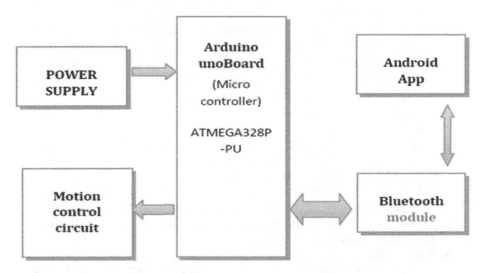

FIGURE 2.2   System architecture.

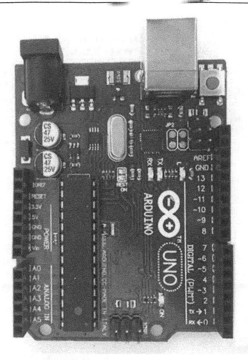

FIGURE 2.3   Uno R3 by Arduino.

An Android smartphone device with the Bluetooth module HC-05 and the ATMEGA328P CPU can control the lawnmower. A microcontroller is used to manage the entire system. The microcontroller is connected to a Bluetooth module and DC motors. The Bluetooth module gathers data from an Android phone and transfers it wirelessly to the controller [11,12]. The controller controls the robot's DC motor. The Android phone allows the robot to move in all four directions [13,14]. The detailed figures are shown in Figure 2.3 to Figure 2.7.

2.3.1 Arduino Uno Board

The Arduino Uno is an open-source microcontroller board. Other circuits and shields are connected to it using digital and analog input/output (I/O) pins. The board can be programmed using Arduino IDE, which has 14 digital I/O pins (six of them utilized for output) and 6 analog I/O pins (integrated development environment) [15].

The pinMode(), digitalRead(), and digitalWrite() routines can be used to utilise the 14 digital input/output pins as input or output pins in Arduino programming. Each pin may deliver or receive up to 40 milliamperes and has a 5-volt operational voltage with 20–50 kOhm resistors, as depicted in Table 2.1.

With 10 bits and 1024 possible values, there are 6 analog input pins and 14 digital input pins. They measure from 0 to 5V, though the analog Reference () function on the

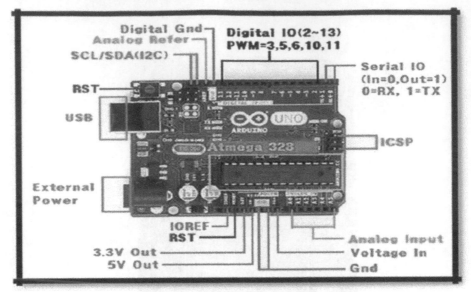

FIGURE 2.4   Uno R3 by Arduino pinout.

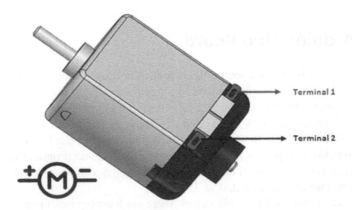

FIGURE 2.5   Direct current motor.

FIGURE 2.6   Direct current motor pinout.

FIGURE 2.7 L293D IC for motor drivers.

TABLE 2.1 Parameters

CATEGORY OF PINS	NAME ON A PIN	DESCRIPTION
Electricity	V_{input}, 3.3V, 5V, Ground	V_{input} acts as an external power source. For CPU and other components 5V supply is used. Voltage generated is 3.3V. and current is 50 mA.
RESET	RESET	The microcontroller is turned off and on again.
Analog Pins	A0–A5	It will produce analog input of 5V.
IO Pins	Digital Pins D0–D13	Input or output pins
TTL Serial Pins	(Rx)0, (Tx)1	This device receives and sends data.
Exterior Interrupts	2, 3	Make a disturbance
PWM	3, 5, 6, 9, 11	8-bit output option
SPI	(SS)10, (MOSI)11, (MISO)12 and 13 (SCK)	This gadget is capable of SPI communication.
Built-in LED	13	To activate the built-in LED
Two-Wire Interface	(SDA)A4, (SCA)A5	It's for communicating with TWI.
AREF	AREF	A reference voltage is used to provide input voltage.

AREF pin can increase this limit. The library, which uses analog pins 4 (SDA) and 5 (SCL), also supports TWI communication (SCA). The extra pins are

- **AREF:** When used with analog Reference() providing a reference voltage for analog inputs.
- **RESET Pin:** used to reset microcontroller.

Multiple devices, such as a microcontroller, computer, or another Arduino board, can all be connected to Arduino. ATmega328P microcontroller supports UART TTL (5V) serial communication, accessed via digital pins 0 (Rx) and 1 (Tx) (Tx). On the digital pins of the Uno, t Serial library will communicate serially. The serial connection is channeled over USB, with an ATmega16U2 on the board. The ATmega16U2 firmware uses regular USB COM drivers. The ATmega328P supports I2C (TWI) and SPI communication. The Wire library is included in the Arduino software.

2.3.1.1 Arduino programming

An Arduino Uno uses the Arduino programming language in Wiring. The board is connected using a USB link. Choose appropriate board and port from Tools menu. And from the File menu load the model code. Model code is loaded from Files>Examples>Basics>Blink to start the Arduino Uno board and see underlying Drove. Go to the top bar and click the 'transfer' button once you've stacked the model code into your IDE.

2.3.2 DC (Direct Current) Motor

Electromagnetism governs the operation of an electric motor. A motor changes electrical energy into mechanical energy. An electric motor that runs on a direct current is known as a direct current motor (DC motor) [16]. When a current-carrying conductor is put in an external magnetic field, it is exposed to a force proportional to the conductor's current and the external magnetic field's intensity. Field windings supply magnetic flux in a functional DC motor, while the armature serves as the conductor, as shown in Table 2.2.

2.3.2.1 Motors' specifications

- The motor is a conventional DC motor of the 130 type.
- No-load current: 70 mA
- Normal voltage: 4.5V to 9V
- Rated voltage: 6V (max)
- No-load speed: 9000 rpm
- Loaded current: 250 mA
- Rated load: 10 g*cm (estimated)

The L293D IC is an extensively used motor driver IC allowing a DC motor to rotate in any direction. This IC contains 16 pins that can control 2 DC motors in any direction at any time. It indicates that an L293D IC can operate two DC motors; see Figure 2.8.

This IC can also drive small and silent huge motors. The H-bridge principle is used in this L293D IC, allowing electricity to flow either way. As we already know, the voltage must be altered for the DC motor to revolve in both directions. As a result,

TABLE 2.2 Terminal details

SL. NO.	TERMINAL NAME	DETAILS
1	T1 & T2	There are only two connections on a conventional DC motor. A coil connects them, and hence, no polarity. On reversal of the connection, the motor reverses direction.

FIGURE 2.8 L293D IC for motor drivers pinout.

a motor can be controlled using an H-bridge circuit based on L293D ICs. The H-bridge principle is used in this L293D IC [17,12], allowing electricity to flow either way. As we already know, the voltage must be altered for the DC motor to revolve in both directions. As a result, a motor can be controlled using an H-bridge circuit based on L293D ICs, as shown in Table 2.3.

TABLE 2.3 Pin details

PIN NO.	NAME ON A PIN	DETAILS
1	EN 1,2	Input pins 1 and 2 are enabled via this pin (7).
2	In 1	Control of the Output 1 pin. The power is in the hands of digital circuitry.
3	Out 1	One of Motor 1's ends is connected to this wire.
4	Gnd	The circuit is connected to ground.
5	Gnd	The circuit is connected to ground.
6	Out 2	The opposite end of Motor 1 is attached to this.
7	In 2	Control of the Output 2 pin. The power is in the hands of digital circuitry.
8	Vs2	Motor 2 has one end connected to it.
9	EN 3,4	Enabling input pins.
10	In 3	The power of digital circuitry will control output 3 pin.
11	Out 3	Connected to one end of Motor 2.
12	Gnd	The circuit is connected to ground.
13	Gnd	The circuit is connected to ground.
14	Out 4	Other end of the motor Is connected by motor 2.
15	In 5	Control of the output 4 pin. The power is in the hands of digital circuitry.
16	Vss2	To make I.C. operation possible with +5V.

2.3.2.2 Features

- Possible to run two DC motors on the same IC
- The vehicle's speed and direction can be controlled
- The motor voltage Vs2 is 4.5V–36V
- Maximum peak motor current is 1.2 A
- Maximum continuous motor current is 600 mA
- 4.5V–7V Vcc1 supply voltage (VSS)
- Time between transitions: 300 ms (at 5V and 24V)
- A programmed thermal stoppage choice is available

The H bridge is a system and drives motors both clockwise and anticlockwise. As previously indicated, this IC can simultaneously run two motors in any direction; the circuit to do so is shown in Figure 2.9.

The Vcc1 power pin must receive +5V. The other power pin for this I.C. is Vcc1, which gives the voltage required for the IC to work. The other pin, Vcc2, supplies voltage to the motors. According to the motor's specifications, this pin can be linked to any voltage between 4.5 and 36V; however, it is attached to +12V in this case.

Input pins 1 and 2 control motor 1, while input pins 3 and 4 control motor 2. The motor's speed and direction are maintained through a micro controller [16,11]. Toggle input pins follow the order described below to start the motor; see Table 2.4.

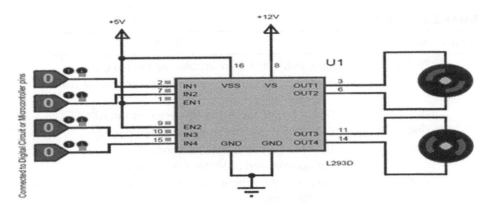

FIGURE 2.9 Working of L293D motor driver.

TABLE 2.4 Toggle input pins

In1=5V	OUT1=5V	MOTOR 1 remained
In2=5V	OUT2=5V	
In3=5V	OUT1=0V	MOTOR 1 doesn't move
In4=5V	OUT2=5V	

2.3.3 Module of Bluetooth HC-05

The HC-05 module [18] is a simple SPP (serial port protocol) module to create a secure wireless serial connection and may be used in both master and slave mode as shown in Figure 2.10 & 2.11. The key details as shown in Table 2.5.

2.3.3.1 HC-05's technical specifications

Serial Bluetooth modules can be used with Arduino and other microcontrollers. Operating voltage and current is of 4 to 6V and 30 mA, respectively. Its length is about 100 m and is compatible to TTL and supports serial connection (USART). The protocol followed is IEEE 802.15.1 and uses FHSS. It can also be used as a master/slave and can be connected to any devices through Bluetooth; it also supports baud rates of different range.

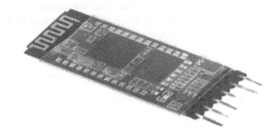

FIGURE 2.10 Module of bluetooth HC-05.

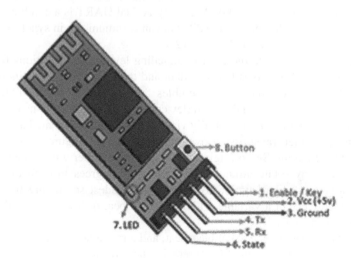

FIGURE 2.11 HC-05 module pinout.

TABLE 2.5 Key details

NUMBER	NAME	EXPLANATION
1	Enable/Key	This is used to switch between Data and Voice mode (set low).
2	Vcc	Connect to a +5V power supply.
3	Gnd	Connect the pin to the system ground.
4	TX	Serial data is sent by this device. This pin will output any serial data received via Bluetooth.
5	RX	The data is received in serial format. This pin will use Bluetooth to transmit all serial data it receives.
6	Status	The onboard LED is connected to the status pin, which can be used as feedback to confirm that Bluetooth is working properly.
7	LED	Indicates the module's current state. To signal that the module has entered, blink once every 2 seconds. Commanding mode Repeated blinking indicates that you are in Data mode and are awaiting a connection. Blink twice in one second: The connection was successful in Data mode.
8	Button	Toggle between Data and Command mode by controlling the Key/Enable pin.

2.3.3.2 UART

A universal asynchronous receiver/transmitter (UART) is a single integrated circuit that allows a computer to communicate serially with a peripheral device. The term "universal" refers to altering the data format and transfer speeds. UARTs are frequently used in microcontrollers [19,20,21,22]. A dual UART is a combination of two UARTs. Many modern ICs have a UART that can communicate in synchronous mode; these are UARTs, as shown in Figure 2.12.

A driver circuit controls the electric signaling levels and operations (differential signaling). The UART receives bytes of data and then distributes the bits in order. A second UART at the destination reassembles the bits into complete bytes. A shift register is the most basic serial-to-parallel conversion mechanism in every UART. Digital data (bits) are transmitted serially via a single wire or other media, which is less expensive than parallel transmission over several lines; see Figure 2.13.

The SG90 Miniature Servo Engine is a small, light server with a powerful output [23]. The servo may rotate around 180 degrees (90 degrees in each direction) and works similarly to standard types; however, more modest servos are limited by the control line's delivery of a variable-width electrical beat or heartbeat width balancing (PWM), as shown in Table 2.6.

A basal heartbeat, an excessive heartbeat, and a redundancy rate are all present. A servo engine may normally spin 90 degrees in one direction or the other, resulting in 180 degrees of development [23].

FIGURE 2.12   Servo motor SG-90.

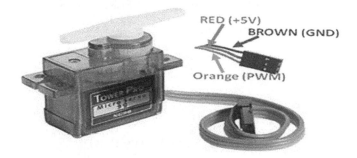

FIGURE 2.13   Servo Motor SG-90 pinout.

TABLE 2.6   Wire colors

WR. NO.	COLOR	DETAILS
1	Red	Powers the engine repeatedly with +5V utilized
2	Orange	This wire receives a PWM signal used to run the engine
3	Brown	Ground wire related with the ground of framework

2.3.3.3 Highlights from the SG-90

- Working voltage: Normally, +5V
- Force: 2.5 kg/cm
- Working rate: 0.1 s/60°

- Gear type: Plastic
- Revolution: 0°–180°
- Engine weight: 9 g

2.4 IMPLEMENTATION OF THE SYSTEM

The system was put in place by categorizing the operations into different categories, such as main activity, login, and home activities. The following sections go over the code snippets and graphic representations.

2.4.1 Lawn_Main_Activity

The Lawn_Main_Activity option is used to save state information of a created instance. It is also possible to set a content view by changing its layout and add animation effects for the main_activity; see Figure 2.14.

```
userId= sharedPreferences.getString(Constants.PREFERENCE_KEY_USER_ID,"");
new Handler().postDelayed(new Runnable() {
@Override
public void run() {
 Intent intent = null;
 if(userId.equals("")) {
 intent = new Intent(MainActivity.this, LoginActivity.class);
 }
 else{
 intent = new Intent(MainActivity.this, HomeActivity.class);
 }
 startActivity(intent);
 finish();
 }
 },SPLASH_SCREEN);
 }
```

Lawnmower
Controller via Bluetooth

FIGURE 2.14   Main activity.

2.4.2 Login Activity

The user can connect to the mobile app[2] and lawnmower using the login activity system. It uses the user's email address as the username and password, as seen in Figure 2.15.

A type field can be specified in a JSON object script key definition, indicating that the field is a secret key. The value presented in the user interface should be darkened for security reasons. A content key needs to be provided as a secret phrase to ensure that the incentive for that field is buried in the user interface when defining script keys in JSON data [24,25]. The content key can be defined to include a type field with a secret word value to indicate that this field should be protected in this scenario.

2.4.3 Home Activity

Figure 2.16 shows the options available to the lawnmower operator, which include the ability to move the machine arm in the left, right, forward, and backward directions [26]. Furthermore, the operator can send a cut signal to trim the grass to the desired height [27].

2.4.4 Microcontroller Program Snippet

Programming Arduino Uno is done using wiring-based Arduino programming. Connect board via USB once the Arduino IDE has been installed on the computer [28,29]. Select the appropriate board in the Arduino IDE by going to Tools>Boards>Arduino/Genuino Uno, then Tools>Port in the Tools menu. Open Files>Examples>Basics> and load the basic code sample.

```
#include <Servo.h>
#define mot A0
#define mott A1
```

FIGURE 2.15   Login screen.

```
#define mottt A2
#define motttt A3
Servo lawnmotor:String dta;
void setup( {
Serial.begin(1 15200);
lawnmotor attach(9);
pmode(mot. out);
pmode(mott, out);
pmode(mottt, out);
pmode(motortttt, out);
lawnmotor.write(15);
dwrite(mot, L);
dwrite(mott, L);
```

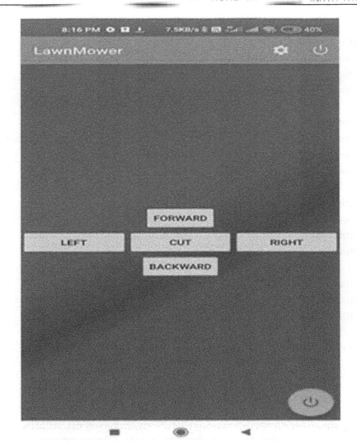

FIGURE 2.16 Home activity screen.

```
dwrite(mottt, L);
dwrite(motttt, L);
void loop(){
while (Serial. Avail() {
dta = Serial readString Until("\n");
Serial.println(dta);
if (dta == "f" | dta == "F") {
d_write(motor 1 a L):
d_write(motor1b, H);
d_write(motor2a L):
d_write(motor2b, H);
if(dta=="6" || dta == "B") {
d_write(motorla, H);
d_write(motor1b, L);
d_write(motor2a, H);
d_write(motor2b, L);
```

```
if (dta= "1" || dta== "R") {
d_write(motor1a, H):
d_write(motor1b, L);
d_write(motor2a, L);
d_write(motor2b, H);
if (dta== "1" dta== "L") {
d_write(motor1a L);
d_write(motor1b, H):
d_write(motor2a, H):
d_write(motor2b, L):
if(dta== "0" || dta== "0") {
d_write(motor1a, L);
d_write(motor1b, L);
d_write(motor2a, L);
d_write(motor2b, L);
if(dta= "s" || dta == "S") {
d_write(motor1a, L);
d_write(motor1b, L);
d_write(motor2a, L);
d_write(motor2b, L);
for (inti = 0;i<= 180;i++) { delay(20);
for (inti = 180: i>= 0; i--) { lawnmotor.write(i);
delay(20):
}
```

2.5 CONCLUSION

Designing and constructing a workable model, partially controlled lawnmower, via Bluetooth communication, are among the framework's primary aims. Several Android-powered smartphones and tablets were used to test a Bluetooth network successfully. This paradigm was examined in contrast to the examination goals and test information collected through interviews. The majority of the population liked the model, and it performed well in terms of precision, security, adaptability, and efficacy. It showed consistency in terms of movement and similarity 1–2,3,7–23,30.

REFERENCES

[1] Al-Fuqaha, A., Guizani, M., Mohammadi, M., Aledhari, M., & Ayyash, M. (2015). Internet of Things: A Survey on Enabling Technologies, Protocols, and Applications. *IEEE Communications Surveys & Tutorials*, 17(4), 2347–2376.

[2] Evan. W Patton, Michael Tissenbaum & Farzeen Harunani (May 3rd 2019). MIT App Inventor: Objectives, Design, and Development Computational Thinking Education, 2019.

[3] Bodke, D., Gosavi, V., Choudhari, R., & Nivedita, P. (October 2018). Smart Home Automation System Using Mobile Application. *International Research Journal of Engineering and Technology (IRJET)*, 5(10), 1093–1098.

[4] Hicks, R.W. & Hall, E.L. (11th October,2000). A Survey of Robot Lawn Mowers. *Proceedings of the SPIE 4197, Intelligent Robots and Computer Vision XIX: Algorithms, Techniques, and Active Vision.*

[5] Flora, H.K. & Chande, S.V.A. (January 2014). Systematic Study on Agile Software Development Methodologies and Practices. *International Journal of Computer Science and Information Technologies*, 5(3), 3626–3637.

[6] Priyanka, L., Nagaraju, J., & Reddy, V.K. (July 2015). Fabrication of Solar powered Grass Cutting Machine. *International Journal & Magazine of Engineering, Technology, Management, and Research*, 2(7), 1–5.

[7] Pandey, S., Munj, T., Panchal, K., Paralkar, R., & Kumar. (April 2018). Fabrication of Automatic Solar Lawn Mower. *International Journal of Innovative Research in Science, Engineering, and Technology*, 7(4), 3729–3736.

[8] Ramos, D. & Lucero, J. (2009). *Solar Powered Automatic Lawn Mower.* San Jose State University, California, USA. 1–22.

[9] Patil, P., Bhosale, A., & Jagtap, S. (May 2017). Fully Automated Solar Grass Cutter. *International Journal of Science Technology and Engineering*, 3(9), 104–106.

[10] Jain, S., Khalore, A., & Patil, S. (December 2015). Self-Efficient and Sustainable Solar Powered Robotic Lawn Mower. 2, 3729–3756.

[11] Olawale O.E., Ajibola and Sunkanmi , Olajide Member, IAENG, October 20-22, 2021, Hong Kong ,Design and Implementation of Autonomous Lawn Mower. *Proceedings of the International MultiConference of Engineers and Computer Scientists 2021*, 1–6.

[12] Mulla, A.I., Sushanth, K., Mranila, P., Mohammed, H.S., Mohammed, S., Mohammed, A., & Mohammed, Y.U. (2016). Dual Mode Lawn Mower Using Sensors and GSM. *International Journal of Advanced Research in Computer and Communication Engineering*, 5(5), 556–559.

[13] Franzius, M. et al. (2017). Embedded Robust Visual Obstacle Detection on Autonomous Lawn Mowers, *Proceedings of the IEEE Conference on Computer Vision and Pattern Recognition (CVPR) Workshops*, 2017, 44–52.

[14] Rambabu, V., Rao, K.S., Rao, P.K., & Rao, D.V. (2014). Mobile Operated Lawn Mower. *International Journal of Mechanical Engineering and Robotics Research*, 3(4).

[15] Hertzog, P.E. & Swart, A.J. (March 2016). "Arduino — Enabling engineering students to obtain academic success in a design-based module." *2016 IEEE Global Engineering Education Conference (EDUCON) (2016)*: 66–73.

[16] Hariya, A., Kadachha, A., Dethaliya, D., & Tita, Y.D. (2017),Fully Automated Solar Grass Cutter. *International Journal of Science Technology & Engineering*, 3(9), 104–106.

[17] Yusof, N.B.R. & Bin, M.K.A. (2013). *Integrated Design – Grass Cutter and Collector Machine.* Mohd Khairrul Amry Bin Romli Universiti Teknikal Malaysia Melaka.

[18] Kumar, R., Ushapreethi, P., Kubade, P.R., & Kulkarni, H.B. (April 2016). Android Phone Controlled Bluetooth Robot. *International Research Journal of Engineering and Technology (IRJET)*, 3(4), 104–114.

[19] Bulski, P., Yu, S., & ED, D. (2008). Investigation of Sound Induced by Grass Cutting Blades. *Journal of Engineering and Applied Science.*

[20] Manheche, F. (2011). *Automated Lawn Mower.* University of East London, London, UK.

[21] Ghahrai, A. (4th August 2019). Difference between Iterative and Incremental Development in Agile, https://devqa.io/iterative-incremental-development-agile.

[22] Gibson, D.J. (2009). *Grasses and Grassland Ecology*. Oxford University Press, New York.

[23] Secchi, Cristian, Levratti, Alessio, & Fantuzzi, Cesare. (2013). A Low Cost Localization Algorithm For An Autonomous Lawn Mower. *IEEE International Workshop on Robot Motion and Control, 9th Annual Conference Poland.*

[24] Aponte-Roa, Collazo, X., Goenaga, M., Espinoza, A.A., & Vazquez, K.,7th to 9th Jan, (2019). Development and Evaluation of a Remote Controlled Electric Lawn Mover. 2019-IEEE 9 th Annual Comuting and Communication Workshop and Conference, (CCWC), pp: 1–5.

[25] Baloch, Taj Mohammad & Kae, Timothy Thien Ching. (2008). Design and Modelling a Prototype of a Robotic Lawn Mower. *2008 International Symposium on Information Technology*, 1–5.

[26] Dipin, A. & TK, C. (April - June2014). Solar Powered Vision Based Robotic Lawn Mower. *International Journal of Engineering and Reviews*, 2(2), 53–56.

[27] Sujendran, S. & Vanitha, P. (2014). Smart Lawn Mower for Grass Trimming. *International Journal of Science and Research (IJSR)*, 3(3), 299–303.

[28] Lin, Hsiung-Cheng, Huang, Uo-Shing, Lin, Keng-Chih, & Kao, Shih-Hung. (2010). Intelligent Auto saving energy Robotics Lawn Mower. 2010 IEEE International Conference on Systems, Man and Cybernetics (2010), pp: 4130-4136.

[29] Wasif, Muhammad.. (2011). "Design and implementation of autonomous Lawn-Mower Robot controller." 2011 . 7th International Conference on Emerging Technologies (2011), pp: 1-5.

[30] Wu, Xinyu, Guo, Huiwen, Sun, Jianquan, Wei Feng, Yongsheng Ouand, & Nicole, B.R. (2017). Robust Grass Boundary Detection For Lawn Mower with Novel Design of Detection Device. *2017 IEEE International Conference on Real-time Computing and Robotics (RCAR)*, 218–222.

Intelligent Optimized Delay Algorithm for Improved Quality of Service in Healthcare Social Internet of Things

3

Anija Starry B and Nismon Rio R

*Department of Computer Science, Christ University,
Bangalore, India*

Contents

DOI: 10.1201/9781003282990-3

3.1 INTRODUCTION

Internet of Things (IoT) interconnects billions of devices by establishing a network. The devices that are connected communicate with each other by sharing data regulated by the application and accomplishing the task based on the application. The social or human-like behavior is adapted in the IoT environment, forming the Social Internet of Things (SIoT). The advancement in IoT has created an effect on machine-human relations [1–10]. The large-scale applications adapt IoT due to advancements in networking, Intelligent network management, battery management, remote sensing, sensors, and other technologies. The data involved through IoT devices are enormous. IoT network merges physical and virtual things [11].

Figure 3.1 describes the applications that benefit the usage of IoT for their computation. IoT has taken a leap in usage of technology and has set up a trend in many applications like medical, industries, agriculture, traffic signal management, etc.

3.1.1 IoT in Medical Application

People today have become health conscious, especially the elderly and injured sick people who need continuous health monitoring. Medical applications adapt to IoT

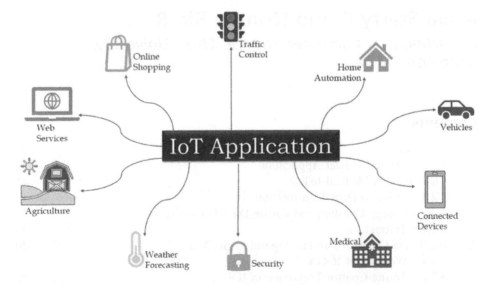

FIGURE 3.1   IoT devices and application.

usage due to the advancement in technology. Continuous monitoring of one's health, updating the medical details to the connected medical station, and sending an alert message in case of emergency should be taken care by IoT-connected devices and their application [12–19]. The medical IoT also focuses on the patient's health, patients' waiting time, improved services by eliminating redundant manual processes, and providing another automated services. The real-time healthcare monitoring wearables make a strong case for implementing SIoT in medical applications. The network should provide a better quality of service (QoS) to have efficient data transfer within the IoT devices connected with the medical application. Achieving higher QoS is necessary for healthcare services, especially during medical emergencies and in the intensive care unit (ICU). The critical data from the sensor devices sent over the network are lost or delayed at the transmission path due to various environmental conditions and abnormal functionality of Edge or Gateway devices. The medical application cannot afford errors and delays in data transfer. The sending and receiving of accurate data with reduced delay and improved latency must be top priority.

In healthcare, one of the most fundamental aspects of medical IoT applications is the IoT that incorporates cloud recourses and IoT functionalities. The cloud provides a standard protocol to support the connection between the medical equipment and the transmission resources like sensors and computation devices [20]. But this traditional method faces a few challenges in delay, security, data loss. Intelligent network management has become unavoidable in the above-stated health and medical services to achieve a higher degree of QoS system, which indirectly improves the critical data transfer time.

The challenges in medical IoT to transfer the data are as follows:

- Low usage of bandwidth
- Delay during the data transmission
- Data loss due to device or link failure
- Resource limitations such as battery consumption memory
- Security
- Heterogeneity network

This chapter is divided into three sections. Section 3.2 discusses the challenges in medical IoT applications researchers proposed previously. Section 3.3, introduces the proposed intelligent optimized delay algorithm (IODA). 3.4, conclusion, discusses the future work of the proposed algorithm.

3.2 CHALLENGES IN MEDICAL IOT

In the current world scenario of medical application, monitoring and managing people's health continuously with all facilities has become a trend and practice. Since there is an increase in requirements for medical services, providing a good QoS has become uncompromised. In many cases, QoS and medical service have become stringent in delivering the services to the users.

With the medical IoT application perspective, the network operator faces the major challenge of providing QoS in network functionalities and end-user requirement computations. Allocation of bandwidth, network resources, delay in data transmission, energy consumption in deviceshave become the primary concern.

3.2.1 Delay in Data Transmission

SIoT has a complicated network where various equipment is connected and deployed as the user devices that communicate to exchange information complexly. The generation of a massive amount of data from various devices like sensors, medical equipment, etc., results in delays during data transmission. The data transmitted over the network must be reliable, and thus, QoS must be enhanced to achieve better real-time service in medical IoT.

1. Proposed SWARM-based data delivery in SIoT. The fault-tolerance routing algorithm is developed to achieve multiple objective optimization problems (MOP) to establish connectivity with the disjoint path, even after the failure of the path. The algorithm operates based on the set of constraints given. This model is deployed in heterogeneous wireless sensor networks (WSN). The nodes with higher battery capacity are set as the super node, and the nodes with the lower battery capacity become the sub-nodes.

The network topology with k-disjoint multiple-path routing increases the number of alternative paths. The objective function of the multiple paths is evaluated by the parameters and derived to solve functions such as delay, energy consumption, and throughput. The optimal hop number defines the delay. A multipath is established when there is a more significant number of nodes, and simultaneously, the packets can be routed to the destination with the reduction of delay. The delay can be minimized by optimizing the hops and the successful transmission of packets to the destination. One hop for the nearest node is generated for each node between the source node, destination node, and the intermediated nodes—the lesser the number of hops, the lesser the delay. Queuing, transmission, retransmission, propagation, idle time, and processing of data can increase the delay.

2. Defined a framework for minimizing delay based on WSN for IoT applications. A protocol is proposed to maximize the spectrum allocation effectively and minimize the delay. A genetic algorithm based on delay reduction is proposed to enhance the QoS of the routing algorithms. The optimum path is generated by utilizing the ideal spectrum in the sensor networks, and then the data are transmitted through the optimum path.

The genetic algorithm calculates the initial population of the network nodes, and an alternative solution is defined using the routing table.

  i. The fitness function is calculated for the set of chromosomes, and three
     operators are calculated for reproduction selection, crossover, and path
     mutation.
 ii. The selection reproduction process compares the chromosomes with the
     fitness value of the entire population.
iii. The process uses certain limitations to overcome the network interference
     and produce the optimal path. When the value of conflict vectors are dif-
     ferent in parent chromosomes, "NO" conflict vector value is taken by the
     child chromosome from the value of the parent. If the "YES" conflict vector
     is chosen, there is a chance of having the same nodes for different routing.
     So "NO" conflict vector is preferred for allocating the route for data
     transmission.
 iv. The mutation process randomly alters the genes for the selection process.
     According to the ratio generated by the algorithm, the process will shift the
     values. The crossover process doesn't work along with selection and muta-
     tion processes.

The transmission rate depends on the node distribution and node degree; thus, the delay
is reduced to 3%. When additional nodes have been added, the algorithm's efficiency and
routing should be enhanced.

3. Determined the sensor-initiated healthcare packet priority in congested IoT
   networks. At the router, the healthcare packet header is at the sensor level to
   prioritize the healthcare data routing, and the QoS of the software is modified at the network level. The proposed method reduces the cost and risk of
   human life. The system works based on the embedded sensors and sends the
   data IoTcloud network. The packet data contain the header and the information following IEEE 802-15.4 standards. The bits are reserved for storing
   specific information. The identifier in the application is used to set to
   information related to healthcare data, so when the data arrive, the system
   checks for the data. If the dataare from the healthcare, the data packet is set
   to the priority and then transmitted. The software QoS is modified using the
   proposed system model. The other processing in the network system stops
   for the time being to transmit the high-priority healthcare data.

Various delays are discussed, in which queuing delay, transmission delay, hop delay,
and route discovery latency were analyzed, and a solution for queuing delay was
proposed. By prioritizing the healthcare data in the queuing table, the delay is minimized by setting a low waiting time in the queue. The test was conducted by setting the
transmission range, nodes, channels, packets, frequency, packet size, and time
parameters. The system identifies the medical data with the standard data, and the end-
to-end delay of the data packet is calculated. The proposed system model works better
when compared with the traditional system model. Overall implementation of this
project may cost a lot and become expensive in both hardware and software implementation. Figure 3.2 showcases the comparison of the techniques applied to reduce
delay during data transmission. The data are compared among the research papers that

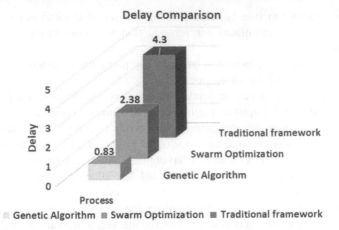

FIGURE 3.2   Comparison of methods to reduce delay.

used swarm optimization technique in multi-path routing, genetic algorithm to transmit the data, and framework that uses the traditional algorithm.

The network that used the genetic algorithm for data transmission to select the optimal path has reduced delay compared with swarm optimization technique and traditional framework. After analyzing the results, the network embedded with intelligence outperforms the traditional method and is reliable for critical data transmission for healthcare applications.

3.2.2 Energy Consumption during Data Transmission

4. Proposed a secure and energy-efficient framework using the Internet of Medical Things (IoMT) for e-healthcare. Insufficient or unbalanced energy consumption of biosensors nodes placed on the patient's body fails to send the patient's report to the nearest medical center, which creates a negative impact on the medical system. To overcome these issues, secure and energy-efficient framework using IoMT was developed. The framework has two working algorithms in which the first algorithm forms a graph between the edge and nodes. Queue delay, distance, link node information, hop count, and energy consumption are calculated. Using Kruskal's algorithm, a sub-graph is constructed. It optimizes the neighbor node list, which has the healthcare information that is sent to the sink node, and the sink node sends the information to the healthcare center. The optimal cost learning is done based on the intelligence in the algorithm.

The biosensors connected with the network use the residual energy, hop count, distance, and queue delay. The computation is done to calculate the cost function. When the data transfer becomes overloaded, the hop count changes, and there is a change in the routing table. By calculating the ratio of the energy consumption for the particular interval of time, the transmission of every consumption of the nodes connected with the network is calculated. The sensor nodes are re-constructed by eliminating certain routes and balanced by obtaining the shortest, consistent and secured routes. The energy consumption of sensor nodes is calculated and results are saved for further analysis. The mobility-based medical sensor does not support SEF-IoMT framework and needs to improve the energy consumption level.

5. A joint deep learning and IoMT-driven framework for elderly patients. An enhanced approach is developed, a self-adaptive power control-based algorithm that improves the battery life, reduces energy consumption, and is reliable. A deep-learning algorithm examines the data correlation in IoMT.

The data flow pattern is identified and learned by the algorithm. The system adapts the transmission mechanism according to the number of packets, buffer size, and the acknowledgment received through the packets. The battery model is developed to manage battery consumption in the sensor nodes. The battery's rated capacity and the battery's recovery effect are calculated to improve the battery charge and the power discharge of the devices connected to the IoT. The algorithm considers the acknowledgment from the receiver node and adapts its transmitter power levels. The routes are established based on the power levels in the IoT devices. The algorithm considers the lowest and the latest biosensor nodes due to the dynamic wireless channel and the adaptive allocation in the power. By implementing the algorithm, the reduction of energy consumption is achieved. The project is applied for the biosensor nodes attached with the patient, the sensor transfers the data that are being sensed, and the battery level is optimized for these restricted functions. But when more features are added, energy consumption will become challenging.

6. Discussed the energy-efficient edge-based real-time healthcare support system. The computing of data is done in the cloud, which results in the usage of more energy. During an emergency of the patient, sufficient resources may not be available due to energy constraints. The deep-learning technique unleashes the computation of the cloud at the edge level, which increases the battery life, and thus, the energy is used efficiently. Energy-efficient smart edge-based healthcare support system (EESE-HSS) monitors the patient's health and provides instantaneous response to critical events. The algorithm sends the critical data to the cloud to further diagnose the disease, and the sensed data are sent immediately to the concerned user. The deep-learning algorithm and the intelligence edge work on a three-tier architecture.
   i.   WPAN is a wearable device consisting of IoT sensors.
   ii. The edge device is incorporated with intelligence and has deep-learning technology embedded in it. The local decisions are handled at the edge, and immediate reaction action is done in an emergency.
   iii. The cloud does the complex computation and stores the medical record for future diagnosis and analysis of the patients' health data. The global hypothesis is built to identify the disease in the future, and the deep-learning technology embedded in the cloud improvise disease detection concerning the sensed data collected from the sensors.

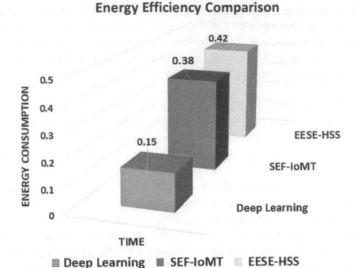

FIGURE 3.3 Energy efficiency comparison chart.

The computation is done at the edge level, so the energy constraint of the device connected is overcome by using this technique EESE–HSS.

Figure 3.3 describes the comparison of the algorithms developed to improve the energy efficiency of the network and the connected devices in the IoT. Energy is a critical resource essential for the healthcare application where critical data transmission is done.

Among the three algorithms compared, the algorithm which implements the deep-learning technique outperforms the other two algorithms. The deep-learning algorithm optimizes the system to learn through the input received via the IoT-connected devices. Even though it initially shows high energy consumption, as the application works, the system learns, adapts, and utilizes energy efficiently.

3.2.3 Throughput

At the time of critical data transmission, it is necessary to understand the rate of data delivery over a period. The applications that work with real-time measurement of data should understand the actual traffic of the data in the network.

7. Determined artificial intelligence (AI). Powered decentralized framework for IoT in healthcare. AI framework is developed to access the data in the nodes at the real time. The framework works on four different layers under the control of r rule-based AI system, hospital, clinics, and remote patients' layers.
    i. Rule-based AI systems integrate smart contract between the blockchain network and the remote sensors nodes. Smart decisions, detection of failure nodes, and malicious nodes are identified at this layer.

    ii. Remote sensor nodes sense the BP/BT level of the patient on routine and transfer the data through IoT network.

    iii. Clinic layer acts as an additional layer between the hospital and the remote sensors, such as the remote patients. The layer gets activated at the time of critical call and updates the medical data over the network to the hospital.

    iv. Hospital layer stores the patient information with unique identification. Emergency data will be handled at the clinic; extra information or the previous records are accessed by the clinic with the hospital. The hospital layer is synchronized with the clinic layer.

The time consumption of the data transfer between the clinic and hospital layer is calculated at four levels. The computation power manipulates the time consumption based on the data registered with the network and the data requests sent between the layers. Throughput transaction is calculating dividing the number of seconds by the total number of successful transactions. The framework can be enhanced in reliability, energy efficiency, and time.

    8. Determined a perception mechanism based on throughput rate constraint in intelligence IoT. The mechanism claims to achieve efficient data perception to eliminate instability and uncertainty and ensure transmission efficiency of the network; the accuracy of the data transmission is obtained. The data pattern is observed through the data shared over the network for the particular unit of time. The load of the network is evaluated through the analysis of the computing system's robustness. The capability of each node's communication is limited considering the characteristics of the scale-free network will make some nodes encounter network congestion, delaying the communication process. The performance of the throughput data is calculated to verify the throughput rate constraint. As the communication process occurs, the data are transferred through the network where the nodes are connected. The throughput rate gradually increases when the communication load is decreased. The framework that is being developed for optimization works well with an improved throughput rate, even when the communication traffic is high.

    9. Proposed a QoS provisioning framework for service oriented IoT. At the application user end, it is necessary to deliver reliable service at the acceptable cost at the computational time. QoS provisioning (QOSP) framework is developed to improve the service quality in the application layer. Optimization algorithm is developed along with QOSP framework to evaluate the performance of throughput, jitter, and delay time. The QOSP framework has three phase llayers:

    i. The preparation phase collects and stores the sensed data, and the data collector accepts the service requests and holds them in the queue. The received request of service is sent to the next phase for further analysis and processing.

ii. The computation phase handles multiple services for the requested service sent from the preparation phase. Computation phases the studies and differentiates between their service states. The IoT composite services are rescheduled based on the priority and decision type.

iii. The validation phase is based on application type and the service priority. Service quality is measured in the step using QOPF. QoS is estimated based on two categories; the first is task-based, which includes a response time metric, and the second is evaluation based, which provides for the performance.

The QOPF framework developed breakdown the complexity of the calculation. Service reliability and the cost are balanced by maximizing the composite service quality in the IoT application layer. The framework should improve its effectiveness at the real-time service concerning power consumption.

Figure 3.4 compares the mechanism that enhances the throughput rate in IoT in medical devices, which improves the QoS for the application users.

The chart compares the mechanism based on time and throughput rate. The throughput rate is calculated at 60 seconds, and the performance of each mechanism is estimated. QOSP framework has a higher throughput rate when compared with the AI-decentralized network and intelligence IoT.

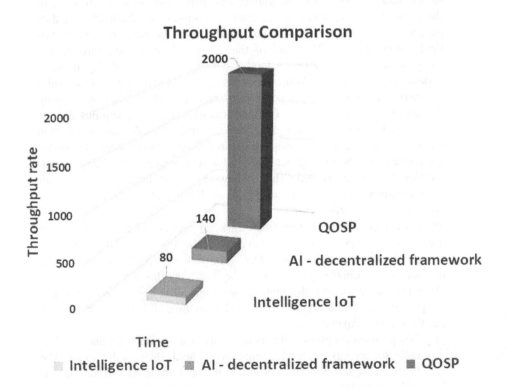

FIGURE 3.4 Throughput rate comparison.

3.3 INTELLIGENT OPTIMIZED DELAY ALGORITHM (IODA)

Most of the healthcare application deals with the real-time data needed to provide good QoS at the user end application. End-to-end delay is more important, and discrete QoS is necessary for each traffic category in IoT. The critical data at time of emergency cannot afford delay and data loss; it needs a guaranteed delivery. The network framework should be designed to intelligently select the shortest path that reduces delay during data transmission [21–31]. Delay can occur due to traffic load, link failure, network congestion, node failure, queue, and buffer. The node failure may result from low power in the connected devices, malicious attacks in the node, and physical damage in the nodes. Intelligence algorithm must be developed to identify the failure or the distraction if it from the node or the link.

The proposed IODA uses the swarm-optimization technique to identify the shortest path to route the data with reduced delay and data loss. The intelligence technique must be applied at the router to do the path selection efficiently considering the factors that will affect the data transmission delay. The framework learns as the transmission that takes place over time; later, the framework itself will route the optimized path without link failure and achieve less end-to-end delay during data transmission.

Figure 3.5 describes the framework of the IODA algorithm in which the user application is connected with the router, and the sensed data are transferred to the router via IoT network.

3.3.1 Working of IODA

The IODA algorithm programs the router to select the optimum path and automatically chooses the optimum route at the time of node failure during live data transmission. IODA algorithm implemented in the router assigns the path to transfer the data. The swarm-optimization algorithm selects the path in the network for quick transfer of data. The path must be automated so that the data should flow along with the lowest delay route.

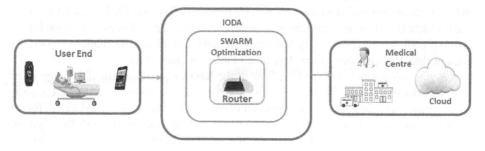

FIGURE 3.5 Framework of IODA algorithm.

Consider an analogy: Wood is resistant to electricity, but when electricity is passed to the wood, the current passes through the low resistant area and burns that particular area. The pattern formed will not be defined. Instead, it varies each time. It automatically chooses the low resistant area in wood and burns it forming a different pattern. Similarly, the framework is designed so that the data will automatically select the available node with the shortest route to reach the destination.

The IODA algorithm works based on an optimization technique incorporated with intelligence. Particle swarm-optimization (PSO) technique is embedded within the IODA algorithm since the algorithm deals with enormous data. PSO works well where the population is high, and that population tends to achieve the common goal. Based on the application used, the population is considered to be the data d that needs to be transferred. The nodes in the network are calculated as N. Power p, Bandwidth b, Latency l, and Throughput t are the parameters that influence the data transmission. IoT uses various topologies; based on the topology, the optimization technique is implemented, and data transmission occurs. The IODA algorithm and the optimization technique choose the optimum path for reducing transmission delay during data transmission. During data transmission, the IODA algorithm parallelly checks for the critical parameters in the network p and b and the link failure to prevent the data loss; this feature enables the data to transmit without transmission delay. The value of l and t are calculated and stored in a database on which analysis is performed; the outcome of the analysis will be used as feedback to improvise the algorithm to fine-tune the optimization.

3.3.2 Traffic Control Technique in IODA

The IODA algorithm will alert the arrival of the critical data cd during an emergency by analysing the incoming data with the threshold value and pausing other data transfers until the critical data are transferred. Critical data cd is defined based on the source where the data are received. For example, the data from an ambulance, ICU, and alert notification from the medical device are critical data. Thus, the alert notification is given to the nearest medical centre at the time of emergency. The records of the patients are stored in the cloud for future reference and further diagnosis of the patient's health. Figure 3.6 Flowchart of IODA the proposed Traffic Control Technique (TCT), used in IODA, alerts the system in case of critical data cd arrival. When multiple critical data arrives, the TCT assigns flags $f1, f2, f3, \ldots, fn$ for each critical data based on the application's priority. The flagged cd does not check for the optimal path; instead, it directly transmits the data toward the destination. During the critical data transmission, other data transmission is paused for a while.

Figure 3.6 explains the working flow of the IODA algorithm. The IODA algorithm was initialized at first. When the data d arrives at the source point, TCT checks whether the incoming data are a critical cd or not. If the data are checked "Yes" for cd, then the other data transmission is paused for a while, transmitting cd directly, surpassing the optimal path check. In case of the arrival of multiple cd, then a priority flag is given to each cd based on the application it is using. TCT checks "No" Power p, and bandwidth b is estimated to calculate the optimal path. This feature enables the data to

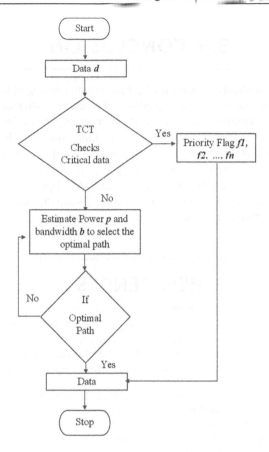

FIGURE 3.6 Flowchart of IODA.

transmit without delay in transmission. Latency l and throughput t values are calculated and stored for further algorithm optimization.

3.4 RESULTS

The proposed IODA algorithm is embedded with intelligence and an optimized technique, which enhances the QoS of the application. The unique TCT technique implemented in IODA makes the algorithm work efficiently for the data transmission of critical data. The power of the nodes, bandwidth, latency, and throughput are considered the parameters for efficient data transmission by reducing the delay. TCT technique efficiently transmits the data by reducing the delay. The algorithm needs to be further developed mathematically and implemented under various scenarios.

3.5 CONCLUSION

SIoT has leaped the medical application where remote monitoring of the patients is done. The challenges in SIoT are discussed based on delay, energy efficiency, and throughput parameters. The comparative study of the intelligence algorithm based on the above-mentioned parameters is done and the outperformed intelligence technique is estimated. The framework of the IODA algorithm is proposed in this paper. IODA algorithm will provide QoS to the application users by reducing the end-to-end delay of the data transmission. In the future, the intelligence-embedded IODA algorithm should be developed mathematically. Simulation and testing should be done to implement the framework in the real-time scenario.

REFERENCES

[1] Hasan Mohammed Zaki, & Fadi Al-Turjman. SWARM-based data delivery in Social Internet of Things. *Future Generation Computer Systems*. 2017:92:821–836.
[2] Sankayya Muthuramalingam, Sakthivel Rakesh Kumar, Gayatri N, Fadi Al-Turjman, Wireless sensor network- based delay minimization framework for IOT applications. *Springer* 2021: 1-9.
[3] Besher Kedir Mamo, Baitedspacher Sara, Nieto-Hipolito Juan Ivan, Ali Mohammed Zamshed Sensor initiated healthcare packet priority in congested IoT network. *IEEE xplore*. 2020:21:10:11704–11711.
[4] Saba T, Haseeb K, Ahmed I, et al. Secure and energy-efficient frameworks using Internet of Medical Things for e_ healthcare. 2020.
[5] Zhang Tianle, Sodhro Ali Hassan, Luo Zongwei, Zahid Noman, Pirbhulal Sandeep, Nawaz Muhammad Wasim, Aoint deep learning and Internet of Medical Things driven framework for elderly patients. *IEEE Access*. 2020:8:75822–75832.
[6] S Abirami, P Chitra, Energy Efficient edge based real-time healthcare support system. *Advances in Computer*. 2020:117:1:339–368.
[7] Puri Vikram, & Kataria Aman Sharma Vishal. Artificial Intelligence-powered decentralized framework for Internet of Things in Healthcare 4.0. 2021:1-18.
[8] Fei Jiang, & Ma, Xiaoping. Fog computing perception mechanism based on throughput rate constraint in intelligent Internet of Thing. *Springer Nature*: 2019:23:563-571.
[9] Badawy Mahmoud M, Zainab H. Ali Ali Hesham A, QoS provisioning framework for services-oriented internet of things (IoT), *Springer Link*, 2020:23:575-591.
[10] Kamel H Rahouma, Aly Rahad Hamed, Hamed Hesham F, Challenges and solutions of using the Social Internet of Things in healthcare and medical solutions–A survey. *Toward social internet of things (SIoT): enabling tecnologies, architectures and applications*: Springer Link 2020:846:13-30.
[11] Miori Vittorio, & Russo Dario. Improving life quality for the elderly through the Social Internet of Things (SIOT). 2017:1-6.
[12] Ruggeri G, & Briante O., A framework for IoT and E-health systems integration based on the Social Internet of Things paradigm. *IEEE xplore*. 2017:426–431.
[13] Kumaran P, & Sridhan R. Social Internet of Things (SIOT): Techniques, applications and challenges, 2020:445-450.

[14] Baburao D, Pavankumar T, & C S R Prabhu. Load balancing in the fog nodes using particle Swarm optimization-based enhanced dynamic resource or location method, *Springer*: 2021.

[15] Adhikari Mainak, Srirama Satish Narayana ,Multi objective accelerated particle Swarm optimization with a contained-based scheduling for Internet of things in cloud environment, *Science Direct*: 2019:137:35-61.

[16] Farrokhi Alireza, Farahbakhash Reza, Rezazadeh Javad, Minerva Roberto, Application of Internet of Things and artificial Intelligence for smart fitness: A survey. *Science Direct*: 2021:189:107859.

[17] Guo Z, Li Y, Srivastavan G, K. Yu, Lin. J C W Deep learning embedded Social Internet of Things for ambiguity-aware social recommendation, *IEEE Transactions on Network Science and Engineering*: 9:3:2021:1067–1081.

[18] Nandan Aridaman Singh, Singh Samayveer, & Awasthi Lalit K, An efficient cluster head election based on optimized genetic algorithm for movable sinks in IoT enabled HWSNs, *Science Direct*: 2021:107:107318.

[19] Kashyapa Neeti, Kumari A Charan, & Cnhikara Rita. Service composition in IoT using genetic algorithm and particle Swarm optimization. 2020:10:1:56-64.

[20] Pradhan Bikash Bhattacharyya Saugat, Pal Kunal, IOT-based applications in healthcare devices. *Hindawi Journal of Healthcare Engineering*. 2021; 2021:1–18.

[21] Bakshi Mohana, Chowdhury Chandreyee, & Maulik Ujjwal. Energy-efficient cluster head selection algorithm for IoT using modified glow-worm optimization. 2021:77:6457-6475.

[22] Lakshamaprabu SK, K S, Khanna DAB, et al. Effective features to classify it big data using Social Internet of Thing. *IEEE Access*. 2018;8:1–9.

[23] Xu Q, Su Z, Zhang K, et al. Fast containment of infectious diseases with E-healthcare mobile Social Internet of Things. *IEEE Internet of Things Journal*. 2015;8:16473–16485.

[24] Ghorpade S N, Zennaro M Saeed R A, Chaudhuri BS, Abdel Khalek S, Alhumyani H, Enhanced differential crossover and quantum particle Swarm optimization for IoT application. *IEEE Access*. 2021:9:93831–93846.

[25] Hussain Azham, Manikanthon SV, Padmapriya T, Nagalingam Mahendran Genetic algorithm based adaptive offloading for improving IoT device communication efficiency. 2020:26:2329-2338.

[26] Jyotsna, & Nand Parma. Fog computing and edge computing: an edge over cloud computing, *Turkish Journal of Computer and Mathematics Education*,2020:12:11:4887:4894.

[27] Pervaiz Sobia, Ul-Qayyum Zia, Bangyal Waqas Haider, Gao Liang A systematic literature review on particle swarm optimization techniques for medical diseases detection, *Hindawi*, 2021:5:1-10.

[28] Sefati S, &, Navimipour. A QoS-aware service composition mechanism in the Internet of Things using a hidden-Markov-model-based optimization algorithm. *IEEE Internet of Things Journal*, 2021:8:20:15620-15627.

[29] Sun Weifeng, Wang Zun, & Zhang Guanghao. A qos-guaranteed intelligent routing mechanism in software-defined network, *Science Direct, Computer Network*, 2021: 185:107709.

[30] Chai Zheng-Yi Du Meng-Meng, Song Guo-Zhi. A fast energy-centered and QoS-aware service composition approach for Internet of Things. *Science Direct, Applied Soft Computing*, 2021:100:106914.

[31] Kil Hyunyoung, & Nam Wonhong. Efficient anytime algorithm for large-scale qos-aware web service composition, *International Journal of Web and Grid Services, ACM Digital Library*, 2013:9:1:82-106.

Trust Management

4

Architecture, Components with Emerging Domains in SIoT

Deepak P[1], Ajay A V[1], Raghavendra K[1], and Puneeth S P[2]

[1]Department of Computer Science and Engineering, The National Institute of Engineering, Mysuru, Karnataka, India
[2]Department of Information Science and Engineering, Bapuji Institute of Engineering and Technology, Davanagere, Karnataka, India

Contents

4.1 INTRODUCTION

Electrical and electronic devices have become smart and intelligent in recent years. Sensors, actuators, and RFIDs are all getting ingrained in our fabric. Not only has greater pervasiveness resulted in human-to-device communication, but it has also resulted in device-to-device communication. In recent years, a new paradigm combining IoT with Social Networks termed the Social Internet of Things (SIoT) has evolved, in which objects are not only intelligent but socially conscious. The social network of intelligent devices is akin to the Social Internet of Things (Abdelghani et al., 2016).

In the SIoT, trust plays a critical aspect for devices to establish a dependable self-contained communication. Trust between objects is calculated using Direct Observations, Indirect Recommendations, Centrality, Energy, and the object's Score. In order to tackle the key issues such as Data discovery and composition, Network navigability, Trust management, and so on, SIoT facilitates device-to-device interaction and provide a platform for items to autonomously associate with devices in networks.

4.1.1 Trust Management System (TMS)

Indeed, in the IoT, the trust management system (TMS) has been regarded as an effective solution for security as shown in Figure 4.1. As a result, many research studies were conducted in order to present prediction and trust evaluation approaches. In a standard TMS, previous behavior of device data is used to anticipate the network entity's trust value, but the network entity's context is rarely considered. Three characteristics of the approach's originality might be summarized:

i. Highly scalable trust model should be designed properly.
ii. The system's ability to deliver the most reliable service provider while taking into consideration the dynamic aspects of the internet of things such as context, Object capacity, and object social relationship.
iii. The use of a decision tree to examine the relationship between the many components of a network and object behavior, as well as to improve decision-making.

When creating these inter-object social interactions, trust is crucial, and it is also necessary to assess an object's trustworthiness before relying on device information offered by them. For SIoT, a number of trust evaluation model has been created but due to a lack of adequate datasets, most of these approaches struggle to validate and verify their models. To solve the problem, we propose the Scalable and Robust Trust Platform for SIoT (SCART- SIoT), a scalable trust platform with plug-and-play that would provide a dataset for researchers to test and compare alternative trust models (Sagar, Subhash, Adnan Mahmood, Quan Z. Sheng, and Sarah Ali Siddiqui, 2020).

Security and privacy needs, such as privacy and trust management among people and things, have played a critical role in detecting rogue nodes in SIoT and thereby promoting IoT applications. We focus on IoT network security issues and present a survey on trust evaluation for trustworthy IoT based on specific criteria. Furthermore, we discuss the research issues of trust evaluation in the IoT, as well as research directions in the future field.

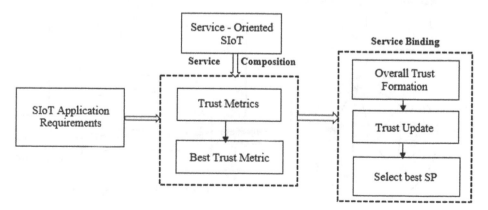

FIGURE 4.1 Components of a Service- Oriented SIoT System.

Sensor nodes in IoT networks are typically low-capability devices that are subject to a variety of security attacks. Many security techniques and solutions have been presented in recent years to address this issue.

The IoT is growing in popularity with the enormous number of IoT devices increasing the potential of threats like viruses and cyber-attacks, to name a few. Enabling a trustworthy environment in the Internet of Things, where interactions are based on the communication nodes trust value which is one possible strategy to achieving IoT security. Although trust management and evaluation have been explored extensively in networks that are distributed, we still have urgent difficulties like badmouthing trust values that prohibit them from being deployed in actual applications of IoT. In addition, much research has to be done to ensure that current trust solutions will be scalable over trillions of devices in SIoT.

4.1.2 SIoT Relationships Parental Object Relationship (POR)

By incorporating elements of social networks in IoT, the developing paradigm of the SIoT has turned the classic notion of IoT into a social network of trillions of networked smart items. In the IoT, devices can form social relationships on their own and interact with other in the network based on its social behavior. Establishing these interactions in a trusted and reliable manner, i.e., Establishing relationships and building trust among things, is a fundamental challenge that requires attention. It is necessary to determine and forecast device behavior in the network over time. As a result, to solve this issue, propose a time-aware machine learning approach for driving the trust evaluation model efficiently.

The model suggested (as shown in Figure 4.2) can effectively separate trustworthy and untrustworthy objects inside the network, and it also shows how an object's trust varies over time, as well as the impact of each trust parameter on score value.

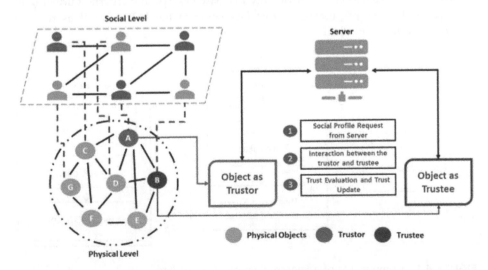

FIGURE 4.2   SIoT components and trust evaluation process.

4.1.3 SIoT Architecture – Relationship Management

Rapid advances in network communication and computing technology has resulted in expansion of trillions of intelligent devices like intelligent machines, smart watches, and autonomous cars with processing (Venkatesan and Kumar, 2021), sensing and communication capabilities, which not only enable device-to-device communication over the network paradigm. This has unquestionably generated substantial revenue and opened the door to a plethora of applications and services in a variety of key areas, as well as a massive increase in connected smart items, which is predicted to reach 75.44 billion by 2025. Furthermore, various research projects have examined the possibility of incorporating the concept of social network into the ecosystem during the last decade in IoT. As a result of this integration, a new paradigm has emerged (Cai et al., 2022).

Furthermore, each object in SIoT can form relationships shown in Figure 4.2 with other objects in terms of ownership (relationships with objects belongs to the Same Owner), Social relationships (relationships with objects belongs to Friends in a Social Network), Parental relationships (relationships with objects from the Same Manufacturer), co-location and work relationship (relationships with objects from the same location and its Environment), and parental ties (relationships with object from same location and its environment). Because social objects will only enter into a connection if the other object is trustworthy to reduce likelihood of a risky decision, trust is critical in forming and maintaining social partnerships. It is simple for them because they have strong bonds with the things around them (Khan et al., 2020).

4.1.3.1 Objects mimic human social behavior

We employ social information (Friends, Interest Groups, Working relationships etc.,) and object interactions as major data to assess trustworthy of an object in SIoT ecosystem. In terms of multicast interactions, Social information is collection of an object's friends (F), social interest communities (C), and co-work relationship (CW) information, whereas object-object interactions provide insight into cooperativeness (CoP) in the form of successful - unsuccessful interaction among the participating objects. The data sources are defined as triplets F, C, and CW, as well as Object-Object interactions cooperativeness (CoP) (Wang and Zhang, 2016).

Let $O = \{o_1, o_2, ..., o_n\}$ represent the set of objects and given the set of triplets $\{F, C, CW\}$ for each object, and the object-object interactions, the target problem can be formulated as quantifying the trust of an object O_i towards another object O_j at any time interval T by using the given set of triplets and cooperativeness, and expressed as composition of all the trust parameter as follow:

$$\text{Trust } (O_i, O_j) = \langle F, \ C, \ CW, \ CoP \rangle$$

4.1.3.2 The proposed solution

We present a computational model depicted in Figure 4.3 for assessing object trustworthiness based on social knowledge and interactions. This model addresses all of the important components of trustworthiness management. As shown in the diagram, the

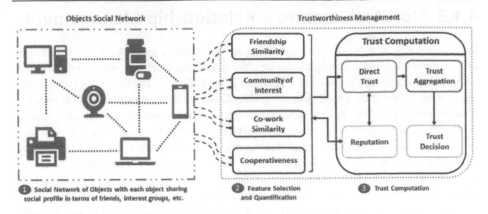

FIGURE 4.3 Trust evaluation model in SIoT.

first stage in calculating trustworthy is to obtain trustee's social info, after which the following step is to quantify the selected attribute using the information obtained in the first step. The component of feature extraction covers challenge of picking an appropriate trust measure while quantifying for a specific Social IoT application, and metrics designated like Cooperativeness, Community of Interest, Friendship Similarity and Co-work Similarity. The object trustworthy is calculated using direct trust and reputation, followed by its aggregation procedure.

4.1.4 Trust Management Model

The SIoT bridges the gap between social media - IoT. Core idea is a big group of people connected in social network can provide far more precise responses to complex problem than individuals. Thus, publishing services/information, identifying them, and discovering new resources will be one of the most important goals is better implementation services in a given network of objects. Instead, relying on normal Internet search approaches which are unable to expand future trillions of devices, which performed by viewing social network site of "friend" things (Chen et al., 2021).

IoT networks were created with the goal of connecting billions of devices to machines, humans and intelligent objects for data collection, control, and actuation. Device-to-Device communications have cleared the way for true ubiquitous computing (UC), which is smart and capable of making its own decisions without the need for human participation. For future networks, this necessitates a connection between humans and robots directly. Human interactions, on the other hand, are primarily determined by need-based connections, trust, and networks. As a result, it's critical to recognize that meaningful human-machine interaction necessitates more connectedness between users and things. Furthermore, it necessitates a direct link of things to humans as a social relationship, resulting in the evolution of omnipresent technology.

According to the present situation, propose a decentralized case, where node stores information, calculates about other nodes to have its self-opinion in network where malicious attack that can change the behavior based on the request, like Direct Attacks in this way, are identified easily by Parental Objects Relationship (POR), which form between products in same categories products, and Ownership Objects Relationship (OOR), which form between different goods belonging to same network, are at the heart of SIoT. Human intervention should be avoided in the formation and management of such interactions where the laws for devices and their social interactions are primarily determined by humans. SIoT, in a nutshell, connects present social networks with a network of things in future.

4.1.4.1 Deriving trust

Presents a new secure approach for determining the trustworthiness of SIoT nodes. Figure 4.4 depicts the framework. We extract four aspects of trust from the user's experience based on Direct and indirect trust calculated using the attributes like honesty, cooperativeness, communal interest, and energy. To enhance application performance and establish secure connection, the trust computed is examined based on many variables weighed properly (Um et al., 2019).

4.1.4.1.1 Developing trust metrics

The parameters are useful for describing a node's attitude, experience and its behavior. Each property trusted is mutually beneficial and hence must be evaluated separately (Sagar, Subhash, Adnan Mahmood, Michael Sheng, Munazza Zaib, and Wei Zhang, 2020).

a. **Honesty:** An honest node is supposed to deliver proper recommendations in its neighbor network with the range (0, 1) for honesty of a node which is regarded as a prime factor. This ensures that node is not malicious and improves the trustworthiness of networks. A node uses personal information, or direct trust, to assess honesty. Direct Trust is earned when node interacts directly with another.

b. **Cooperativeness:** Whether trust node is cooperative socially with the trustor is represented by cooperative trust. Nodes with mutual friends are

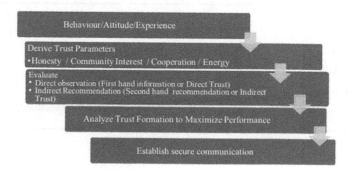

FIGURE 4.4 Process of deriving trust.

expected to be cooperative and behave differently than others. The cooperativeness of nodes in the SIoT environment can be anticipated by their network links. The application's performance is improved by socially cooperative nodes. Each device/object has a group of pals who are inclined to cooperate. Owners will update this list on a regular basis.

c. **Community interest:** The Other component which promotes communication between items of common interest is community interest. The items are categorized based on their parent-child, co-worker, or relationships that are co-located. Objects with similar community interests are expected to interact frequently, resulting in improved application performance.

d. **Energy:** The energy of a node is very essential in network/data communication and information sharing. All SIoT devices have power low and inefficient energy. As a result, a node's energy should be prioritized for collaboration reasons. The product of power and time is used to calculate the energy of a node.

4.1.4.2 Evaluate direct observations and indirect recommendations

Two sorts of trusts are reviewed to promote trustworthiness among SIoT nodes: observations that are first-hand or Direct and second-hand advice or Indirect. The calculated parameters for trust are shown in Table 4.1. The trust is calculated by equation (4.1) as follows when i and j nodes directly interact with one other (Subash and Rethnaraj, 2021).

$$T_{ij}^{X}(t) = \alpha T_{ij}^{X}(t)(t - \Delta t) + \alpha D_{ij}^{X}(t) + \beta G_{ij}^{X} + \alpha\beta DP_{ij}^{X} \qquad (4.1)$$

Where X = cooperativeness, honesty, energy and community interest and Δt is time elapsed since the last trust update.

TABLE 4.1 List of parameters used

PARAMETERS	DESCRIPTION
$D_{ij}^{x}(t)$	Direct trust of i towards j at time t in x
$D_{kj}^{x}(t)$	Recommendation of k from j at time t in x
$T_{ij}^{x}(t)$	Trust between i and j at time t in x
$G_{ij}^{x}(t)$	Centrality of a node
$D_{ij}^{x}(t)$	Direct trust of i towards k at time t in x
DP_{ij}^{x}	Dependability factor
α, β, λ	Weighing factors

4.1.5 SIoT Paradigms

Social media is integrated with the IoT and necessitates demanding developed measures that may extend its work beyond existing solutions. Core IoT is a confluence of heterogeneous gadgets and offerings that lacks enterprise standardization and is accepted as true with compliance. As a result, it's critical to grasp important distinct views that require both comprehending devices and human behavior in the ecosystem. The deployment of SIoT is examined via the angles.

4.1.5.1 Human-device interaction

IoT integration with social networks necessitates both device-to-device communication and human engagement. Machine-to-Machine (M2M), Human-to-Human (H2H), and Human-to-Machine (H2M) network communications are all part of this. Currently, the IoT technical landscape allows for ubiquitous D2D communication. However, flawless H2D integration still necessitates updated designs and middleware. This connection is essential for ambient intelligence based on human-to-human interactions which brings IoT networks one step closer to being fully omnipresent.

4.1.5.2 Collaborative-awareness

In contrast to traditional IoT networks, collaborative awareness is a significant aspect in SIoT networks. Traditional networks rely on proactive and reactive data from machines to execute activities. The SIoT ecosystem, on the other hand, will necessitate the need for human-to-human interactions that will govern machine to machine and human to machine connectivity. To improve quality of experience and its collaboration with humans, SIoT must appear as social networks that are an extension.

4.1.5.3 Privacy and data protection

Pervasive computing in SIoT environment is based on human data. Sensors, active - passive internet devices, and other devices are commonly used to collect data, which can appear in numerous form. SIoT networks, in general, the nature of data must balance both reactive and proactive which is critical to ensure data security and privacy throughout the network, including both data at rest and in motion. To proactively assess situation-based learning, acquisition data can invoke crawling data and learning different methodologies. Reactive data acquisition, on the other hand, may necessitate a real-time query. As a result, data collecting in the SIoT environment must adhere to security, data protection, and privacy regulations.

The holistic viewpoints should be investigated in the framework context in order to build an ecosystem SIoT which lets SIoT-enabled smart machines engage with humans and networks using architecturally neutral methods which can integrate existing applications, enterprise solutions and different IoT-services into its networks which necessitates an understanding of key components.

4.1.5.4 Integration of social network

The smart objects (SO) integrated with the current systems (SN) are critical for facilitating data collecting and the generation of ambient intelligence. All of this stuff are required: provider discovery, operability inside consumer belief roles (TR), and Such hyperlinks to SNs may be executed via means of integrating SN APIs to retrieve reactive information that may in the end be shared with clever items with higher decision-making. An important challenge at this degree is permissions compliance and consumer roles as hooked up via means of the SNs able to ensure information Integrity and the SN to SO relationship. By increasing the SNs, information update along with status, position and activity update may be used to govern SO for SIoT networks.

4.1.5.5 Ambient intelligence

The way to harvest ambient intelligence in SIoT is to dynamically link devices to SN. Human actions on UC devices' SNs are often used to control them automatically. Regulation is critical to make certain a constant hyperlink among era and humans. In addition, the idea of intelligence is crucial for D2D connections that comply with SN provider standards. According to a few research, middleware components could be utilized to control SIoT network trust and data flow policies.

4.1.5.6 Smart objects and social networks combination

Link between devices and SNs is dictated by the SN and SO combination, which is the center of SIoT technologies landscape. Majority of today's devices are designed on embedded platform that communicate wirelessly with one another and with gateway devices. Because the nature of these embedded devices is constrained, efficient communication protocols are required. SNs, usually cloud based IT solution that have more processing and memory capacity. As a result, in order to appropriately interact with SNs, SIoT systems may require ground-up modeling. We'll go through these architectures in greater depth in the next section (Zhukova et al., 2020).

4.1.5.7 XaaS – Everything-as-a-service

Cloud Computing "as-a-Service", or the provision of services over the internet, is a growing global trend. Customers are increasingly accessing services, goods, and corporate solutions through Software-as-a-Service (SaaS) choices. PaaS (Platform-as-a-Service) and IaaS (Infrastructure-as-a-Service) are two more service type that use the same pay-as-you-go approach (IaaS). All of these cloud business models can be considered to be part of the XaaS model. The concept of transforming things and SNs into services and allowing them easily discover and connected with different services is at the heart of SIoT. Future SIoT networks will leverage devices and its analytics to improvise the value and quality of experience (Dhelim et al., 2021).

4.1.5.8 Device heterogeneity

Sensor networks, which provide a variety of computing and networking resources, are commonly used to build IoT networks. Human integration, on the other hand, adds still the technical stack now has even another layer of variability. Furthermore, different devices have diverse technological stack implementations, including protocols. Finally, a lack of standards for heterogeneity is exacerbated by a plethora of IoT application options. As a result, ensuring device interoperability for SIoT ecosystems is critical. Smart object clustering based on roles and resources can successfully tackle this challenge, allowing groups of related tasks/resources smart objects to form direct linkages. Manufacturers may be able to produce cost-effective IoT devices as a result of the implementation flexibility. The absence of standardization, on the other hand, will stymie the effective application of these regulations.

4.1.5.9 Interoperability

Data integrity and interoperability may be hampered by technology heterogeneity in SIoT networks. Intelligent interoperability will be ensured, in particular, via uniform data management and storage systems. One approach to the challenge is to use metadata heuristics to determine type of data that can turn into action able information to model resource-based operations. Middlewares can be used to set up resources managing and descriptive framework, especially systems like ontology based, to allow for data interchange between smart object.

4.1.5.10 Mobility

SIoT ecosystems are made up of constantly moving smart objects. One of the most difficult issues in preserving service discovery and fixed links between devices is the need for dynamic mobility. Furthermore, devices may dynamically adjust their functionality based on their location, putting network convergence and fixed device trust borders in jeopardy. Smart object relationships this difficulty can be solved by using a system based on proximity. Based on their locations, connected services and functionality, dynamic, tiny sub community of smart objects can be developed. Based on the position finding, the network can swiftly converge by discovering neighboring items.

4.1.5.11 Service discovery

In SIoT networks, data volume, device mobility and interoperability necessitates effective speedier convergence in network, trust connections, and hence service discovery is necessary for information flow. Discovery algorithms and Service advertisements for SIoT networks may not scale as effectively as IP-based solutions. As a result, middlewares can use service advertisement rules based on artificial neural networks to start role-based and location-based services discovery by preemptively promoting the remaining resource based on location and resource characteristics of smart objects; these strategies will dramatically minimize service discovery times.

4.1.5.12 Context management

Consumers' adoption of technology gave them more options when it came to acquiring data. On the other hand, it posed a huge problem for information and process context management. Consider a typical workplace scenario in which a person utilizes a variety of internet-connected devices simultaneously and the devices may be use to access SN with related data, resulting in context switching issues. To ensure a balanced exchange of information across numerous devices while also organizing this data for brilliant context and devices switch, seamless context management is essential. Semantic-based context modeling techniques can considerably improve device compatibility, context switching, and scaled application availability across a number of devices in the vicinity (Alshehri et al., 2018).

4.1.5.13 Application development

In order to gain meaningful insights and intelligently automate corporate activities, Often IoT networks are utilized for analysis and data sensing. This information is mostly accessible in SN situations by a variety of apps that tailored the roles, needs, and requirements of the users. Programmes are usually designed to install on devices or to run in Cloud Environment. Differences in processing, networking, and storage capability compound the issues of network architecture and device compatibility. As a result, Lightweight APIs that offer unified access across several devices can aid in application development with deployment. Middleware can also be used to manage APIs, bridging the gaps between devices with IT solution and allow for smooth resource integrate across SIoT ecosystem.

4.1.6 Types of Attacks and Its Roles with Management in Trust SIoT

In today's IoT technology, which deals with the interaction of things, trust issues are among the most urgent. Unauthorized access, loss of Privacy, Safety and Security, as well as information manipulation for individuals are all problems brought on by a lack of confidence in socially collaborative object. In order to have reliable communication, every object in the SIoT technology stacks must have a high level of confidence in its surrounding objects. On the amount of confidence, a trust-based relationship also makes it easier to discriminate between trustworthy and hazardous objects (Wang and Zhang, 2016).

Two significant design issues in SIOT TM Architecture are Data protection and confidentiality and it's crucial to keep in mind that these objects are heterogeneous which introduces a host object-level vulnerabilities and problems in security. As a result, to protect the network from access control system threats, a security plan is required. As a result, it's necessary to create an effective TM control in SIoT networks to protect objects and the data they contain from illegal access. In the creation of TM solutions, the identification of trust types among smart objects is critical (Abidi and Azzouna, 2021; Narang and Kar, 2018).

Trust Attacks for Security and privacy:

Malicious with Everyone (ME): a node behaves in a malicious manner towards everyone. This is the most fundamental attack: regardless of the requester, a node provides bad advice and services.

A Discrimination Attack: occurs when node changes it's behavior depending on who is requesting services which means a node could distinguish between nodes that are not friends and nodes that have weak social relationship.

On-Off Attack (OOA): a node alternates between being benevolent (ON) and malicious (OFF) on a regular basis (OFF). The node builds up its trust during the ON state, after then, it's use to assault network.

A Whitewashing Attack: When a node with bad reputation leave network and returns with new identity, this is known as a Whitewashing Attack (WA). When a node rejoins the network, its reputation is reset to default number.

Self-Promotional Attack: To be chosen as a service provider, a node that is malicious makes best suggestions for itself. It only provides poor services after being chosen as a provider.

Other attacks focus on a particular target, such as malicious nodes that exclusively give harmful services/a bad reputation.

Bad Mouthing Assault: A attack seeks to smear the other nodes reputation; a node i.e., malicious will offer fake proposals in order to diminish chances of benevolent nodes chosen as provider. Although it carried out by single node, attack is frequently part of a collusive conduct in which the group nodes cooperate to devastate an expert node's reputation.

Ballot Stuffing Attack: A collusive attack in which a node i.e., malicious sends good suggestions to another in order to improve its reputation, boost its chance of being chosen as provider.

Sybil Attack: A rogue node utilizes multiple identity to offer various types of proposals on the same service (SA) and the identities are virtually always false, and are all part of attack.

Opportunistic Service Attack: When hostile nodes recognize that its trust reputation is degrading, it launches an opportunistic service attack (OSA). As a result, in order to choose a service provider, the node strives to maintain a reasonable degree of confidence.

To recap, the chart above depicts how trust-related attacks are classified according to the two factors mentioned. To our knowledge, existing trustworthy model can only separate a subset of the assaults outlined, i.e., design to recognize and separate a subset of attacks specifically but none can effectively combat all of them.

Given the diversity of devices and services accessible, For SIoT ecosystems, security the most crucial building block. To protect against a range of assaults, whether network, access or data-based, SIoT networks must be secure and reliable. This delicate requirement will ensure that SIoT interactions are reliable and robust. It's critical to infer that without robust and secure SIoT systems/networks, the Internet of Things would fail. SIoT is likely to fall short of its potential before it even gets off the ground. As a result, data governance in SIoT ecosystems need the aforementioned schemes to assure platform integrity, compliance and data confidentiality (Khanfor et al., 2020).

4.1.7 Emerging IoT Domains, Existing State-of-Art and Unresolved Issues in Research

Aside from the aforementioned Internet of Things categories, the growing ecosystems in IoT promise incredible technology opportunities that has a direct impact on human quality of life. For example, the Internet of Space Things (IoST) aims to bring high-speed, low-latency internet to every corner of the globe. The Internet of Nano Things (IoNT) has the potential to revolutionize the healthcare business by permitting telemedicine and inter wireless body area network (WBAN) connectivity. The Internet of Underwater Things (IoUT) has already aided in improving the condition of our seas, accelerating search and rescue operations, and establishing effective crisis governanace, systems (such as Tsunami, oil leakage notifications) (Aljubairy et al., 2021).

The Social Internet of Things (SIoT) aims to connect IoT networks with humans and social networks (SNs) in order to provide understandable insights in real time and require a comprehensive technological revamp, despite technology breakthroughs and a wide range of technical platforms. These new ecosystems have unique operational characteristics that necessitate extensive study and development of IoT technology stacks. Privacy, security and governance policy are very important in SIoT environments. Not just technological advancements, but also a unified, scalable architecture are required in these expanding ecosystems. As a result, it's crucial to examine the open research questions in each of these fields separately (Iera et al., 2015; Narang and Kar, 2018).

- Emerging IoT domains and ecosystems should be identified.
- A thorough examination of current IoT ecosystems and accompanying technologies.
- Examples of application-specific deployments and growing IoT ecosystem trends.
- For SIoT, there are security, privacy, and trust needs.

4.1.7.1 Research questions

Furthermore, we established research questions to uncover study gaps in these domains, as provided by Oliver, Gough, & Thomas and Cherry, Boland, & Dickson. As a result, (RQ1) was born: "What are the quickly evolving IoT areas that could establish an independent ecosystem?" This prompted us to pursue (RQ2): "How do the architectural and technical requirements in these IoT domains differ from those in other application domains?" We looked at how these ecosystems fit into the existing IoT landscape in the steps that followed. As a result, (RQ3) was born: "How can these ecosystems be integrated into the existing digital blueprint?" Finally, what are the technological difficulties that must be handled, that are specified, if existing methods are used to adapt these ecosystems? And the technological issues which need to be addressed and expressed in terms (RQ4): "What open research challenges exist in this domain?" (Floris et al., 2022)

4.1.7.2 Emerging technologies

The expanding coupling of IoT with 6G will open up a wealth of options for a wide range of applications, from telecommunications to automobile safety and e-healthcare, to address human society's challenges as the next phase of the social Internet of Things (Ali et al., 2021).

The Internet of Nanothings (IoNT) is an Internet of Things/nanotechnology hybrid. IoNT appears to be a scaled-down application extension of Internet of Things networks in its most basic form. This, on the other hand, is unusual since it uses nanoscale sensors and ultra-small scale devices for sensing and actuation. Environmental monitoring and medicinal applications are two areas where IoNT has a lot of space for development (Dong et al., 2022).

Threats to security and goals to be optimized in IoNT:

CHALLENGES AND GOALS	RESOLUTION
Data encryption	Because of their small size and restricted calculating capabilities, most nanodevices lack encryption. There are a lot of safety issues if critical data between nanodevices, whether on a single nanodevice or across nanonetworks, cannot be encrypted. This is especially true as nanodevices grow more integrated into our bodies. Embedded and lightweight cryptography encryption algorithms which are genetic-based might be able to encrypt IoNT data while consuming less energy.
Malware Injection	Most nanosensors and wearable electronics communicate with internal gateways via plain text due to a lack of on-board processing power with multi-hop wireless connections with gateways expanding the surface threat externally, increasing the likelihood of code injection and man-in-the-middle attacks which could compromise not only personal information, but potentially turn the sensors into rogue objects. Data breaches and code injection can be detected in real time using time-access and token-based data relaying in conjunction with identity management control.
Denial of service (DOS) attacks	DOS attacks on network resources and traffic are depleted, resulting in a communication breakdown and to prevent DOS attacks is by analyzing traffic and isolating malicious activities. External micro-gateways can employ the lightweight, scalable DOS attack prevention technology to stop known attackers.
Access control	Authentication is frequently ensured using traditional symmetric and asymmetric cryptography. Biochemical cryptography is a novel and unexplored field that uses biological molecules such as DNA/RNA evidence to encrypt data and safeguard its confidentiality and integrity.

The Internet of Space Things (IoST) aims to provide low-cost global networking while retaining a network coverage of a high-bandwidth umbrella for delivering internet connectivity via satellite networks in LEO (LEO). The demand for larger bandwidth and data rates is increasing in lockstep with the advancement of wireless networks devices that are continually progressing. The extremely intertwined nature of the internet is already producing issues with address. As billions of these gadgets transmit massive quantities of data around the clock, the situation will only become worse (Pandharipande, 2021).

The overall goal of IoUT research is developing a system of networked sensors, underwater devices and autonomous vehicles that connect and relay data over internet, as depicted in Figure 4.5. Scientists will be able to implement catastrophe biosensors to

FIGURE 4.5 SIoT ecosystems map and open challenges.

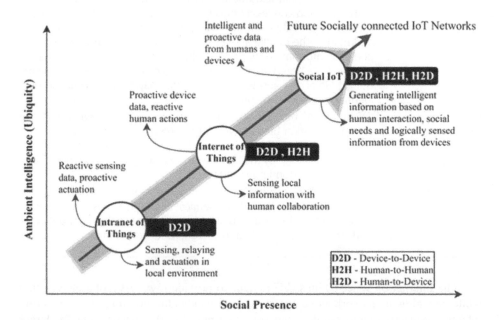

FIGURE 4.6 Device Interaction with Humans towards SIoT.

detect ocean bed quality and explore reef and ocean species, as well as recovery and identification solutions for oil spills, tsunamis, and notable shipwrecks.' health via the network of underwater objects. Underwater networks could gain a substantial edge for armed forces applications if ocean geo-fencing becomes the weapon of choice for international sea management and monitoring (Pandharipande, 2021; Kumaran and Sridhar, 2020).

4.2 CONCLUSION

The Internet of Things has come a long way in the previous decade, from ultra-low-power hardware to cloud-based solutions, edge computing in IoT devices will soon have a new horizon with the arrival of 6G technology. In recent years, a huge array of communication technologies has steadily grown, reflecting a range of subject areas and requirements and its purpose is to connect trillions of things to humans, devices, and smart things for data collection, actuation and its control. True ubiquitous computing (UC), which is brilliant, capable of making decisions without the assistance of a human, is now possible thanks to device-to-device (D2D) connectivity. Figure 4.5 shows how to obtain UC to which SIoT as a service model can be formed for future networks which necessitates a direct connection between humans and robots. Human interactions, on the other hand, are primarily determined by need-based connections, trust, and networks. As a result, it's critical to recognize that meaningful human-machine interaction necessitates more connectedness between users and things (Rad et al., 2020).

Due to the diversity of technology and interconnectivity, several dynamic integration challenges are presently delaying the full implementation of the IoT ecosystem. Several new IoT areas require considerable re-modeling, design, and standardization from the ground up in order to achieve seamless IoT ecosystem integration (Iqbal et al., 2019).

REFERENCES

Abdelghani, Wafa, Corinne Zayani, Ikram Amous, and Florence Sèdes. (Sep 2016). "Trust Management in Social Internet of Things: A Survey."15th Conference on e-Business, e-Services and e-Society (I3E), Swansea, United Kingdom. pp. 430–441. 10.1145/3446999.3447635430–441

Abidi, R. and N. B. Azzouna. (2021). "Self-adaptive trust management model for social IoT services." 2021 International Symposium on Networks, Computers and Communications (ISNCC), pp. 1–7 doi: 10.1109/ISNCC52172.2021.9615856

Ali, Omer, Mohamad Khairi Ishak, and Muhammad Kamran Liaquat Bhatti (Aug. 16, 2021). "Emerging IoT domains, current standings and open research challenges: a review." *PeerJ Computer Science, 7.*

Aljubairy, A., A. Alhazmi, W. E. Zhang, Q. Z. Sheng, and D. H. Tran (2021). "Towards a Deep Learning-Driven Service Discovery Framework for the Social Internet of Things: A Context-Aware Approach." In: Zhang W., Zou L., Maamar Z., Chen L. (eds). Web Information Systems Engineering – WISE. 2021.

Alshehri, Mohammad Dahman, Farookh Khadeer Hussain, and Omar Khadeer Hussain. (2018). "Clustering-Driven Intelligent Trust Management Methodology for the Internet of Things (CITM-IoT)."*Mob. Netw. Appl.*, 23(3 (June 2018)): 419–431.

Cai, B., X. Li, W. Kong, J. Yuan and S. Yu. 2022. "A Reliable and Lightweight Trust Inference Model for Service Recommendation in SioT." In *IEEE Internet of Things Journal*, 9(1), 10988–11003, doi:10.1109/JIOT.2021.3125347.

Chen, Y. et al. (2021). "Graph-based service recommendation in Social Internet of Things." *International Journal of Distributed Sensor Networks*.

Dhelim, S., H. Ning, F. Farha, L. Chen, L. Atzori, and M. Daneshmand. (Dec. 15, 2021). "IoT-Enabled Social Relationships Meet Artificial Social Intelligence." In IEEE Internet of Things Journal, 8(24), 2625–2647, 15, doi: 10.1109/JIOT.2021.3081556

Dong, P., J. Ge, X. Wang, and S. Guo. (Feb. 2022). "Collaborative Edge Computing for Social Internet of Things: Applications, Solutions, and Challenges." In *IEEE Transactions on Computational Social Systems*, 9(1): 291–301.

Floris, Alessandro, Simone Porcu, Luigi Atzori, and Roberto Girau. (2022). "A Social IoT-based platform for the deployment of a smart parking solution." *Computer Networks*, 205. 108756, ISSN 1389-1286.

Iera, A., G. Morabito, and L. Atzori. (2015). "The Social Internet of Things." *2015 IEEE International Conference on Cloud Engineering*, pp. 1–1. doi: 10.1109/IC2E.2015.68.

Iqbal, R. et al. (2019). "Trust management in social Internet of vehicles: Factors, challenges, blockchain, and fog solutions." *International Journal of Distributed Sensor Networks*.

Khan, Wazir, Qurat-ul-Ain Arshad, Saqib Hakak, Khurram Khan, and Saeed-Ur-Rehman. (2020). "Trust Management in Social Internet of Things: Architectures, Recent Advancements and Future Challenges."*IEEE Internet of Things Journal*, 1–1. 10.1109/JIOT.2020.3039296

Khanfor, A., H. Friji, H. Ghazzai, and Y. Massoud. (2020). "A Social IoT-Driven Pedestrian Routing Approach During Epidemic Time." 2020 IEEE Global Conference on Artificial Intelligence and Internet of Things (GCAIoT), pp. 1–6. doi: 10.1109/GCAIoT51063.2020.9345900

Khanfor, A., H. Friji, H. Ghazzai, and Y. Massoud. (2020). "A Social IoT-Driven Pedestrian Routing Approach During Epidemic Time." 2020 IEEE Global Conference on Artificial Intelligence and Internet of Things (GCAIoT), pp. 1–6. doi: 10.1109/GCAIoT51063.2020.9345900

Kumaran, P. and Sridhar, Rajeswari. (2020). "Social Internet of Things (SIoT): Techniques, Applications and Challenges." *2020 4th International Conference on Trends in Electronics and Informatics (ICOEI) (48184)*, pp. 445–450. doi: 10.1109/ICOEI48184.2020.9142908

Malekshahi Rad, M., A. M. Rahmani, A. Sahafi et al. (2020). Social Internet of Things: vision, challenges, and trends. *Human-centric Computing and Information Sciences* 10, 52.

Narang, Nishit, and Subrat Kar. (2018). "Utilizing Social Networks Data for Trust Management in a Social Internet of Things Network." In Proceedings of the 24th Annual International Conference on Mobile Computing and Networking (MobiCom '18). Association for Computing Machinery, New York, NY, USA, 768–770

Pandharipande, A. (June1, 2021). "Social Sensing in IoT Applications: A Review." In *IEEE Sensors Journal*, 21(11), 12523–12530, 1. doi: 10.1109/JSEN.2021.3049714

Rad, Mozhgan, Amir Rahmani, Amir Sahafi, and Nooruldeen Qader. (2020). Social Internet of Things: vision, challenges, and trends. *Human-centric Computing and Information Sciences*. 10. 10.1186/s13673-020-00254-6

Roopa, S., Puneetha, Vishwas, Buyya, Rajkumar, Venugopal, Iyengar, and Patnaik, Lalit. (2020). "Trust Management for Service-Oriented SIoT Systems." 216–222. 10.1145/3446999. 3447635.

Sagar, Subhash, Adnan Mahmood, Quan Z. Sheng, and Sarah Ali Siddiqui. (2020). "SCaRT-SIoT: towards a scalable and robust trust platform for social internet of things: demo abstract." *Proceedings of the 18th Conference on Embedded Networked Sensor Systems.* Association for Computing Machinery, New York, NY, USA, 635–636.

Sagar, Subhash, Adnan Mahmood, Michael Sheng, Munazza Zaib, and Wei Zhang. (2020). "Towards a Machine Learning-driven Trust Evaluation Model for Social Internet of Things: A Time-aware Approach." In *MobiQuitous 2020 - 17th EAI International Conference on Mobile and Ubiquitous Systems: Computing, Networking and Services (MobiQuitous '20).* Association for Computing Machinery, New York, NY, USA, 283–290.

Sangoleye, F., N. Irtija, and E. E. Tsiropoulou (2021). "Data Acquisition in Social Internet of Things based on Contract Theory." *ICC 2021 - IEEE International Conference on Communications,* pp. 1–6.

Shafi, J. and A. Waheed. (2018). "S-IoT: A new platform for Online Social Networks Using IoT." 2018 1st International Conference on Computer Applications & Information Security (ICCAIS), pp. 1–6. doi: 10.1109/CAIS.2018.8441970

Subash, Rajendran and Jebakumar Rethnaraj. (2022). "Friendliness Based Trustworthy Relationship Management (F-TRM) in Social Internet of Things.", *Wireless Personal Communications,* 123. 10.1007/(11277-021-09256-8): 2625–2647. 10.1007/s11277-021-09256-8

Um, Tai-Won, et al. (2019). "Design and implementation of a trust information management platform for social internet of things environments." *Sensors,* 19(21): 4707.

Venkatesan, Geetha, and Avadhesh Kumar. (2021). "Enhanced adaptive trust management system for socially related IoT." *International Journal of Internet Technology and Secured Transactions,* 11(5-6): 584–596.

Wang, Pu and Peng Zhang. (2016). "A Review on Trust Evaluation for Internet of Things." In *Proceedings of the 9th EAI International Conference on Mobile Multimedia Communications (MobiMedia '16).* ICST (Institute for Computer Sciences, Social-Informatics and Telecommunications Engineering), Brussels, BEL, 34–39.

Zhukova, N., A. M. Thaw, M. Tianxing, and M. Nikolay. (2020). "IoT Data Collection Based on Social Network Models." 2020 26th Conference of Open Innovations Association (FRUCT), pp. 458–463. doi: 10.23919/FRUCT48808.2020.9087350

Security Threats in SIoT

5

Ajay A V[1] and Pramod H B[2]

[1]*Visvesvaraya Technological University, Department of Computer Science and Engineering, Rajeev Institute of Technology, Hassan, Karnataka, India*
[2]*Department of Computer Science and Engineering, Rajeev Institute of Technology, Hassan, Karnataka, India*

Contents

DOI: 10.1201/9781003282990-5

5.1 INTRODUCTION

Because of the current rapid growth in the connection area, a new level of technology has emerged that will redefine how network devices interact with the physical world. This is the Internet of Things. The Internet of Things is a term that refers to the interconnection of various smart devices that have unique access. With the unique networking capabilities of intermediary devices, the Internet of Things is altering the method of interaction between users and devices (Afzal et al. 2019). As a result, our lives will be transformed into a socially hyperconnected environment. We can see three generations of the Internet of Things: tagged things, web services and internetworking, and social and cloud computing. Figure 5.1 depicts the three generations of the IoT, with SIoT included as the rise of the third generation of IoT.

Today, the notion of social technology with IoT to establish social relationships is becoming more popular because of the properties of social things, which enhance the composition and information discovery of objects by interacting with their physical environment (Hou et al. 2019). The need to combine the concepts of both Internet of Things and social networks became necessary because of the growing appreciation that a "Social Internet of Things" model can bring various inferences to a future global population permeated by sensible objects pervading human life. In reality, adopting the social networking concepts to the IoT can result in a slew of advantages: (a) the structure of SIoT can be constructed to ensure navigability of the network, with effective creation of objects and services while maintaining scalability, similar to the social network of human beings, and (b) the social network analysis models developed can be applied to SIoT-related concerns.

The SIoT devices are socially tied between humans and things, as well as between the things that function like social circles. This system creates profiles based on data from a variety of IoT applications (Lin et al. 2017). These profiles are exchanged within a SIoT

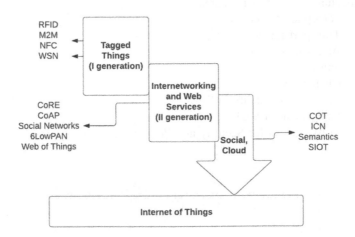

FIGURE 5.1 Generation of IoT.

network, which is accessible to a wide range of IoT applications. SIoT networks offer recommendation services to improve the performance of IoT applications by sharing and utilising IoT application records. Furthermore, the profiles generated by SIoT networks can help a specific IoT application by locating similar situations that have previously been addressed for the same IoT application (Mawgoud et al 2020).

The following are examples of object relationships in SIoT:

- **Relationship among parental objects:** establishment of relation among goods from the same category of manufacture batch, usually same objects produced by the similar producer within the equivalent time period.
- **Relationships among co-location objects are** created between objects (similar or dissimilar) that are used in the same location. In other circumstances, these relationships are formed between items to work together to achieve a common aim. They are, nevertheless, valuable for populating the network with "short" links.
- **A collaboration relationship among co-work objects** will be accomplished together by objects to create a shared application.
- **An ownership object relationship** is formed between disparate things belonging to the same user.
- **Social object relationship:** When interaction takes place among items, irregularly or continually, a relationship is formed among owners throughout their lives.

In terms of Social IoT, three key characteristics distinguish the relationship between social networks and the IoT (Atzori et al. 2012).

1. Instead of just establishing and exploiting social interactions between owners or humans, the SIoT creates and exploits social relationships between things. Humans may be worried about mediation; yet, things play the most important roles.
2. Things can identify assets and services on their own through social ties with the IoT, providing a pre-determined solution and reducing human labour.
3. The SIoT is no longer reliant on internet technology; instead, social networking services (SNSs) serve as a platform that deals with objects but not with people. SIoT software is already being used in industries such as higher education, healthcare, and telecommunications (Jia et al. 2019).

5.2 SIOT APPLICATIONS

The following are some of the ways SIoT is used in various industries:

1. **Education:** In schools and institutions, IOT means increased connectivity and educational quality. These gadgets assist students in gaining greater access to

learning materials through effective communication channels; they also assist teachers in assessing their students' learning abilities in real time.

2. **Industry:** A business owner who is experiencing a technical issue with a machines can find a remedy using their co-worker relationship by contacting devices of other comparable industry owners who have already confronted the same difficulty. Troubleshooting services can be provided by combining equipment from diverse industries.

3. **Farming:** An agriculturist with a vegetable farm who is looking for advice on a new crop can use social connections to solve the difficulty by consulting other farmers who have worked with the same crop.

4. **Retail management:** The proprietor of a retail store can keep track of inventory by connecting to the warehouse's smart devices.

5. **Health:** SIoT is used in the health business when a person is dealing with a health problem and does not know where to find a good health specialist. The person can consult a specialist by instructing their device to locate the doctor. This scenario employs co-location and social relationships in this scenario.

5.3 SIOT ARCHITECTURE

We use an architectural model for the IoT comprised of three layers to explain the proposed system. It consists of: (a) the sensing layer, which is responsible for collaboration of nodes for data acquisition in short-range and local networks; (b) the network layer is in charge of data transfer across multiple networks; and (c) the application layer is where IoT and middleware applications are implemented (Jabangwe and Nguyen-Duc, 2019). The objects, gateway, and server are the three main components of the proposed system.

5.3.1 Server in SIoT

Indeed, the network and application layers are covered by the SIoT server, not the sensor layer. The application layer consists of three sublayers. The management of data storage, as well as the associated descriptions, are part of the base sublayer. These keep track of the number of members' profiles and their relationships, as well as the behaviours of actual and virtual world objects.

The relevant ontologies are kept separate from the rest of the social activities and database, which is used to denote a semantic view. Appropriate semantic engines are used to extract such a view. A framework to interpret a machine for expressing features like functional, non-functional, and IoT device operations, ontology, and semantic services is required. Several studies in this area have already been conducted, and they could serve as a starting point for developing an ontology for use in the system (Mendhurwar and Mishra, 2021). Adopting the ontology web language for services model, which offers rich, descriptive, and well-defined semantic descriptions, is one option. Services are used as an interface in this framework to represent resources of the IoT (i.e., physical devices) and to enable operation access and its capability. An ontology is a core IoT property that aids the agent (human or machine) in reading a tag electronically and comprehending the data contained inside it. Ontological classification and semantic annotation techniques will be impossible to discover automatically.

As shown in Figure 5.2, tools that implement the SIoT system's essential functionality are found in the sub-layer component. The goal of ID management is to assign an ID that can be used to identify all potential object categories. The goal of profiling is to configure static or dynamic information both manually and automatically for objects. The owner control (OC) component allows you to define the kinds of actions that an object can undertake, the data that can be shared (between the set of objects that can access the information), and the types of associations that can be established. Because objects lack the intellect of humans when it comes to selecting friendships, relationship

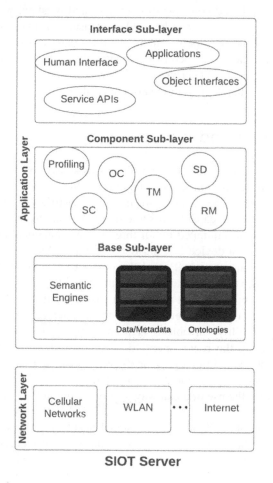

FIGURE 5.2   SIoT server.

management is a critical unit in a network. As a result, this intelligence must be implemented into the SIoT through which a part of the essential capacity is to be permitted among objects to start, update, and conclude friendships with different items.

The service discovery [SD] component plays a critical component that aims to discover which object can supply the desired facility in the similar manner that individuals search for friendships and data on networking sites that are social.

The service composition [SC] module allows objects to communicate with one another. The interaction is usually about an item that wants to retrieve data about the world or locate an object that provides a service. The ability of SIoT to support such information retrieval is the key potential in deployment. The service discovery technique uses entity relationships to find a preferred service, which is subsequently triggered by the component.

Finally, the trustworthiness management (TM) component aims to understand how the data provided by other members will be treated. Reliability is based on an object's behaviour, and it is intimately linked to the relationship management component. The literature-based concepts of centrality and prestige, which are critical in the learning of social networks, can be used to measure trustworthiness.

The interface sub-layer, which contains the third-party crossing point for humans, objects, and services, can be mapped to a solo site, distributed across multiple sites in a federated manner, or deployed on the cloud. We do not propose any specific implementation solution in this document (Skarmeta et al. 2014).

5.3.2 Gateway and Objects

In the case of systems like gateways and objects as shown in Figure 5.3, layer combination depends primarily on device features, which can be predicted in three eventualities. In a basic one, a fake object like an RFID tag or a sensing device presence with lowest-layer capable to send simple signals to other element (i.e., the gateway), which remains equipped by all three levels' functionalities.

In a different case, a device like a video camera is able to sense physical world data and transmit it via network IP, and the object can be configured with network layer capabilities rather than application layer functionality. As a result, a gateway with application layer capabilities is not required. It would be sufficient to have a server at the application layer on the internet with gateway application layer capability.

In the third possibility, an object, i.e., smart, may integrate the three levels of functionality, obviating the requirement for a gateway, but only for some message capabilities aimed at maintaining the device's internet connectivity. This situation with smart devices has sufficient computational capacity to conduct entirely three-layer processes but requires the use of a gateway to provide ubiquitous network connectivity (Tawalbeh et al. 2020).

The applications of SIoT, along with social agents and the service management agent, are all part of the application layer, regardless of the scenario used. The social agent's job is to communicate with SIoT servers to maintain its profile, friend-relationships, and identify and request services from the social network, which includes the ways of communicating directly with other objects.

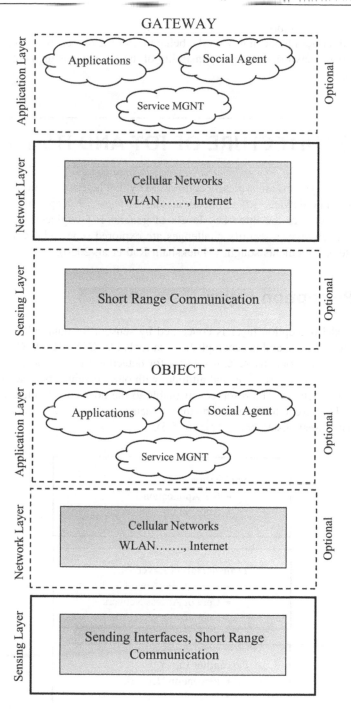

FIGURE 5.3 Gateway and object.

If the service composition requires it, or when they are physically close together, the human interfaces that can govern the behaviour of the objects when interacted with inside the social network are the responsibility of the service management agent (P and Sridhar, 2020).

5.4 ARCHITECTURE OF IOT AND ITS THREATS

Traditional IoT systems are typically epitomised by five layers, like: (a) perception, (b) network, (c) middleware, (d) application, and business. Perception, transport, and application layers are the three key levels of general IoT engineering, as shown in Figure 5.4. Each layer's security challenges are explored separately, with new robust and feasible arrangements sought (Malekshahi Rad et al. 2020).

5.4.1 Perception Layer

The IoT model perception layer is concerned by sensors for data collection and processing in IoT devices and is accomplished via tools like GPS, RFID, RSN, and WSN. The physical layer contains several sensors for detecting measurement quantities like humidity, temperature, pressure, and altitude, with other parameters as well as position identification functions. The resources available to the nodes are limited, and they are also required to have a distributive structure in their organisation, as well as the physical layer security threats listed below (Figure 5.5).

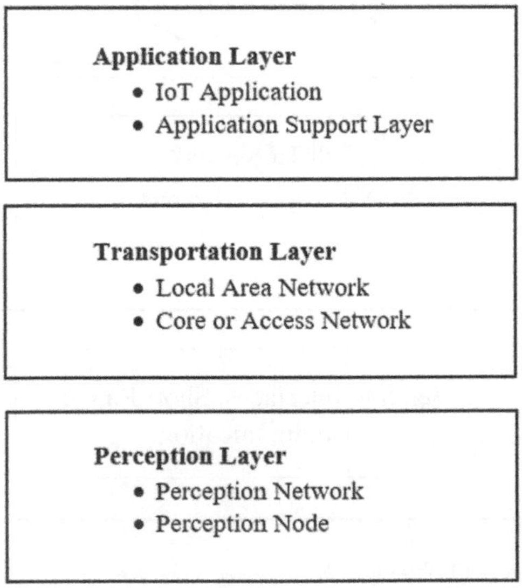

FIGURE 5.4   Three key levels of IoT engineering.

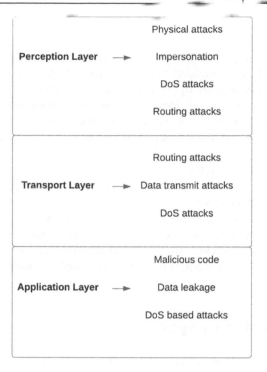

FIGURE 5.5   List of probable attacks in each layers.

  a. **Physical attacks:** The hardware-based attacks on IoT devices put distance
     between the attacker and the IoT system that needs close physical prox-
     imity to succeed. The following are some examples of known assaults of
     this type.
     i. **Tampering:** The attack is carried out by either physically replacing the
        nodes or a portion of the hardware or by interrogating electronically to
        access and modify critical information, such as routing data and keys.
    ii. **Malicious code:** Malicious software is injected materially for theft
        access to an IoT system, which compromises the nodes here.
   iii. **Impersonation:** The process of authentication in a distributed system
        is difficult, and hostile nodes will be utilised to generate an incorrect
        identity to commit collusion.
    iv. **DoS attacks:** Attackers have compromised the processing capability of
        the nodes, rendering them unavailable.
     v. **Routing attacks:** The hacked nodes in the middle of the data gathering
        and transmission process change the correct path for routing. WSNs are
        more likely to be affected by these events.
    vi. **Data transmission attacks:** These attacks compromise the confidentiality
        and integrity of data transmission mechanisms. Sniffing and MITM are
        examples of this type of attack.

5.4.2 Transport Layer

This layer ensures omnipresent access to the initial level. This level's major purpose is to send the acquired data from level first to another system level for processing across the network, which is utilised by all access networks (WiFi, 4G, MANET) or the internet. When compared to previous generations of cellular networks, many open frameworks of an LTE network are typically IP-based and are vulnerable in terms of security. The following are the key security risks that may develop at this time:

i. **Routing attacks:** Malicious programmes in the central area might change routing decisions, tables, and even cause harm throughout the data collection and transmission process.
ii. **DoS attacks:** The transport layers are especially vulnerable to assaults because of the IoT's involved and heterogeneous nature.
iii. **Data Transit Attacks:** Attacks can compromise sensitive data confidentiality and integrity while it is being transmitted via access grants or open networks.

5.4.3 Application Layer

This layer is suited to customer needs. For example, when consumers query the layer, it offers data such as temperature, atmospheric pressure, and other measurements. This data is critical for the development of IoT since it serves as the foundation for displaying the various needs of customers to create IoT devices in a multipurpose way. This layer can be used to build and implement various IoT ecosystems. Support for applications is subjected to support at its sub-level in all services that provide intelligent computing for better realization. In terms of application layer security, the following are the most significant threats:

i. **Data leakage:** Knowing about the security flaws in the application makes data theft fairly simple (for both attackers and users).
ii. **DoS-based attacks:** Attacks have the potential to harm the application entirely or the node service.
iii. **Malicious code:** Through knowledge of current vulnerabilities, certain malicious codes can be injected into the programme.

5.5 SIOT SECURITY

5.5.1 Challenges

SIoT integrates social technologies with the Internet of Things infrastructure, which comprises a wide range of devices/objects, networks based on distributed (fog or edge) or central computing (cloud) and storage, also a various systems and its applications including analytical tools. While increasingly powerful smart objects are anticipated for SIoT, evolutionary implementation architectures may regard these as co-located or cooperative value clusters of IoT devices with varying capacities. Numerous IoT-related components remain limited in terms of energy of node, high mobility, nodes' self-organization, short range connectivity, and intermittent dynamic routing necessitating stimulation incentives (P and Sridhar, 2020). The following are the many facets of security at various levels of SIoT:

1. **Perception layer:** Unauthorized access to the device or its data, as well as duplicating and blocking, are all possibilities along with the above. Side channel attacks on the perception layer (viruses, trojans, and so on) include attacks on the environment, crypto-analysis attacks, and software attacks. To prevent these types of attacks, we need to include security measures such as hash functions, encryption techniques, and anonymity, as well as assessment of risk and detection of intrusions, which are all available. We can also have embedded security by combination of techniques of hardware and software by security experts ensuring an efficient footprint while balancing energy and velocity using elliptic-curve-cryptography-based security solutions (ECC). Strange behaviour can be detected by identifying attack signatures and sensitive and infected nodes, part of network, can be cordoned off. Smart objects device security reinforced by network security managed by in house or third party.

2. **Network layer:** Security requirements at the network layer include integrity, anonymity, non-repudiation, and message recency; security requirements at the access level include access control, authentication, and authorization. Functional security needs are challenged when the number of devices, complexity, mobility, and distribution of entities grow, widening the attack surface. Intrusion detection, P2P encryption, routing security, and data integrity are some of the security methods that would likely benefit from the introduction of IPv6 since it will provide unified standards-based interfaces and architecture for the IoT network layer. For resource-limited entities, the edge/fog computing architecture allows security approaches such as the use of proxies to ensure integrity, authentication, access control, confidentiality, trust, non-repudiation, and privacy at the edge.

3. **Application layer:** Spear-phishing, malicious code injection, DoS, sniffing, and other attacks are common in this layer. Fault tolerance, identity management, energy-efficient security, management of keys, trust, governance, end-to-end security, big data, and transparency of data and group membership are some of the issues that affect this layer. IoT security and IoT forensics are becoming increasingly important. Centralized and collaborative IoT, connected and distributed Intranets of Things with IoT are some of the numerous types of IoT designs. However, a security architecture that includes the usage of encryption mechanisms, federated identity management, risk assessment, firewalls, and intrusion detection is recommended.

MQTT and COAP are two IoT communication protocols. From trusted gateways to edge devices, protocols are in charge of security. By combining stateless access tokens to enforce blockchain technology-based security, hash functions used in cryptography can enhance the security even further. Individual device firmware should be pre-computed using cryptographic hashes to overcome resource limits in IoT devices, avoiding masquerading, and assuring non-repudiation.

4. **Analytics layer:** SIoT's intelligence sets it apart from similar networks and other apps, allowing objects and humans to develop by sustaining interactions on their own for achieving ecosystem goals and creating value. This intelligence could be incorporated within the smart objects themselves or accessed externally by the CPSS cluster's objects. Adapting evolutionary computation intelligence methodologies from fields such as bioinformatics, financial engineering, cybersecurity and Internet of Things, where the main goal is to combat persistent, well-equipped invaders attempting to compromise cyber-physical systems, because they are commonly accepted that every system's security is only as good as its weakest link. Few perceive block chain technologies as serving as the foundation for several initiatives of digital transformations. A blockchain creates an auditable ledger, which is secure, distribute, transparent and immutable by allowing participants to implement routing, storage, wallet services, and mining that is completely examined from the beginning system transaction. The core idea is to leverage SHA 256 or Merkle tree and ECC hashed as strong proofs of nonrepudiation, authentication, and integrity to drive distributed trust via majority-consensus voting. As a result, SIoT leverages blockchains to establish appropriate levels of security, trust and privacy for data in transit while accounting for processing overheads such as payload transfers, computing delays, and so forth.

Because of its unique characteristics, SIoT is sensitive to multidimensional threats. Effective management, procedures, governance policies, guidelines and tools and techniques, as well as careful evaluation of architectural and technological choices, can all help to improve overall system security over time.

5.6 PRIVACY AND CONFIDENTIALITY IN SIOT

Researchers now have a better understanding of the vulnerabilities that exist in various IoT devices. Attacks of new kinds on IoT structures require a comprehensive security strategy to secure the system and data from beginning to end. Threat attacks that make use of flaws in individual devices to get access to devices that are more secure from the external are a driving force behind comprehensive security answers that cover work on best approaches in cryptography for non-cryptographic security techniques, system data security, and frameworks that make it easier for developers to create safe systems on heterogeneous devices. We need further exploration to enable people of completely skill levels to communicate and practice IoT systems, despite the restricted user interface available on most IoT equipment (Mawgoud et al. 2020).

Privacy in the IoT is one of the most important factors for storing personal information safely in an IoT context. To provide a physical or logical entity, it is hoped that a unique identifier and the capacity to talk separately over the internet would be provided. Since things transmit data on their own, privacy is essential in the IoT ecosystem (Roopa et al. 2018). The interoperability of items is also critical to the IoT's success. On its own, the data transmitted by an endpoint is unlikely to cause privacy concerns. Even fragmented information from various endpoints can yield sensitive information when assembled, grouped, and analyzed. A person or entity has the right to verify how much information they are willing to share with others.

The Internet of Things connects hundreds of billions of things to the internet. These items generate a large amount of personal information that must be handled, transmitted securely, and stored. In this endeavor, traditional confidentiality algorithms face various challenges. High requirements for scalability, heterogeneity of relevant building blocks and resource constraints in embedded devices, such as energy and processor restrictions, must all be addressed in IoT security solutions. Data confidentiality is a major constraint in the Internet of Things, ensuring access to and modification of certified entities via an access control system, as well as object authentication practise with an associated identity supervision system. In terms of confidentiality, defining an object authentication method and an access control system are two critical components (Zhang et al. 2022).

5.7 TRUST MANAGEMENT IN SIOT

Indeed, in the IoT, the trust management system (TMS) has been regarded as an effective solution for security, and many research studies were conducted to present prediction and trust evaluation approaches. When creating these inter-object social interactions, trust is crucial, and it is also necessary to assess an object's trustworthiness before relying on device information they offer. For SIoT, a number of trust evaluation models have been created, but due to a lack of adequate datasets, most of these approaches struggle to validate and verify their models.

In today's IoT technology, which deals with the interaction of things, trust issues are among the most urgent. Unauthorized access, loss of privacy, safety, and security, as well as information manipulation for individuals, are all problems brought on by a lack of confidence in socially collaborative objects. To have reliable communication, every object in the SIoT technology stacks must have a high level of confidence in its surrounding objects (Jabangwe and Nguyen-Duc, 2020). On the amount of confidence, a trust-based relationship also makes it easier to discriminate between trustworthy and hazardous objects.

Two of the most significant design issues for SIoT TM architecture are data protection and confidentiality. It's crucial to remember that these objects are heterogeneous, which introduces host object-level vulnerabilities and security problems. As a result, to protect the network from access control system threats, a security plan is required. As a result, it's necessary to create an effective TM control in SIoT networks to protect objects and the data they contain from illegal access. In the creation of TM solutions, the identification of trust types among smart objects is critical.

5.7.1 Trust Attacks for Security and Privacy

A. **Malicious with everyone (ME):** A node behaves in a malicious manner toward everyone. This is the most fundamental attack: regardless of the requester, a node provides bad advice and services (Faqihi et al. 2020).

B. **A discrimination attack:** This attack occurs when a node changes its behavior depending on who is requesting services. This means a node could distinguish between nodes that are not friends and nodes that have a weak social relationship.

C. **On-Off attack (OOA):** A node alternates between being benevolent (ON) and malicious (OFF) on a regular basis (OFF). The node builds up its trust during the ON state; after then, it's use to assault network.

D. **A whitewashing attack:** When a node with a bad reputation leaves a network and returns with a new identity, this is known as a whitewashing attack (WA). When a node rejoins the network, its reputation is reset to default number.

E. **Self-promotional attack:** To be chosen as a service provider, a malicious node makes best suggestions for itself. It only provides poor services after being chosen as a provider.

F. **Other attacks** focus on a particular target, such as malicious nodes that exclusively give harmful services/ a bad reputation.

G. **Bad-mouthing assault:** An attack seeks to smear the other node's reputation; a node, i.e., a malicious one, will offer fake proposals to diminish chances of benevolent nodes chosen as provider. Although it is carried out by a single node, the attack is frequently part of a collusive conduct in which the group nodes cooperate to devastate an expert node's reputation.

H. **Ballot stuffing attack:** This attack is a collusive attack in which a node, i.e., a malicious one, sends good suggestions to another to improve its reputation, boost its chance of being chosen as provider.

I. **Sybil attack:** A rogue node utilizes multiple identities to offer various types of proposals on the same service (SA). The identities are virtually always false, and are all part of attack.

J. **Opportunistic service attack:** When hostile nodes recognize that their trust reputation is degrading, they launch an opportunistic service attack (OSA). As a result, to choose a service provider, the node strives to maintain a reasonable degree of confidence.

5.8 CONCLUSION

There is a need for exponential research on the implications of present SIoT security frameworks. We feel that further study should be conducted on the fresh roles of attacks and new knowledge methodologies for researchers on invention, thoughts, and originality in a secure environment with machine-human interaction through the machine-learning techniques that connect to the real world of things using the Social Internet of Things. Future challenges like technical (connectivity, compatibility, and longevity), business (investment, modest revenue model etc.), and societal (changing demands, new devices, expense, customer confidence etc.) are to be compared for a better Social IoT.

REFERENCES

Bilal Afzal, Muhammad Umair, Ghalib Asadullah Shah, and Ejaz Ahmed. (2019). "Enabling IoT platforms for social IoT applications: Vision, feature mapping, and challenges." *Future Generation Computer Systems*, 92, 718–731. ISSN 0167-739X. doi: 10.1016/j.future.2017.12.002

Pooja Anand, Yashwant Singh, Arvind Selwal, Pradeep K. Singh, Raluca A. Felseghi, and Maria S. Raboaca. 2020. "IoVT: Internet of Vulnerable Things? Threat architecture, attack surfaces, and vulnerabilities in Internet of Things and its applications towards smart grids." *Energies*, 13(18), 4813.

Luigi Atzori, Antonio Iera, Giacomo Morabito, and Michele Nitti. (2012). "The Social Internet of Things (SIoT) – When social networks meet the Internet of Things: Concept, architecture and network characterization." *Computer Networks*, 56(16), 3594–3608. ISSN 1389-1286.

P.M. Chanal and M.S. Kakkasageri. (2020). "Security and privacy in IoT: A survey." *Wireless Personal Communications*, 115, 1667–1693.

Raddad Faqihi, Jayabrabu Ramakrishnan, and Dinesh Mavaluru. (2020). "An evolutionary study on the threats, trust, security, and challenges in SIoT (social internet of things)." *Materials Today: Proceedings*, ISSN 2214-7853.

Jianwei Hou, Leilei Qu, and Wenchang Shi. (2019). "A survey on internet of things security from data perspectives." *Computer Networks*, 148, 295–306. ISSN 1389-1286. doi: 10.1016/j.comnet.2018.11.026.

Ronald Jabangwe and Anh Nguyen-Duc. (2020). "Siot framework: Towards an approach for early identification of security requirements for internet-of-things applications." *e-Informatica Software Engineering Journal*, 14(1), 84.

Mengda Jia, Ali Komeily, Yueren Wang, Ravi S. Srinivasan. (2019). "Adopting Internet of Things for the development of smart buildings: A review of enabling technologies and applications." *Automation in Construction*, 101, 111–126. ISSN 0926-5805.

J. Lin, W. Yu, N. Zhang, X. Yang, H. Zhang, and W. Zhao. (Oct. 2017). "A survey on Internet of Things: Architecture, enabling technologies, security and privacy, and applications." *IEEE Internet of Things Journal*, 4(5), 1125–1142. doi: 10.1109/JIOT.2017.2683200

M. Malekshahi Rad, A.M. Rahmani, A. Sahafi et al. (2020). "Social Internet of Things: vision, challenges, and trends." *Human-centric Computing and Information Sciences*, 10, 52.

Ahmed A. Mawgoud, Mohamed Hamed N. Taha, and Nour Eldeen M. Khalifa. (2020). "Security threats of Social Internet of Things in the higher education environment." In Hassanien , A., Bhatnagar, R., Khalifa, N., Taha, M. (eds.) Toward Social Internet of Things (SIoT): Enabling Technologies, *Architectures and Applications*, pp. 151–171. Springer, Cham.

Subodh Mendhurwar and Rajhans Mishra. (2021). "Integration of social and IoT technologies: Architectural framework for digital transformation and cyber security challenges." *Enterprise Information Systems*, 15(4), 565–584. doi: 10.1080/17517575.2019.1600041

Kumaran P. and R. Sridhar. (2020). "Social Internet of Things (SIoT): Techniques, Applications and Challenges." *2020 4th International Conference on Trends in Electronics and Informatics (ICOEI)*(48184), pp. 445–450, doi: 10.1109/ICOEI48184.2020.9142908.

K.H. Rahouma, R.H.M. Aly, and H.F. Hamed (2020). "Challenges and solutions of using the Social Internet of Things in healthcare and medical solutions—A survey." In Hassanien A., Bhatnagar R., Khalifa N., Taha M. (eds.), Toward Social Internet of Things (SIoT): Enabling Technologies, Architectures and Applications. *Studies in Computational Intelligence*, vol. 846. Springer, Cham.

Pandharipande, Ashish (2021). Social Sensing in IoT Applications: A Review. IEEE Sensors Journal, 21, 12523–1253010.1109/jsen.2021.3049714.

M.S. Roopa, D. Valla, R. Buyya, K.R. Venugopal, S.S. Iyengar, and L.M. Patnaik. (2018). "SSSSS: Search for Social Similar Smart Objects in SIoT." *2018 14th ICINPRO*, pp. 1–6. doi: 10.1109/ICINPRO43533.2018.9096686.

M.S. Roopa, Santosh Pattar, Rajkumar Buyya, K.R. Venugopal, S.S. Iyengar, and L.M. Patnaik. (2019). "Social Internet of Things (SIoT): Foundations, thrust areas, systematic review and future directions." *Computer Communications*, 139, 32–57. ISSN 0140-3664.

A.F. Skarmeta, J.L. Hernández-Ramos and M.V. Moreno. (2014). "A decentralized approach for security and privacy challenges in the Internet of Things." *2014 IEEE World Forum on Internet of Things (WF-IoT)*, 67–72. doi: 10.1109/WF-IoT.2014.6803122.

Lo'ai Tawalbeh, Fadi Muheidat, Mais Tawalbeh, and Muhannad Quwaider. (2020). "IoT privacy and security: Challenges and solutions." *Applied Sciences*, 10(12), 4102. doi: 10. 3390/app10124102.

Zhang, Peiying, Wang, Yaqi, Kumar, Neeraj, Jiang, Chunxiao, & Shi, Guowei (2022). A Security- and Privacy-Preserving Approach Based on Data Disturbance for Collaborative Edge Computing in Social IoT Systems. *IEEE Transactions on Computational Social Systems*, 9, 97–10810.1109/tcss.2021.3092746.

Ivan Zyrianoff, Alexandre Heideker, Dener Silva, João Kleinschmidt, Juha-Pekka Soininen, Tullio Salmon Cinotti, and Carlos Kamienski. (2020). "Architecting and deploying IoT smart applications: A performance-oriented approach." *Sensors*, 20(1), 84.

Challenges and Solutions of Using Social Internet of Things (SIoT) in Healthcare and Medical Domains

6

Arulkumar N

Department of Computer Science, Christ Deemed to be University, Bangalore, India

Contents

DOI: 10.1201/9781003282990-6

6.1 IOT IN HEALTHCARE

Internet of Things (IoT) technologies can allow remote monitoring in hospitals to assist patients as well as physicians. This mode of communication could be made more convenient and productive by increasing patient participation. Hospital admissions and stays will be reduced when IoT is implemented in the healthcare and medical domains. Between 2022 and 2027, the global structural health monitoring market is expected to grow at a CAGR of around 15% to 17% concerning IoT adoption [1]. Additionally, the Internet of Things has a substantial influence on reducing healthcare expenses but also enhancing treatment outcomes. Unquestionably, the Internet of Things has been transforming the heath industry through facilitating the interaction of people with technology to provide healthcare services. The Internet of Things offers benefits, mainly in the healthcare business, that benefit patients and doctors.

6.1.1 SIoT in Healthcare

The Social Internet of Things (SIoT) is a subset of the Internet of Things (IoT) that enables social interactions between objects in hospitals when they are in the presence of humans. SIoT attempts to address IoT's sustainability, trustworthiness, and information identification challenges in healthcare and medical domains using social computing [2]. SIoT aims to maintain a barrier between people and things, allowing objects to use their own social networks while also allowing humans to impose privacy-protecting limitations and obtain access to just the results of autonomous inter-object interactions. The key challenges of implementing SIoT in healthcare and medical domains are given in Figure 6.1.

The University of Pittsburgh Medical Centre cut the chances of going back to the hospital by 76% and kept patient satisfaction levels above 90% by putting in remote patient-monitoring systems [3]. So, apart from some challenges, there are some significant advantages when the SIoT is considered for healthcare. They are:

- Collecting extra data about patients without placing an undue strain on patient care
- Improving the efficiency of patient treatment and management by eliminating manual data collection

FIGURE 6.1 Challenges of implementing SIoT in healthcare domains.

- Increasing patient participation in their treatment, leading to decreased hospital readmissions
- Using data from IoT devices to help people make good decisions and help healthcare operations run efficiently
- Using continuous patient-monitoring and real-time data to help doctors find illnesses before they show up, even if patients have no symptoms
- Facilitating improved outcomes and assuring that healthcare services operations function smoothly with minimal errors, waste, and operational costs by using information generated by sensor nodes [4].

6.2 RELATED WORKS ON SIOT IN HEALTHCARE

The SIoT is on its way in the healthcare domain to become customized for social media usage, enabling intelligent, connected gadgets in hospitals to create automatic updates and allow users to communicate regularly. This will create opportunities for better social-monitoring technologies that maximize the potential of thousands of linked smart devices in hospitals. Trayush T et al. surveyed the advances and challenges associated with IoT in healthcare [5]. Additionally, this article discusses the numerous devices and applications used in IoT healthcare. IoT healthcare technologies such as connectivity, location, sensing, and cloud computing improve management.

Khan M M et al. proposed an IoT-based method for a health screening that uses patients' recorded temperature, pulse, and oxygen levels, representing the vital metrics necessary in healthcare [6]. It can also be readily synced with a smartphone app for immediate access. The suggested Internet of Things-based technique is based on an Arduino Uno and was tested and confirmed. Comparing the system's results to those obtained from other commercially available equipment validated the accuracy of the system's findings.

Bouazza H et al. developed a Social IoT-based hybrid IoT service recommender system [7]. It is a hybrid system that involves implicit innovative filtering and ontology to provide consumers with individualized IoT services recommendations. The SIoT is modelled using an ontology in which we add the social links between items into the recommender system beside the evaluations, while collaborative filtering predicts ratings and creates suggestions. Regarding personalization and recommendation accuracy, the assessment findings suggest that the suggested recommendation method outperforms collaborative filtering without SIoT.

Gulati N. et al. conducted the research by deploying socially enabled IoT systems in an ambient assisted living (AAL) environment and developing FriendCare-AAL, a robust Social IoT-based AAL system for the elderly [8]. In addition, it introduces the concept of duty offloading across devices and gives a picture of how to set up a partnership between intelligent devices. The suggested technology can assist senior residents who live in intelligent home environments. In an emergency, the system sends out notifications right away to tell the right people about what is going on. To test the performance, an intelligent home AAL scenario for an elderly person is recreated using the human motion model 'home sensor simulator', and then a dataset of the elderly person's routines is constructed. Both Naive Bayes (NB) and Random Forest (RF) techniques are used to examine the data and predict the older person's well-being.

AI-Turjman F et al. completed an analysis of 5G-enabled devices in Social IoT [9]. It provides the primary reasons for carrying these smart gadgets in this research study and the association between the user's surrounding environment and application use. It also covers context-awareness in intelligent systems and paradigms for space exploration, online vs. offline, energy considerations, and continuing social IoT applications. Additionally, it identifies the most recent open research problems in this field.

The IoT could have more problems and attacks than benefits if it is not properly run. Marche C et al. showed the many ways that trust attacks could harm the IoT. They propose a trust governance model that could protect the IoT from many threats [10]. Analyses demonstrate how such a developed scheme can successfully distinguish practically whatever malicious devices are in the topology at the cost of increasing the frequency of activities required to focus on the design.

Gulati N et al. introduced a unique model design in SIoT systems, including argumentation [11]. The suggested approach serves as a conceptual basis for future applications in the aforementioned field. In addition, a game-theory weighted voting mechanism solves the challenges of dispute resolution in argumentation-based decision-making process. An intelligent residential supported-living scenario is simulated in MATLAB and verified. Consequently, the proposed method exhibits its effectiveness as a decision-making scheme in the Social IoT system. The proposed approach demonstrates its usefulness as a decision-making scheme in SIoT systems.

6.3 SUGGESTED COMMUNICATIONS AND MODELS FOR SOCIAL IOT

SIoT is about connecting many different devices and sensors to the internet to form a social network, but sometimes it is hard to see how they are connected. In SIoT, IoT devices connect to and interact with one another through the respective conceptual communication models of the organization. A successful and secured data transmission model depicts how the system operates and explains how the connection might be achieved [12,13]. The SIoT allows people and devices to connect regardless of their location, network, or service provider. There are different connectivity models used in the SIoT [14]. The purpose of the connections may vary from place to place and also based on the plan's necessity. These connection models are given in Figure 6.2. The following sections adds more information about the various connectivity models suggested for the Social IoT in healthcare and medical domains.

6.3.1 Device-to-Device Connectivity

It refers to two or more devices on a hospital network using IoT that can communicate directly. They interact over various networks, including IP networks and the internet, but almost always use Bluetooth, Z-Wave, and ZigBee protocols to connect using intelligent objects [15,16]. Home automation systems often use such a paradigm to transport communication signals in short data packets at a comparatively low rate. This might include light bulbs, thermostats, and door locks exchanging uncertain quantities of data by enabling IoT platforms for SIoT.

6.3.2 Device to the Internet (Cloud)

A Social IoT ecosystem is made up of web-enabled intelligent devices that collect, transmit, and analyse data from their respective hospital environments through integrated systems such as processors, sensor systems, and smartphones. Connecting devices to the cloud can be done by the admin in the hospital in a variety of ways, depending on how well they connect. For example, when you use the "device-to-cloud" data transmission method, your devices in the hospital could automatically connect to an internet cloud provider through wi-fi and the IP network to exchange

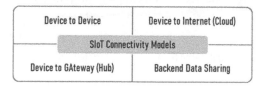

FIGURE 6.2 SIoT connectivity models.

data of the faculty and patients. The cloud concept lets admins in the hospital keep an eye on their devices from afar, such as smartphones or web browsers. In the hospital, these technologies consist of cellular, satellite, wi-fi network, low-power wide area networks, including direct ethernet internet access.

6.3.3 Device to Gateway (Hub)

The SIoT gateway, in its simplest terms, is an intelligent central hub for IoT devices in healthcare domains. Gateways in the hospital environment could connect devices and the cloud, transforming connectivity between mobile devices and data into useful information [17]. These can be virtual or physical devices. The IoT gateway functions as a network router for the hospital, connecting IoT devices to the internet. Several benefits of gateways are given in Figure 6.3.

Standard protocols: Gateways in the hospital may interface with sensors or devices through various connection methods and then convert the data to a standard protocol, including MQTT, for transmission to the cloud [18].

Unfiltered data: Gateways may pre-process patient data generated by sensors or devices, lowering the quantity of data sent, processed, then maintained by the SIoT system.

Delays: By executing operations on the gateway instead of in the clouds, gateways may minimize delays to maintain hospital records in time-critical activities.

Security: Because sensors or devices in SIoT are only linked to the gateway, the number of sensors or devices connected to the internet is reduced. Therefore, it makes gateways both targets and the first line of defence. That is why every gateway's security must be a top concern to care for a patient's record.

6.3.4 Cloud-Based Data-Sharing Model

The back-end (cloud-based) data-sharing model is the communication model for all the data services in the SIoT for the hospital concept. It is a connection framework that allows users to export as well as analyse large volumes of data from some cloud servers in conjunction with data from numerous healthcare sources. This design satisfies "the (user) wishes to provide third-party vendors access to the submitted sensor data." When patients and providers migrate from one IoT service to another, an efficient cloud-based data-sharing healthcare system framework facilitates the transmission of data. Extending the notion of device-to-cloud, this technology enables users to get and examine data from a large variety of intelligent devices. For example, a hospital business model may use this

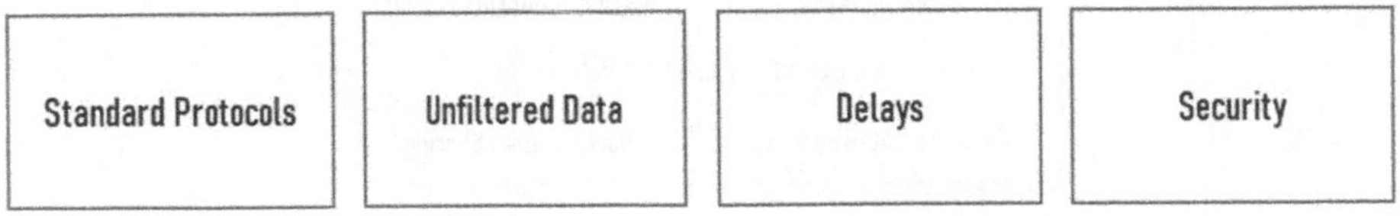

Standard Protocols	Unfiltered Data	Delays	Security

FIGURE 6.3 Benefits of gateways in SIoT.

paradigm to access patient information from all devices that operate inside the hospital. Additionally, this paradigm helps resolve data availability difficulties in maintaining hospital records.

6.4 HIERARCHICAL NETWORK DESIGN FOR SIOT IN HEALTHCARE

Flat network architecture is still used today in healthcare domains, but it is mainly used for minimal networks or for people who want to save money by using a few routers or switches. A hierarchical architecture breaks a network into different levels of operation management in healthcare, each with its functions [19]. In this way, a network designer for the hospital sector can choose the best hardware, software, and features for each network level.

6.4.1 Types of Layers

Usually, the levels in hierarchical network architecture are based on how the network is laid out. They may, however, vary, which is why it is better to think of them as logical levels. Although a three-layer form is the most popular, it is not required. There is no globally accepted architecture for the IoT. Numerous scholars have suggested various designs. These Internet of Things elements establish the basics of almost every IoT system worldwide. However, they are broken up into many different architectural layers to make the Internet of Things network even better [20]. Typically, a three-layer hierarchical network consists of the following:

- *Access layer:* The SIoTs' access layer network is a wireless sensor network (WSN), which consists of sensors as end devices. It allows workgroup or individual network access to the hospital.
- *Distribution layer:* This level of the SIoT enables connection based on policy and manages the boundary between the other two or more layers. It is sometimes called the "workgroup" layer because it is where routing and data filtering happen, so people call it that. It establishes a policy-based connection and manages the border between the access and core layers.
- *Core layer:* This is the network's backbone in the hospital for the proposed SIoT model. It enables rapid transfer across network distribution switches placed to share the data. It enables rapid transfer among distribution switches located across an organization's location.

6.4.2 SIoT Relationship Models for Hierarchical Design

The SIoT paradigm introduces new ways of managing object and devices interactions, allowing for expanding the functionality of SIoT in healthcare domains beyond the

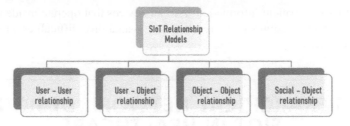

FIGURE 6.4 Possible SIoT relationship models.

current deterministic and limited processes that drive hospital communications. A SIoT network still requires the definition of a concept of social relationship between objects, the design of an architectural reference model [21–23]. The possible SIoT relationship models for the proposed SIoT model are given in Figure 6.4. The possible relationships should be established and managed automatically in the proposed healthcare domain using SIoT.

User–User relationship: This model creates a social network that helps to connect the users. Here, patients can connect with doctors through this SIoT network. Patient health monitoring and management are done quickly using this social network [24].

User–Object relationship: In this method, a user could connect with the IoT devices to create a social network. Here, patients, doctors, and admins could communicate using the objects (IoT devices). IoT devices help to connect the physical level to the social level. In addition, if an IoT module is linked to a patient, it receives information through its sensors, which are then monitored by the physicians.

Object–Object relationship: Objects in the SIoT network could process the data and send it directly to the remote device or a server using the wi-fi network. This process is performed automatically without any human interaction. Further, it also makes it more advantageous to monitor the patient. This method is also called the relationship of physical objects.

Social–Object relationship: This model connects the IoT devices with their owners to form a social network. Communication is formed by connecting the social level with the physical level.

6.5 PROPOSED SIOT MODEL FOR HEALTHCARE AND MEDICAL DOMAINS

Before incorporating SIoT into any business process like healthcare and medical domains, it is critical to understand how the network designer would build the design. Among other things, finding a reputable supplier of IoT solutions is easier and more successful than dealing with all of the different things that affect IoT design, like how many different things there are. This choice will result in a massive reduction in the number of resources spent on the sensors for the hospitals. In its simplest form, the SIoT architecture is a collection of disparate components: sensors, protocols, actuators, cloud services, and layers.

6.5.1 Five-Stage SIoT Solution Architecture for Healthcare

The architecture of the SIoT is broken up into layers so that admins in the hospital can make sure the system is working correctly for both faculty and patients. This should be considered before initiating the hospitals' IoT architecture procedure. In addition, long-term SIoT architectures must-have essential features like functionality, scalability, availability, and maintenance [25]. The SIoT architecture would fail to take care of the SIoT relationship models without solving these issues. Stages in implementing a social IoT architecture for healthcare and medical domains are given in Figure 6.5.

Connecting sensors and actuators: The distinguishing characteristic of sensors is their capacity to turn data from the external environment into data for analysis in hospitals that can save people. This process has moved forward thanks to the addition of sensors and actuators in hospital environments. Actuators go even further than this; these devices can change the world around them. They can, for example, turn off lights and modify the temperature in a room. Designers for hospitals may use hardware to elicit the data essential for further research about the hospital's requirements to create.

Monitoring using gateways (Hubs): Gateways connect sensors and other IoT modules and devices to the cloud. Gateways act as wireless access points on the campus for internet-connected IoT devices.

Report analysing: It is essential to include sensors in the early stages of the SIoT architectural framework to get the data used for analysing patient healthcare information. Admins could make decisions and take action based on their data from programs.

Data pre-processing: Sensors could be used in many different ways to get data in the healthcare field. Numerous data preparation procedures may account for most issues encountered throughout the analysis process. This enormous dataset is far from ideal; it contains several errors, like noise and outliers. It is unsuitable for analysis due to the possibility of inaccurate results. Choosing or building a SIoT system for healthcare domains is critical for enabling the efficient creation and execution of such scripts. This stage is intended to address various issues in the hospital, including data purification and

FIGURE 6.5 Five-stage SIoT solution architecture.

the creation of domain-specific functionality. It is commonly referred to as data wrangling, defined as iteratively exploring and transforming data to facilitate analysis. Thus, preparing digital data transformation is a necessary strategy for such domains.

Data storing: It is becoming more challenging to store healthcare data because more companies use artificial intelligence and analytics based on SIoT data. By using hybrid cloud data storage, healthcare businesses can keep their data onsite and still have control over their IT infrastructure's security. Patient data that has been aggregated and anonymized may be utilized for prediction. In-depth analysis may reveal tendencies that warrant more study, the creation of novel medications, or alternate diagnostic procedures.

6.5.2 Proposed SIoT Model for Healthcare Domain

As an initial stage of the SIoT model design process, the network gateways and switches are implemented using a CISCO packet tracer, given in Figure 6.6. It investigates the appropriateness of established analytical approaches for forecasting future connections in a dynamic and heterogeneous SIoT [26,27]. Gateways are designed for the patient (IPv4: 192.168.25.1), faculty (IPv4: 192.168.26.1), and office (IPv4: 192.168.27.1) for monitoring and management purposes. This model is designed to collect the movement of objects using the gateways and network switch, construct periodic sequence connections for the SIoT, and predict the object movement and associations between IoT devices.

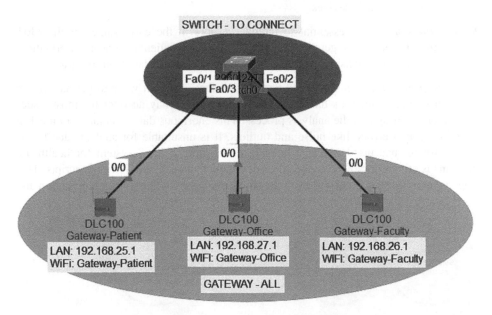

FIGURE 6.6 Gateways and switch in SIoT model for healthcare.

The following are the different IoT devices used in this model to create a Social IoT for the healthcare domain.

- *Laptop:* To wirelessly manage and monitor IoT devices through wi-fi gateways.
- *Door:* To control keyless entry systems that enable customers to enter doors wirelessly.
- *Siren:* To construct an alert profile, which may be applied to any networking location.
- *Fan:* A programmable intelligent fan for improved indoor air quality management.
- *Light:* Could be used in combination with the motion sensor to turn on when someone enters the room automatically.
- *Window:* It is used for ventilation and cooling; the building depends on controllable windows.
- *Webcam:* Its primary use is to send pictures and videos. Furthermore, it can process visual data without human participation, allowing for adopting a wide range of automated operations.
- *Bluetooth speaker:* It may assist doctors in making well-informed suggestions for the business.
- *Smoke detector:* It detects smoke, an essential fire indicator, and sounds an alarm to the building's members.
- *Air conditioner:* It allows the subscriber to monitor and operate the air conditioner from a distance.
- *Solar panel:* It features small solar cells that may be fitted to roofs to generate power from the sun.
- *Temperature monitor:* A hospital can remotely monitor and modify the temperature using an IoT-based temperature sensor. It also enables them to check the temperature of the things from afar and certify the product's quality.
- *Battery:* They have a low self-discharge rate. Therefore, they are ideal for devices that need to operate on minimal power for long periods.

The final proposed model without connection is given in Figure 6.7. IoT devices plays a vital role in monitoring and controlling the patients in hospitals [28–30]. This proposed model has IoT devices, network gateways, and a network switch for data communication. Patient–Room has the IoT devices like siren, light, Bluetooth speaker, laptop-admin, smoke detector, webcam, air conditioner, and door. The Office-Room has the IoT devices like laptop-office, light, door, webcam, solar panel, temperature monitor, siren, fan, window, and battery. IoT devices like door, siren, laptop-faculty, fan, light, window, webcam, and Bluetooth speakers have been used for the Faculty–Room.

6.5.3 Implementation Using CISCO Packet Tracer

The CISCO packet tracer is used to develop the scenario using the following procedures. The next section contains the specific details.

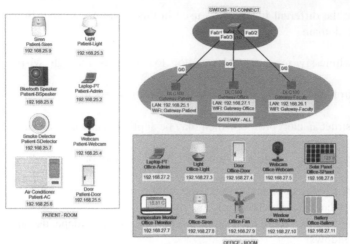

FIGURE 6.7 Proposed model without connection.

1. *Placing a network switch*
   Select Network Devices → Switches → Switch
2. *Employing three network gateways (Gateway-Patient, Gateway-Office, Gateway-Faculty) to connect with Switch0*
   Select Network Devices → Wireless Devices → Home Gateway
3. *Add IoT devices to the gateways*
   Select End Devices → Home → IoT Device
4. *Using a laptop to monitor the IoT network*
   Select End Devices → End Devices → Laptop
   Laptop "Office-Admin" → Connected to Gateway-Office
   Laptop "Patient-Admin" → Connected to Gateway-Patient
   Laptop "Faculty-Admin" → Connected to Gateway-Faculty
5. *Connect all the IoT devices to gateways using Wi-Fi*
   Gateway-Patient: Laptop, Siren, Light, Bluetooth Speaker, Smoke Detector, Webcam, Air-Conditioner, Door
   Gateway-Office: Laptop, Light, Door, Webcam, Solar Panel, Temperature Monitor, Siren, Fan, Window, Battery
   Gateway-Faculty: Laptop, Door, Siren, Fan, Light, Window, Webcam, Bluetooth Speaker
6. *Assign an IP address to all the devices*
7. *Control and monitor the IoT devices through gateways*
   Laptop "Office-Admin" → Gateway-Office → Office-Room
   Laptop "Patient-Admin" → Gateway-Patient → Patient-Room
   Laptop "Faculty-Admin" → Gateway-Faculty → Faculty-Room

6.5.4 IoT Devices Configuration

Configuring each IoT device in the model can secure the system. Table 6.1 gives a completed details of the IPv4 address of the IoT devices used for the proposed model, for example, configuring the IoT device (door) is given in Figure 6.8. Here, gateway is assigned with IPv4: 192.168.27.1, and the "home gateway" is selected as the IoT server.

TABLE 6.1   IP address of the devices

DEVICE	IP ADDRESS	SUBNET MASK	GATEWAY ADDRESS
Room: Faculty-Room			
Gateway-Faculty	192.168.26.1	255.255.255.0	***
Faculty-Laptop	192.168.26.2	255.255.255.0	192.168.26.1
Light	192.168.26.3	255.255.255.0	192.168.26.1
Webcam	192.168.26.4	255.255.255.0	192.168.26.1
Bluetooth Speaker	192.168.26.5	255.255.255.0	192.168.26.1
Window	192.168.26.6	255.255.255.0	192.168.26.1
Fan	192.168.26.7	255.255.255.0	192.168.26.1
Siren	192.168.26.8	255.255.255.0	192.168.26.1
Room: Patient-Room			
Gateway-Patient	192.168.25.1	255.255.255.0	***
Patient-Laptop	192.168.25.2	255.255.255.0	192.168.25.1
Light	192.168.25.3	255.255.255.0	192.168.25.1
Webcam	192.168.25.4	255.255.255.0	192.168.25.1
Door	192.168.25.5	255.255.255.0	192.168.25.1
Air Conditioner	192.168.25.6	255.255.255.0	192.168.25.1
Smoke Detector	192.168.25.7	255.255.255.0	192.168.25.1
Bluetooth Speaker	192.168.25.8	255.255.255.0	192.168.25.1
Siren	192.168.25.9	255.255.255.0	192.168.25.1
Room: Office-Room			
Gateway-Office	192.168.27.1	255.255.255.0	***
Laptop-Office	192.168.27.2	255.255.255.0	192.168.27.1
Light	192.168.27.3	255.255.255.0	192.168.27.1
Door	192.168.27.4	255.255.255.0	192.168.27.1
Webcam	192.168.27.5	255.255.255.0	192.168.27.1
Solar Panel	192.168.27.6	255.255.255.0	192.168.27.1
Temperature Monitor	192.168.27.7	255.255.255.0	192.168.27.1
Siren	192.168.27.8	255.255.255.0	192.168.27.1
Fan	192.168.27.9	255.255.255.0	192.168.27.1
Window	192.168.27.10	255.255.255.0	192.168.27.1
Battery	192.168.27.11	255.255.255.0	192.168.27.1

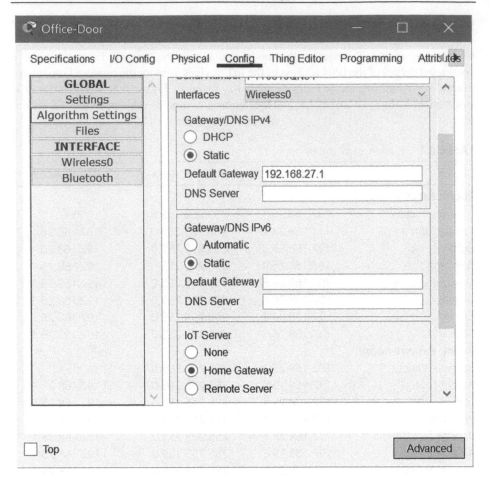

FIGURE 6.8 IoT device configuration (e.g., door).

The following are the general steps to configure all the IoT devices used to create a SIoT model for the healthcare domain. e.g., door.

1. *Add IoT devices to the model*
   Select End Devices → Home → IoT Device
2. *Configuring the IoT device*
   A. *Select IoT Device → Advance→ I/O Config → Select N/W Adapter*
   B. *Select IoT Device → Config → Global Settings → Change: Display Name, Gateway, IoT Server*
3. *Assigning the Wi-Fi network*
   Select IoT Device → Interface → Wireless0 → Configure: SSID, Authentication, and IP Config

The proposed working model with complete configuration is given in Figure 6.9. It has one network switch and three gateways to control the network.

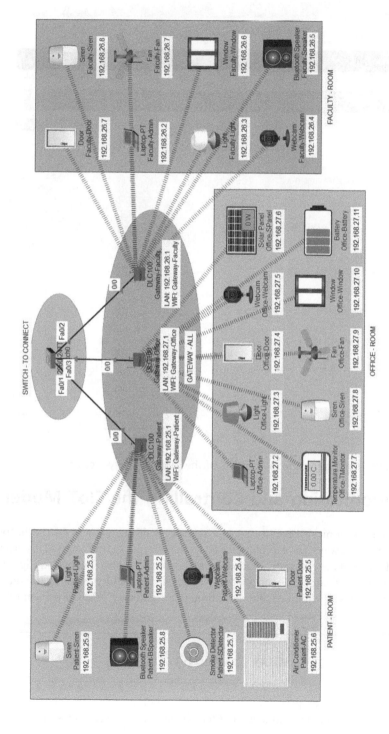

FIGURE 6.9 Proposed SIoT model for the healthcare domain.

FIGURE 6.10   Controlling the SIoT model of the room "Faculty–Admin".

6.5.5 Monitoring and Controlling the SIoT Model

All communication must travel through or connect with the gateway before becoming routed. Hence, gateways serve as entrance and exit nodes for the networks. This proposed SIoT model uses three gateways to monitor and control the social network. Figure 6.10 shows the user interface of the connected IoT devices in the Faculty–Room. The admin can control the IoT devices in this dialog box through the gateway "Gateway–Faculty".

6.6 SUMMARY

Before the Social IoT, patients' contacts and relationships with physicians were restricted to in-person appointments and telephone and text exchanges. There has not been a way for doctors or hospitals to check patients' health regularly and help them make good decisions about what to do about their health. The IoT-connected devices have enabled monitoring and control in the healthcare domains, unlocking the potential to keep people healthy and allowing doctors to give superior treatment. Also, technology has made it easier and faster for patients and doctors to work together, which has made them more involved and motivated. Remote tracking of a patient's condition helps in reducing the length of hospitalisation and preventing readmissions.

The chapter discusses the problems associated with deploying the SIoT in healthcare. Prior to studying alternative SIoT connection models, related papers were studied. A hierarchical network model is established for healthcare that connects to one or more nodes that are one step down in the hierarchy notion. Five-stage solution architecture is proposed to handle and monitor the social network in the healthcare domains. In hospitals, network equipment such as gateways, switches, and IoT devices are utilized to establish social relationships. CISCO packet tracer is used to construct and operate this mainly built social network for healthcare.

In addition, SIoT has a major impact on reducing healthcare costs and improving treatment outcomes. The SIoT is transforming the healthcare industry by redefining the area of technology, human interaction, and connections when offering healthcare solutions. The Internet of Things contains healthcare applications that help patients and physicians [31].

REFERENCES

[1] Franchi, F., Marotta, A., Rinaldi, C., Graziosi, F., Fratocchi, L., and Parisse, M. 2022. What can 5G do for public safety? Structural health monitoring and earthquake early warning scenarios. *Sensors*, Vol.22(8): 3020.

[2] Roopa, M. S., Siddiq, A., Buyya, R., Venugopal, K. R., Iyengar, S. S., and Patnaik, L. M. 2020. Dynamic management of traffic signals through social IoT. *Procedia Comput. Sci.*, Vol.171: 1908–1916.

[3] Holland, J., Kingston, L., McCarthy, C., Armstrong, E., O'Dwyer, P., Merz, F., and McConnell, M. 2021. Service robots in the healthcare sector. *Robotics*, Vol.10(1): 47.

[4] Krishnamoorthy, S., Dua, A., and Gupta, S. 2021. Role of emerging technologies in future IoT-driven Healthcare 4.0 technologies: a survey, current challenges and future directions. *J. of Ambient Intell. and Hum. Comp.*, Vol.2021: 1–47.

[5] Trayush, T., Bathla, R., Saini, S., and Shukla, V. K. 2021. *IoT in Healthcare: Challenges, Benefits, Applications, and Opportunities*. Int. Conf. on Advance Comput. and Innovative Tech. in Eng. (ICACITE). 107–111.

[6] Khan, M. M., Mehnaz, S., Shaha, A., Nayem, M., and Bourouis, S. 2021. IoT-based smart health monitoring system for COVID-19 patients. *Comput. Math. Methods Med.*, Vol.2021.

[7] Bouazza, H., Said, B., and Laallam, F. Z. 2022. A hybrid IoT services recommender system using social IoT. *J. of King Saud Uni. Comp. Info. Sci.*, Vol.2022.

[8] Gulati, N., and Kaur, P. D. 2021. FriendCare-AAL: A robust social IoT based alert generation system for ambient assisted living. *J. of Ambient Intell. and Hum. Comp.*, 1–28. 10.1007/s12652-021-03236-3

[9] Al-Turjman, F. 2019. 5G-enabled devices and smart-spaces in social-IoT: An overview. *Future Gener. Comput. Syst.*, Vol.92: 732–744.

[10] Marche, C., and Nitti, M. 2020. Trust-related attacks and their detection: A trust management model for the social IoT. *IEEE Trans. Netw. Serv. Manage.*, Vol.18(3): 3297–3308.

[11] Gulati, N., and Kaur, P. D. 2020. A game theoretic approach for conflict resolution in argumentation enabled social IoT networks. *Ad Hoc Netw.*, Vol.107: 102222.

[12] Jaishankar, B., Vishwakarma, Santosh, Mohan, Prakash, Pundir, Aditya Kumar Singh, Patel, Ibrahim, and Arulkumar, N. 2022. Blockchain for securing healthcare data using squirrel search optimization algorithm. *Intell. Autom. Soft Compu.*, Vol.32(3): 1815–1829.

[13] Neelakandan, S., Rene Beulah, J., Prathiba, L., Murthy, G. L. N., Irudaya Raj, E. F., and Arulkumar, N. 2022. Blockchain with deep learning-enabled secure healthcare data transmission and diagnostic model. *Int. J. Model. Simul., and Sci. Comput.*, Vol.2022: 2241006.

[14] Khelloufi, A., Ning, H., Dhelim, S., Qiu, T., Ma, J., Huang, R., and Atzori, L. 2020. A social-relationships-based service recommendation system for SIoT devices. *IEEE Internet Things J.*, Vol.8(3): 1859–1870.

[15] Naidu, G. A., and Kumar, J., 2019. Wireless protocols: Wi-fi son, bluetooth, zigbee, z-wave, and wi-fi. *Innovations Electron. Commun. Eng.*, Vol.2019: 229–239.

[16] Lombardi, M., Pascale, F., and Santaniello, D., 2021. Internet of things: A general overview between architectures, protocols and applications. *Information*, Vol.12(2): 87.

[17] Neelakandan, S., Berlin, M. A., Tripathi, S., Devi, V. B., Bhardwaj, I., and Arulkumar, N., 2021. IoT-based traffic prediction and traffic signal control system for smart city. *Soft Comp.*, Vol.25(18): 12241–12248.

[18] Mishra, B., and Kertesz, A. 2020. The use of MQTT in M2M and IoT systems: A survey. *IEEE Access*, Vol.8: 201071–201086.

[19] Jiang, S., Firouzi, F., Chakrabarty, K., and Elbogen, E. B. 2021. A resilient and hierarchical IoT-based solution for stress monitoring in everyday settings. *IEEE Internet Things J.*TechRxiv. Preprint. https://doi.org/10.36227/techrxiv.13728199.v2

[20] Onasanya, A., and Elshakankiri, M. 2021. Smart integrated IoT healthcare system for cancer care. *Wireless Networks*, Vol.27(6): 4297–4312.

[21] Roopa, M. S., Pattar, S., Buyya, R., Venugopal, K. R., Iyengar, S. S., and Patnaik, L. M. 2019. Social Internet of Things (SIoT): Foundations, thrust areas, systematic review and future directions. *Comput. Commun.*, Vol.139: 32–57.

[22] Loscri, V., Manzoni, P., Nitti, M., Ruggeri, G., and Vegni, A. M. 2019. A social internet of vehicles sharing SIoT relationships. In Proc. of the ACM MobiHoc Workshop on Pervasive Syst. IoT Era, (October): 1–6.

[23] Farhadi, B., Rahmani, A. M., Asghari, P., and Hosseinzadeh, M. 2021. Friendship selection and management in social internet of things: A systematic review. *Comput. Netw.*, Vol.201: 108568.

[24] Cai, B., Li, X., Kong, W., Yuan, J., and Yu, S. 2021. A reliable and lightweight trust inference model for service recommendation in SIoT. *IEEE Internet Things J.*

[25] Rahouma, K. H., Aly, R. H., and Hamed, H. F. 2020. Challenges and solutions of using the Social Internet of Things in healthcare and medical solutions—A survey. In *Toward SIoT: Enabling Technol., Archit. Appl.*, 13–30.

[26] AbdulGhaffar, A., Mostafa, S. M., Alsaleh, A., Sheltami, T., and Shakshuki, E. M. 2020. Internet of things based multiple disease monitoring and health improvement system. *J. of Ambient Intell. and Hum. Comp.*, Vol.11(3): 1021–1029.

[27] Abuelkhail, A., Baroudi, U., Raad, M., and Sheltami, T. 2021. Internet of things for healthcare monitoring applications based on RFID clustering scheme. *Wireless Netw.*, Vol.27(1): 747–763.

[28] Pradhan, B., Bhattacharyya, S., and Pal, K. 2021. IoT-based applications in healthcare devices. *J. Healthcare Eng.*, Vol.2021(March).
[29] Woo, M. W., Lee, J., and Park, K. 2018. A reliable IoT system for personal healthcare devices. *Future Gener. Comput. Syst.*, Vol.78: 626–640.
[30] Maktoubian, J., and Ansari, K. 2019. An IoT architecture for preventive maintenance of medical devices in healthcare organizations. *Health Technol.*, Vol.9(3): 233–243.
[31] Mohammadi, V., Rahmani, A.M., & Darwesh, A.M. (2019). Trust-based recommendation systems in Internet of Things: a systematic literature review. *Hum. Cent. Comput. Inf. Sci*, 9, 21. https://doi.org/10.1186/s13673-019-0183-8

Social Aspects of D2D Communications in IoT for 5G and beyond Cellular Networks

7

Pradip Kumar Barik[1], Putul Gorai[2], and Raja Datta[3]

[1]*Department of Information and Communication Technology, Pandit Deendayal Energy University, Gandhinagar, Gujarat, India*
[2]*Department of Electronics and Communication Engineering, NIT Durgapur, West Bengal, India*
[3]*Department of Electronics and Electrical Communication Engineering, IIT Kharagpur, West Bengal, India*

Contents

DOI: 10.1201/9781003282990-7

7.1 INTRODUCTION

With the development of advanced wireless technologies, the data rate requirement of various electronic devices is also increasing. Users often create a social network for sharing information where collaboration among different network entities is essential. Device-to-device (D2D) communication is one of the popular technologies that help in creating such social networks [1]. Proximity users create a direct link using short-range communication technologies such as wi-fi direct or cellular 5G; this allows a high-speed data transfer. D2D communication excludes the requirement of a powerful central controller and hence reduces the capital expenditure (CAPEX) of the network operator. There are several advantages of D2D communication in SIoT (Social Internet of Things), such as enhanced physical layer throughput, lower latency, higher spectral efficiency, lesser energy consumption, and reduced congestion in core networks [2]. However, there are several challenges faced by D2D communication in SIoT, mainly peer discovery, mode selection, resource allocation and management, interference coordination, transmission power control, and upgrading existing infrastructure for supporting the requirements of advanced applications [3].

In the past few years, several advancements have been made on the state-of-art D2D communication technologies with respect to massive machine type communications (mMTC) in IoT, as shown in Figure 7.1. As the number of connected devices in SIoT increases day-by-day, there are requirements for quick and stable updates of the current wireless technologies. Researchers have found innovative ideas on integrating D2D communication for improving the performance of SIoT. Several social networking features, such as interaction among social entities, creation of social links, and the concept of centrality, have been integrated with D2D communication to improve its effectiveness. D2D networks are also inspired by various social networking platforms such as Facebook, Instagram, Google Meet, Twitter, etc., where users collaborate by

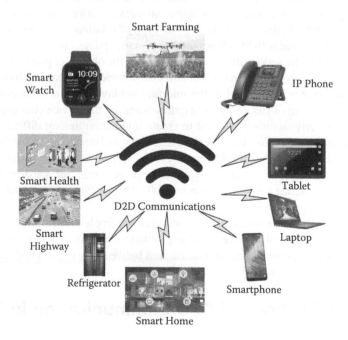

FIGURE 7.1 D2D communications: An integral part of IoT.

sharing their information. Researchers apply such social attributes to many short-range communications to create SIoT networks where D2D communication is an integral part.

7.1.1 Social IoT: Social Networks on IoT

The Internet of Things (IoT) is an integration of electronic gadgets, smart devices, and sophisticated machines that are connected using internet. In this IoT system, various computation capable devices connect and exchange data with other devices and systems. Integration of social networks in IoT (also called SIoT) has been introduced recently to improve network performance. This integration is performed by incorporating the idea of socialization (first introduced by Holmoquist et al. [4]) between different IoT objects. These objects establish a social relationship with each other without human intervention. Such relationships are mainly categorized into 1) parental, 2) co-location, 3) co-work, 4) ownership, and 5) social object relationship [3].

SIoT architecture consists of three layers: i) a sensing layer, which is used for data acquisition in local networks; ii) a network layer, used for transferring data across different networks, and iii) an application layer, where the IoT applications are executed. Each of these layers performs specific tasks based on social interactions of three SIoT elements: the SIoT server, the gateway, and the object [5]. The SIoT server includes the network layer and the application layer. The application layer contains three sublayers. The base sublayer includes a database for the storage and management of data. The social member profiles and their relationships are stored here. The component sublayer contains essential tools that perform the primary function of the SIoT system. ID management is used to assign an ID to the objects. Profiling configures the information about the objects. Owner control (OC) defines the activities and type of relationship between the objects. Relationship management (RM) allows objects to start, update, and end their relationship with other objects. The service discovery (SD) selects the object for providing the desired service. The service composition (SC) enables the interaction between objects. Objects, humans, and services are located in the interface sublayer. The combination of layers varies in gateway and object components, depending on the device characteristics.

Four main activities are processed to create interaction among different SIoT elements: the entrance of a new object, service discovery and composition, establishment of new object relationship, and service provisioning. Concerning the existing D2D communication architecture, a separate layer has been deployed for sensing the physical world for short-distance communication in SIoT. The gateway component and service discovery module are also included in this architecture.

The relationship management functionalities are implemented only into the SIoT server, which does not collaborate with the gateways and objects. Therefore, a problem exists in establishing continuous communication between the objects and the servers in updating their relationship [3].

7.1.2 Applications of D2D Communication in SIoT

There are different application scenarios of D2D communication in social IoT. These applications are mainly categorized into healthcare services, proximity services for sharing content, online gaming, quick disaster management, autonomous vehicle, ubiquitous computing, etc. All such applications require forming a social network where users are connected using peer-to-peer connections. The flow of messages may be either unicast or multicast, depending on the type of application.

7.1.2.1 Healthcare services

These services integrate monitoring sensors with health equipment to enable real-time health monitoring of patients [6]. Doctors from different places may create a network and perform remote treatment using smart devices and robots. Multiple types of equipment are involved here; they may be connected using peer-to-peer D2D links and collaborate by forming social networks.

7.1.2.2 Proximity services

Various social and commercial applications need information sharing between users and users to a central control system. User equiments (UEs) often create a local group for content sharing (such as photos and videos), multiplayer gaming, local multi-casting (sharing promotion messages from shops to neighbor customers), and context-based services [7–9]. D2D communication is the best choice for providing such services as it offers higher data rates, lower delays, and reduced data load on cellular networks.

7.1.2.3 Online gaming

Mobile users often download gaming maps from cloud servers using wireless networks. Content uploading or downloading via cellular networks results in poor user experience due to more latency in accessing the maps. Proximity users may create a social network where one or more users pre-load required content from a server and share the cached data with others using D2D communications. The selection of pre-fetched maps, cloud servers, and users for caching data are the main challenges in implementing such a scheme [10].

7.1.2.4 Disaster management

During a disaster, user devices create temporary ad-hoc IoT networks (where thye computations are performed on cloud) that integrates various electronic devices to share information. D2D communication extends the coverage range of cellular networks and provides essential services to the users when the existing networking infrastructure is damaged [11]. Information sharing via relayed D2D communication is also helpful in disaster management and public safety where the traditional cellular networks are paralyzed.

7.1.2.5 Machine-to-machine communications (M2M)

M2M communication is an integral part of Internet of Things (IoT) in 5G. It involves connectivity between various electronic gadgets starting from low-power hand-held devices to powerful computation- rich devices. For example, smartphones and television may be connected wirelessly for sharing various multimedia contents. A smartphone may also be used as a remote device to control TV programs. A popular application of D2D communication is the vehicular networks, where D2D links are used for sharing information between two or more vehicles (V2V communication). It may also be used in vehicle-to-infrastructure and vehicle-to-pedestrian communications. D2D is a key enabling technology in all such M2M communications [12].

7.1.2.6 Ubiquitous computing

Ubiquitous computing is a crucial factor for future IoT systems. A device with high battery energy and high computational capability may potentially act as a hotspot for the low-battery and low computational capability users in the network. Here, users with low processing capabilities may offload the heavy tasks to the nearby devices having high processing power using D2D communication [13].

7.1.3 Challenges of D2D Communications in SIoT

D2D communication has many use cases for meeting the requirements of upcoming cellular networks. However, introducing D2D communication in existing cellular network infrastructure engenders several design issues and challenges. It requires sophisticated methods and techniques to overcome the problems such as device discovery, synchronization, mode selection, resource allocation, power control, interference management, pricing, mobility management, and security.

7.1.3.1 Device discovery

Peer discovery is an essential aspect of the successful implementation of D2D communication for availing IoT-based services. It may be either user-controlled or network-controlled. In user-controlled peer discovery, a UE finds its partner without the involvement of base station (BS). There are two kinds of user-controlled techniques: restricted and open. A user cannot discover other nearby devices unless they are willing to participate in a restricted case. The frequency of pilot messages plays a vital role in user-controlled discovery methods. In the second case, user permission is not required for finding D2D pairs, whereas, in network-controlled discovery, the BS provides admission control depending on the physical location of the devices and their channel qualities.

7.1.3.2 Synchronization

Synchronization between D2D users and the base stations is another research issue for D2D communication. Local synchronization is necessary here as D2D pairs form a short-range connection. The situation is challenging under the following circumstances [14,15].

i. Intercell D2D communication where the D2D Tx-Rx pairs are located in different cells and the connected BSs are not synchronized.
ii. D2D pair is outside of the coverage range of a BS.
iii. Distances from the BS to the D2D transmitter and to the D2D receiver are not the same, which requires timing adjustment in advance. Synchronization is often necessary to maintain frame and slot time synchronization for device discovery and communication with peers in an energy-efficient manner.

7.1.3.3 Mode selection

UEs can decide the mode of transmission for D2D communication (i.e., direct or via BS) from a number of choices. The best mode may be chosen for optimizing the network performance incorporating network load, interference profile, the channel quality of the D2D links, etc. [16,17]. Users may switch to the cellular mode of transmission if the channel quality of the D2D link is unsuitable for satisfying data rate demand. Different objectives are considered in solving the mode selection problem: energy efficiency, spectrum reuse, throughput maximization, low delay, and minimal power consumption. Here, channel quality measurement and reporting frequency must be kept at a minimum level to avoid more control overhead at the BS.

7.1.3.4 Resource allocation

Resource allocation is an important step for creating a D2D connection and transferring data using the assigned subcarriers. Depending on the availability of free resources, BS can allow a D2D user to use orthogonal or non-orthogonal resources. D2D users may use uplink or downlink resources. In the overlay, D2D users use η fraction of the available spectrum and the remaining $(1 - \eta)$ fraction is used by the cellular users. In contrast, cellular users (CUs) share their allotted resources with D2D users in the underlay mode [18]. There are various optimization techniques in literature that provide optimal resources to the D2D pairs in cellular networks [19].

7.1.3.5 Interference management

Due to the sharing of uplink (UL) or downlink (DL) resource blocks (RBs) between CUs and D2D pairs, interference is created at different entities in the system, as shown in Figure 7.2. Interference can be reduced using a lower transmission power of the D2D transmitters; however, it affects the users' QoS. There are different interference-aware resource and power allocation techniques in the literature that maximize the system's sum rate, subject to QoS and power constraints [20,21]. Mode selection, interference management, and power control are so closely related that these are often jointly optimized [22,23].

7.1.3.6 Pricing and incentives

Finding a pricing and charging rule for D2D users is a pressing issue for cellular operators. Various pricing models are discussed in [24]. For example, the cellular service provider

(a)

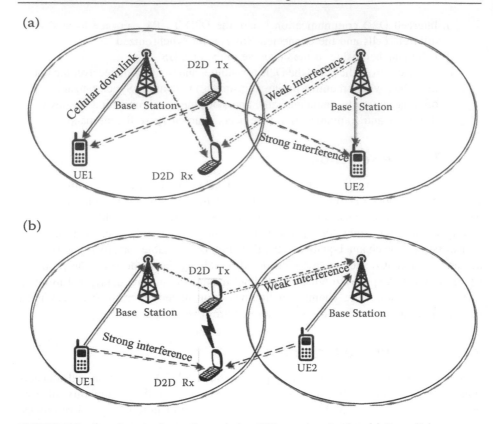

(b)

FIGURE 7.2   Interference issues in underlay D2D communication (a) Downlink resource sharing (b) Uplink resource sharing.

may give incentives such as free data or talk time to the users who participate in D2D relay-based data forwarding procedure. Operators may also include chargeable services such as commercial services, cluster-based communications, security, etc. [25,26].

7.1.3.7 Mobility management

The design of D2D communication protocols in the presence of mobility is still an ongoing research challenge [16]. Most of the work considers static D2D users that may not happen in reality. In many cases, the existing D2D communication protocols fail when the users are mobile, i.e., traveling in vehicles, V2V communications, pedestrian movements, etc. Therefore, sophisticated techniques and algorithms need to be designed to solve such issues [24,27,28].

7.1.3.8 Security

As D2D communications do not need the direct involvement of BS, there is always a possibility of security attacks such as malware attacks, phishing, denial-of-service

(DOS), man-in-the-middle, and eavesdropping, to name a few. A manager is often required to provide security of all applications. Without a central control entity, it is hard to ensure security in all the D2D applications. D2D security is controlled by the *ProSe* application function in three different domains: 1) between 3GPP networks and *ProSe* application servers, 2) between D2D devices and *ProSe* application servers, and 3) between the D2D devices. Security threats are modeled in three different ways based on whether the attacker is active or passive, internal or external, and local or global [27]. Several techniques to ensure security in D2D-enabled cellular networks are discussed in [29].

7.2 SYSTEM DESCRIPTION OF SOCIALLY AIDED D2D COMMUNICATION

As mentioned in the introduction section, D2D communication is a proximity-based data transmission technique where two or more devices create direct links for achieving the following benefits:

- higher bit rate, lower latency, improved spectrum, and power efficiency.
- reduction of base station load by offloading cellular traffic.
- use of both licensed and unlicensed (WiFi-direct) spectrum for achieving better performance.

Social networking may further improve the performance of D2D communication where devices may assist each other by the rules of social relationships. Therefore, the devices form a collaborative group. The key issues that arise when integrating social aspects into D2D communications are as follows:

7.2.1 Peer Discovery

Peer discovery is the most important criterion before the D2D communication takes place. The effectiveness of D2D communication depends on designing an algorithm that selects a D2D pair quickly and efficiently. Peer selection may be centralized where the BS controls the discovery mechanism or distributed where devices themselves may find a suitable partner. A distributed algorithm is time and energy-consuming as network support is unavailable here.

7.2.2 Mode Selection

A device may communicate directly by creating a peer-to-peer connection, or they can offload traffic via a base station. Proper mode selection algorithms help in load balancing, latency reduction, priority-based data services, and energy-optimized transmissions.

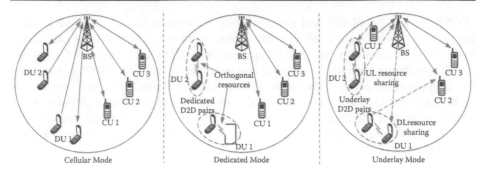

FIGURE 7.3 Modes of D2D communication.

Typically, a DU may transmit data using one of the following modes (See Figure 7.3):

- **Cellular mode:** In this mode, D2D transmitters and receivers get connected via BS without co-channel spectrum sharing with CUs. This mode is very easy to design, but it results in poor spectral efficiency and often, D2D admission fails due to the unavailability of free resources. In Figure 7.3 (leftmost), DU 1 and DU 2 use dedicated spectrum for sending data between Tx and Rx via BS.
- **Dedicated mode:** Here, UEs communicate with each other using dedicated resources. The spectrum efficiency is also very low in this case. DU 1 and DU 2 use orthogonal resources for creating D2D direct links without signal traversal via BS (as shown in Figure 7.3 (middle)).
- **Underlay mode:** In this case, CUs and DUs share their radio resources to achieve better spectral efficiency. However, intelligent admission control, proper resource allocation, and power control algorithms are required for implementing this mode. Here, DU 1 shares downlink resources with CU 2 and DU 2 shares uplink resources with CU 1. Therefore, interference is created at different system entities, as shown in Figure 7.3 (rightmost).

Distance threshold-based approach: A simple distance threshold-based mode selection approach has been used in [19] where a D2D user selects the D2D mode of transmission if the distance between the D2D Tx-Rx pair is less than a predefined threshold. Here the authors have used a tractable approach of the mobile users' location modeled by random spatial poisson point process (PPP) in a hybrid network model.

Channel gain-based approach: A D2D user may use an underlay D2D mode of transmission if the direct D2D link quality is better than the cellular uplink channel [17].

Guard zone-based approach: [30] Uses a concept called guard-zone from the BS where a D2D user is not allowed to transmit in underlay D2D mode as it creates strong interference at the BS. Users outside this guide-zone may choose either D2D or cellular mode depending on the resource availability and SINR requirements of the users.

Daniel Marshall et al. in [31] have shown a performance comparison of these three D2D mode selection techniques. The cellular and D2D interference are modeled based on the PPP assumption. After that, analytical expressions are derived for the success probability of a BS and a typical D2D receiver in a single-tier cellular network. It is shown that distance cut-off schemes outperform the other mode selection methods.

7.2.3 Resource Management

The most important design challenge for the successful implementation of D2D communication is resource management. Efficient resource management can reduce interference, conserve battery or on-grid energy, and maximize the system sum rate. Resource allocation and power control are so closely related that they are often managed one after the other. (Figure 7.4).

There are two types of resource management protocols: i) overlay and ii) underlay. In overlay D2D communication, the cellular resources are orthogonally allotted to CUs and D2D pairs. Although such allocation schemes avoid the interference issues, it results in poor resource utilization that directly impacts the overall system throughput [32,33]. On the other hand, CUs and D2D pairs share uplink or downlink cellular resources in underlay schemes. Underlay resource allocation techniques are prevalent in practice as they improve spectral efficiency by exploiting spatial diversity. However, these needs complex algorithms to eliminate the effect of intracell and intercell interferences [34].

7.2.4 Relay-Assisted D2D Communications (Multi-hop)

The multi-hop D2D communications network is opportunistic. All mobile users can choose the best path for sending data to the given destination nodes and not depend on the centralized routing algorithms. Deeply-faded cellular users (i.e., those with poor

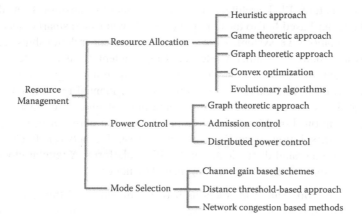

FIGURE 7.4 Solution approaches of resource management problem.

channel quality) can achieve a higher data rate from a relay with better channel gain. D2D relayed communication also helps in extending the cellular coverage. Any inactive cellular user, a fixed relay station, or a movable relay (such as UAV) may participate in relaying data from BS to end-users or between two devices [35]. Selecting a suitable relay device from a group of inactive users needs coordination between D2D users (DUs) and BSs.

Energy-efficient D2D-assisted multimedia transmissions: D2D communication is an integral part of IoT, which has been designed to provide multimedia data services to millions of portable hand-held devices. As these equipment are battery-powered, energy drainage is a crucial issue. D2D communication can eventually reduce battery energy consumption due to short-range communication between proximity devices.

7.3 A SOCIAL D2D ARCHITECTURE FOR PEOPLE CENTRIC IOT (PIOT)

The current state-of-the-art research activities on IoT are concentrated on developing efficient protocols for people-centric IoT. These activities are mainly focused on people-device interaction, social mobile computing, context-aware applications, cloud PIoT, security aspects of PIoT, etc.

7.3.1 Motivation

The motivation of incorporating social D2D architecture for PIoT are as follows:

Dynamic integration: The existing IoT architecture includes connectivity among the smart objects using the internet. The users generally do not collaborate as most of them are selfish in nature. PIoT architecture requires a smooth transition from the present deployed internet-based IoT to the emerging socially connected smart object-based IoT to make a collaborative system. Here, people build social relationships among their peers and then help each other while accessing content from the internet. A more generic and automatic service model might be required for providing services to heterogeneous users that excludes the requirement of manual reconfiguration. Hence, an automated system can make the PIoT environment more user-friendly with less human intervention. For decentralized communication, a classical peer-to-peer (P2P) network gives a solution to combine or depart a service network freely, and smart objects can be integrated dynamically in this PIoT platform. A regular cloud server is also needed to make connections among neighbor nodes.

Directly interaction: Direct interactions between humans and things are required in crowd-sourcing surroundings. PIoT architecture directly supports human-machine interaction. So, dynamics configurable integration and direct interaction are the main features for PIoT.

7.3.2 People-Centric IoT Framework

People-centric IoT architecture has three layers: P2P physical resources layer, distributed service D2D interaction layer, and social D2D enhanced graph layer [36].

7.3.2.1 P2P physical resources layer

This layer integrates several real-world scenarios around us, such as communication between smart objects, sending patient's health status from hospital to doctor remotely, weather forecast information, etc. The P2P model is used for communication in the resources. As the present systems are more susceptible to environmental effects, there is a need for a smart control system. The intelligent control system consists of two types of objects: i) smart objects that are used to communicate with all local objects and ii) unified smart objects that sense the surrounding environment and adapt to the installed control system. The primary purpose of this layer is to build a strong human-machine interaction so that all the components of PIoT system can make socially aware physical connections. Three nodes are mainly responsible for this purpose:

People node: These are the gadgets that are considered as unique smart devices that help to interact people with IoT devices. It reduces the complexity of resources by aggregating services and data on demand. These devices must be user-friendly so that the communication time between users and the data world is minimal.

Local smart object node: It refers to the ability of sensing, computing, communication, self-serving of data sources and smart objects. It can develop a special service model for people's needs. One of the key features of such an in-service model is direct operability. Here, people can provide their interest in selecting a specific application that provides more options and features to meet their demands.

Cloud assistant node contains the regular servers running on the internet. It has the super capability of computation and storage of bandwidth. Privacy and security are the most challenging parts of such cloud-based service management. Therefore, the cloud server node needs to perform specific services with the help of several software and hardware combinations that provide m-services to customers to guarantee privacy and security.

7.3.2.2 Distributed services D2D interaction layer

This layer is an advanced software-controlled entity that includes *unified D2D interaction middleware*. D2D middleware is used to interoperate resource services among people in a society, local smart objects, cloud server nodes, and remote host devices. It is also responsible for hiding various technical information related to the interaction history of the devices.

7.3.2.3 Social D2D enhanced graph layer

Social D2D graph helps to cooperate between people and things in PIoT. A social graph is built to make online social network relationships of people activities and connections of implicit dependencies. The graph model also helps in determining the social relationship among various objects. The dependency of D2D users can be well described using nodes and edges of a graph.

7.3.3 Improvement of D2D Communication Using Social Ties

Social ties significantly improve the performance of D2D communications. Socially-aware peer discovery and relay selection are some of the key design aspects for creating D2D links. Two or more devices (i.e., users) can collaborate and serve as relays for each other. This concept is known as the reciprocal cycle. In the real world, users often form a group for sharing of information. A group leader may communicate to other group members so that everyone in that group may be reached with a guarantee of reliability. Therefore, more robust social ties and faith in the group leader are necessary. All the group members usually select the most trusted cluster user for relaying data; see Figure 7.5.

The concept of the dynamic cluster is presented in [37] where several social attributes, such as interaction among the users and their contact history, users' interest, and workload management functions, are incorporated to select the neighbors dynamically. In [38], various social features are used to optimize the network functionalities. These features are the centrality of the devices (i.e., frequency of forwarding data to other devices), quality of forwarding data, popularity in the society, etc. Therefore, the integration of social attributes helps in finding trustworthy D2D partners among the neighbors.

Social ties can be made possible using three possible functions: trustworthiness management, mobility management, and real use-cases.

Trustworthiness management: Trustworthiness is a major criterion for establishing social relationships among the D2D pairs. A high level of social trust can reduce the end-to-end data delivery delay. Therefore, the relay selection criteria include both the propagation delay (physical length of the wire) and social trust. To express the degree of social relation ship, *trustworthiness social-communication graph* is often used to improve the physical data rate of D2D communication [39]. Trustworthiness management also deals with the detection of malicious devices in the network [40]. If the level of trust for a user is less than a threshold, that particular device is not selected for the D2D relay node. In [41], coalition formation game is used to enhance the uploading services using a trust-based protocol.

Mobility management: It is seen that although the social relationship is stable over a duration of time, the D2D link quality degrades due to the mobility of the users. Therefore, the social network is divided into offline mode (pre-stored social relationship) and online mode (on-demand update of social relationship). The problem of peer selection can be solved by recording the location information of the users. The base station keeps track of the users' location using *location update* messages from them. However, updating the location of the users is highly difficult in a scenario where the user is moving at a very high speed. Integration of social information and their location may improve performance in selecting the best D2D peers. Therefore,

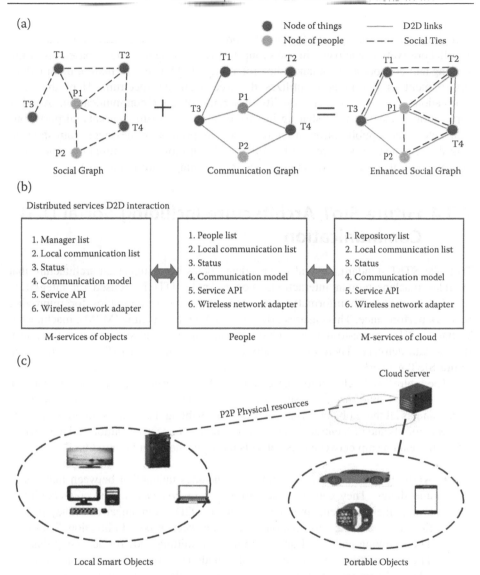

FIGURE 7.5 People-centric IoT framework.

based on the scenario, there are two approaches: ad-hoc (the users themselves do discovery) and centralized (central BS takes control of the peer selection). The ad-hoc method is most popular as it does not consider the user mobility pattern. Nearby users themselves find peers. The best one is selected using their social interaction history or communication benefits (such as gain in terms of throughput and delay). However, the centralized mode is reliable and more secured as compared to the ad-hoc type [42,43].

Real-use cases: There are several real-life applications of social networking in D2D communication, both indoor and outdoor communications. One of such applications is

SoCast [44]. It is a video multicast system that integrates the social relationship of users with a multicast system. *SoCast* also provides rewards for incentives to a user if it collaboratively participates in the group formation. Cognitive radiobased spectrum sensing and collaboration enhance the probability of D2D peer formation in an indoor environment as it efficiently utilizes the free available spectrum. Here the main motivation is to improve the quality-of-service of data communication. Another application is local content sharing in various places like supermarkets, airports, bus stops, etc., where public information (e.g., sharing promotion messages from shops to neighbor customers) is shared with all the users who join the community. The information about their social awareness helps in becoming a group member.

7.3.4 Future SIoT Architecture Including Social D2D Communication

To make SToT standard, several independent bodies have suggested architecture that includes machine-human interactions. For example, ITU-T focused on integrating social awareness with information and communication technologies for improving network performance. This ensures effective machine-to-machine (M2M), machine-to-human (M2H), device-to-device (D2D) communications, and sensor nodes to control station data delivery. Therefore, socially-aware interconnected IoT devices from the future SIoT networks.

The future SIoT architecture may contain the following elements 1) actors (smart IoT objects, such as smart machines, smart cars, smart watches); 2) an intelligent system that interconnects all these objects; 3) an interface for enabling the required interconnections between objects and the central system; and 4) internet connectivity among all the devices [45]. The relationship between these objects has been shown in Figure 7.6.

- **Actors:** The future SIoT architecture includes interaction between humans and things. They can be either *producers* or *consumers*. The connectivity among these elements may be made using D2D communications. They participate in sharing information by creating peer-to-peer bidirectional links. The receiving ends send queries to the transmitting ends for accessing data. The transmitting ends send control signals (i.e., reply message) acknowledging the formation of links, support services that can fulfill the consumer's demand, and other supplementary service information. On the other hand, consumers may accept or reject the offer from the producer. They also prefer nearby producers so that service costs may be as low as possible.
- **Intelligent D2D communication system:** This system is responsible for managing the entire system using four main features: peer discovery, context-aware data management, service management, and recommendation. Peer discovery is one of the crucial steps for D2D link creation. The context-aware system can sense the current situation and adapt its parameters to meet the service requirement. Here context-aware computing enables controllers to manage and provide services that require minimum human interaction.

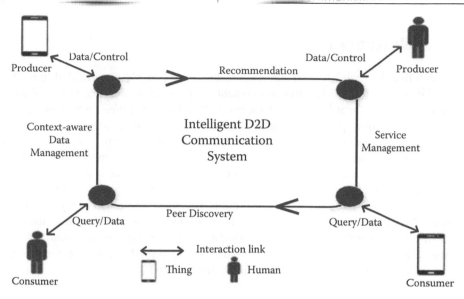

FIGURE 7.6   Future SIoT architecture with D2D features.

- **Interface:** The interfaces act as bridges between various entities in the system. Two possible interfaces are wired (ethernet) or wireless (cellular or wi-fi direct) interface. The supported bandwidth of each link is decided based on data delivery rates and the amount of control signaling. The required control and data channels in each interface are decided accordingly.
- **Future addition:** The architecture has scope of adding new elements and features for enhancement. Sensors, actuators, smart home equipment, etc., are the candidates for adding in the new systems. All these devices interact socially with the help of human-machine communications. The primary goal is to make the system adaptive, re-configurable, auto-tuned, and multi-protocol supported.

7.4 CACHING-BASED SOCIALLY-AWARE D2D COMMUNICATION

Quality of experience (QoE) of a user may be greatly enhanced by using sophisticated caching techniques on mobile devices. Users can cache popular content depending on users' social interests and share it with others by creating direct P2P links. In this context, a hypergraph framework has been proposed by Bo Bai et al. [46] that takes different social tie-ups among users and their interest in accessing content from the cloud. The hypergraph approach solves several problems on proximity node identification, D2D pair creation, resource allocation, and finally, content caching and delivery to the users.

7.4.1 Three Layers of D2D Content Delivery Networks

It is seen that the social domain and interest domain are highly uncorrelated in reality. Therefore, various social features and content interests are included to make a fruitful interaction among the users. This interaction is achieved using three important aspects: location information (physical distance), social ties, and content interest. Users located in close proximity may be socially known to each other. They are more interested in forming peers. Therefore, location information is essential in making social D2D groups. Social ties can be either strong or weak depending on mutual interest and collaborative nature of the users. Strong social ties have more chance of creating D2D communication pair. The bottom layer contains the cached content of every user. Here, a proper load balancing algorithm helps in distributing the content fairly to all the users such that no user will be overloaded with data. A user having more social ties may contain data that is most requested by the users. This three-layer architecture defines the essential components of D2D communication in SIoT.

7.4.2 D2D Caching Using Hypergraph

In this section, we discuss the dependency between hypergraph and D2D communication framework.

7.4.2.1 Hypergraph formation

In D2D-enabled cellular networks, spectral (resource) allocation and interference management are the two important challenges in the physical layer. However, social trust is the key factor for establishing D2D links in the social layer. The duration of maintaining a D2D link also depends on the depth of social ties between the users. As many D2D users are interested in receiving the same content, it is also essential to have a common social interest layer for implementing a content delivery scheme. Therefore, to integrate all these parameters, Hypergraph has been formed that provided a connectivity of all these components of social D2D architecture.

Let X_d is a set of D2D users and $x_d^m \in X_d$ denotes the mth D2D pair. The set of subchannels are X_s and x_s^m indicates the mth subchannel. X_c is a set of commonly accessed content and x_c^m denotes the mth subchannel. A hypergraph is formed with vertices $X = \{X_d \cup X_s \cup X_c\}$. The hyper-edges set D is a subset of X where the ith edge is indicated using D_i. The following considerations are made after the hypergraph is formed:

- Two D2D users in X_d are connected using a hyperedge if they have strong social ties.
- The cached content x_c^m is available with one of the users of a D2D pair, while the other user is interested in receiving the same content.
- The data is downloaded by creating a D2D link where the data rate guarantee has been provided using x_d^m subchannel.

- The interference created to the cellular user using the same x_d^m channel is less than a pre-defined threshold.

7.4.2.2 Caching capacity

The caching capacity Q_m is limited in each device that caches content x_c^m. Therefore the design of caching content would be based on the cache hit ratio of that particular content. The cache hit ratio is denoted as $\eta_m(T, Q_m, P)$, where P is the cache placement matrix when the content x_c^m is present for a duration T. In case the requested content is not present, the optimization goal is to minimize the delay τ incurred in caching the content before it is delivered to the D2D partner. Here, the optimization aim is to maximize $\eta_m(T, Q_m, P)$ and minimize τ. Caching placement policy would include energy optimization, delay minimization, and cache hit ratio maximization. Currently, deep learning and big data analysis are being used to solve efficient cache management in D2D-enabled cellular networks.

7.5 OPEN RESEARCH CHALLENGES

Although many researchers have proposed architecture for SIoT and its integration for human-machine collaborations, it is yet not standardized. There are various challenges in the proposed frame-works that need to be solved before deploying those worldwide. In this section, we briefly discuss the issues and challenges and provide future research directions for improving the SIoT system.

7.5.1 Heterogeneity and Data Management

Electronic devices are presently heterogeneous in terms of computation capabilities, energy requirements, screen resolution, data transfer rate, etc. One single communication technology cannot meet the diverse needs of such devices. Therefore, different technologies have to be merged to meet the requirements. To communicate and cooperate, SIoT must be able to integrate many types of devices and services [47] providing interoperability among all the components. The system should also be open to supporting various applications with diverse characteristics in terms of their scalability, energy requirements, available communication bandwidth, end-to-end latency, and other quality of service requirements.

Data storage and management is another issue of SIoT system. Distributed approaches are often more useful than centralized systems as they do not depend on a unique server to store data. Distributed systems are efficient in case of sudden failure of any particular entity in the system. For data management, various data structure standards, such as metadata structure presented by metadata standards and resource description framework (RDF) proposed by W3C (a worldwide recognized body), will help users and devices with meaningful and valuable information.

7.5.2 Security, Privacy, and Fault Tolerance

Security, privacy, and trustworthiness for the users are considered the sensitive features of the SIoT system. Authentication, confidentiality, and access control are required for SIoT security. There are several lightweight mechanisms for data integrity, effective ID management, and privacy-enhanced technologies in which the trust of SIoT can be managed. The goal of fault tolerance in SIoT is to better adapt to a challenging situation and provide reliable operation of the different components. Some approaches such as [48] and [49] propose a set of possible interactions for specific application. A global set of interactions with devices and users needs to be defined, but it conflicts with privacy issues. The interaction between users and devices is still an open challenge.

7.5.3 Self Operation, Semantic and Context Management

Self operability is another essential aspect for connecting billions of devices together. It is expected that SIoT system will be a global technology that will reduce the distance between people and devices. Intelligent devices can perform automated tasks more efficiently with the help of machine learning algorithms. Therefore, automatic reconfiguration of such devices and controllers can enhance the connectivity and provide a suitable platform for maintaining such a huge connected domain. Self-organizations, self-management, and self-operation are crucial for the SIoT system as they make it automated. The adaption approach used for other technologies may also help automate the SIoT operation system. Therefore, finding sophisticated algorithms for the self-configurable system may be a possible future direction in this domain.

Data analysis, service discovery, and composition provide advanced functionality and enhance the user experience. Proper service management further improves the accessibility of content from the internet. In this context, service orientation architecture (SOA) based system and DPWS [50] are proposed in SIoT system. Unambiguous data interpretation and quick access of user requested content are another two important aspects of SIoT architecture that needs to be guaranteed. Therefore, it is expected that future SIoT system will provide a perception of 99.99% network connectivity anytime and from anywhere in the world. Big data analysis, data interpretations, and automated service management using machine learning are the important aspects for real-time deployment of smart IoT systems. To deal with context and data mining, various semantic approaches such as RDF and OWL [51] are proposed that helps in fast and efficient data access from remote server.

7.5.4 Application Development and New Business Model

The success of SIoT technology depends on the applications and benefits that make use of them. The application process development process will vary based on what devices and services are involved. SIoT technology is quickly becoming vital to business everywhere. To make collaborative nature of SIoT, several considerations are to be taken: 1) offer useful and attractive applications that encourage people to use them, 2) take nonconflicting business models to improve cooperation. When the SIoT-based application benefits users, developers' stakeholders will be interested in investing in marketing and sales, research and developments, advertising, and device commercialization [52].

7.5.5 Efficient Discovery and Search Engines

Device discovery is a process of finding suitable devices that provide meaningful information and services to the end users. Efficient device discovery mechanism makes the SIoT system to offer faster access of data services. Once a suitable device is identified, it can be used for relaying data from cellular base station to users with higher QoS. It is also expected that the search and discovery mechanisms must be energy efficient and reliable. There are several existing discovery approaches such as SPARQL [53], UDDI, DPWS, RESTful [54,55], and other web service-based protocols are used to deal with huge SIoT data management, context awareness, mobile web access, and supplementary services that requires QoS guarantee.

7.5.6 Efficient Energy Management

It is predicted that more than 80% of the users in SIoT will be mobile users that operate with limited battery supply. Efficient energy management may significantly reduce battery drainage and improve network lifetime. These are often critical requirements of wireless sensor networks. The communication range of IoT devices needs to be reduced to transmit data with lesser power. D2D communication helps in reducing the power budget and making the system energy efficient. An energy-efficient solution needs to be implemented at every level, starting from device-embedded software, hardware, monitoring interface, etc. Energy harvesting is one of the recent technologies that help to collect energy from the environment and maintain a good battery backup for small data transfer applications in SIoT. A dual battery system may also be used as a secondary power source, preserving energy for essential data transmissions.

REFERENCES

[1] E. Ahmed, I. Yaqoob, A. Gani, M. Imran, M. Guizani, Social-Aware Resource Allocation and Optimization for D2D Communication, *IEEE Wireless Communications* 24 (3) (2017) 122–129. doi:10.1109/MWC.2017.1600087WC
[2] A. Asadi, Q. Wang, V. Mancuso, A Survey on Device-to-Device Communication in Cellular Networks, *IEEE Communications Surveys Tutorials* 16 (4) (2014) 1801–1819. doi:10.1109/COMST.2014.2319555

[3] L. Atzori, A. Iera, G. Morabito, M. Nitti, The Social Internet of Things (SIoT) When Social Networks Meet the Internet of Things: Concept, Architecture and Network Characterization, *Computer Networks* 56 (16) (2012) 3594–3608. doi:10.1016/j.comnet.2012.07.010

[4] L. E. Holmquist, F. Mattern, B. Schiele, P. Alahuhta, M. Beigl5, H.-W. Gellersen, "Smart-Its Friends: A Technique for Users to Easily Establish Connections between Smart Artefacts", in: G. D. Abowd, B. Brumitt, S. Shafer (Eds.), *Ubicomp 2001: Ubiquitous Computing*, Springer Berlin Heidelberg, Berlin, Heidelberg, 2001, pp. 116–122.

[5] Y. Huang, G. Li, A Semantic Analysis for Internet of Things, in: *International Conference on Intelligent Computation Technology and Automation* 1 (2010) 336–339. doi:10.1109/ICICTA.2010.73

[6] H. Bhatia, S. N. Panda, D. Nagpal, Internet of Things and Its Applications in Healthcare – A Survey, in: 8th International Conference on Reliability, Infocom Technologies and Optimization (Trends and Future Directions) (ICRITO), 2020, pp. 305–310. doi:10.1109/ICRITO48877.2020.9197816

[7] D. Wu, L. Zhou, Y. Cai, Y. Qian, Collaborative Caching and Matching for D2D Content Sharing, *IEEE Wireless Communications* 25 (3) (2018) 43–49. doi:10.1109/MWC.2018.1700325

[8] J. Yan, D. Wu, H. Wang, R. Wang, User Centric Content Sharing Based on D2D Cellular Networks, *IEEE Transactions on Vehicular Technology* 67 (11) (2018) 11208–11218. doi:10.1109/TVT.2018.2870675

[9] X. Lin, R. Ratasuk, A. Ghosh, J. G. Andrews, Modeling, Analysis, and Optimization of Multicast Device-to-Device Transmissions, *IEEE Transactions on Wireless Communications* 13 (8) (2014) 4346–4359. doi:10.1109/TWC.2014.2320522

[10] Z. Lin, Z. Wang, W. Cai, V. Leung, A Smart Map Sharing and Preloading Scheme for Mobile Cloud Gaming in D2D Networks, in: 2017 IEEE International Conference on Smart Computing (SMARTCOMP), 2017, pp. 1–6. doi:10.1109/SMARTCOMP.2017.7946981

[11] P. Pawar, A. Trivedi, Device-to-Device Communication Based IoT System: Benefits and Challenges, *IETE Technical Review* 36 (4) (2019) 362–374. doi:10.1080/02564602.2018.1476191

[12] O. Bello, S. Zeadally, Intelligent Device-to-Device Communication in the Internet of Things, *IEEE Systems Journal* 10 (3) (2016) 1172–1182. doi:10.1109/JSYST.2014.2298837

[13] A. Aijaz, H. Aghvami, M. Amani, A Survey on Mobile Data Offloading: Technical and Business Perspectives, *IEEE Wireless Communications* 20 (2) (2013) 104–112. doi:10.1109/MWC.2013.6507401

[14] N. Abedini, S. Tavildar, J. Li, T. Richardson, Distributed Synchronization for Device-to-Device Communications in an LTE Network, *IEEE Transactions on Wireless Communications* 15 (2) (2016) 1547–1561. doi:10.1109/TWC.2015.2492959

[15] W. Sun, F. Brnnstrm, E. G. Strm, Network Synchronization for Mobile Device-to-Device Systems, *IEEE Transactions on Communications* 65 (3) (2017) 1193–1206. doi:10.1109/TCOMM.2016.2639504

[16] G. Fodor, E. Dahlman, G. Mildh, S. Parkvall, N. Reider, G. Mikls, Z. Turnyi, Design Aspects of Network Assisted Device-to-Device Communications, *IEEE Communications Magazine* 50 (3) (2012) 170–177. doi:10.1109/MCOM.2012.6163598

[17] H. ElSawy, E. Hossain, M. Alouini, Analytical Modeling of Mode Selection and Power Control for Underlay D2D Communication in Cellular Networks, *IEEE Transactions on Communications* 62 (11) (2014) 4147–4161. doi:10.1109/TCOMM.2014.2363849

[18] P. K. Barik, C. Singhal, R. Datta, Throughput Enhancement Using D2D Based Relay-Assisted Communication in Cellular Networks, in: IEEE 28th Annual International Symposium on Personal, Indoor, and Mobile Radio Communications (PIMRC), 2017, pp. 1–6. doi:10.1109/PIMRC.2017.8292340

[19] X. Lin, J. G. Andrews, A. Ghosh, Spectrum Sharing for Device-to-Device Communication in Cellular Networks, *IEEE Transactions on Wireless Communications* 13 (12) (2014) 6727–6740. doi:10.1109/TWC.2014.2360202

[20] P. K. Barik, A. Shukla, R. Datta, C. Singhal, A Resource Sharing Scheme for Intercell D2D CommuniCation in Cellular Networks: A Repeated Game Theoretic Approach, *IEEE Transactions on Vehicular Technology* 69 (7) (2020) 7806–7820. doi:10.1109/TVT.2020.2991476

[21] P. K. Barik, C. Singhal, R. Datta, DAMS: D2D-Assisted Multimedia Streaming Service with Minimized BS Transmit Power in Cellular Networks, *Computer Communications* 144 (2019) 149–161. doi:10.1016/j.comcom.2019.05.019

[22] S. Ali, A. Ahmad, Resource Allocation, Interference Management, and Mode Selection in Device-To-Device Communication: A Survey, *Transactions on Emerging Telecommunications Technologies* 28 (7) (2017) e3148. doi:10.1002/ett.3148

[23] L. Wei, R. Q. Hu, Y. Qian, G. Wu, Enable Device-to-Device Communications Underlaying Cellular Networks: Challenges and Research Aspects, *IEEE Communications Magazine* 52 (6) (2014) 90–96. doi:10.1109/MCOM.2014.6829950

[24] M. N. Tehrani, M. Uysal, H. Yanikomeroglu, Device-to-Device Communication in 5G Cellular NetWorks: Challenges, Solutions, and Future Directions, *IEEE Communications Magazine* 52 (5) (2014) 86–92. doi:10.1109/MCOM.2014.6815897

[25] H. Kebriaei, B. Maham, D. Niyato, Double-Sided Bandwidth-Auction Game for Cognitive Device-to-Device Communication in Cellular Networks, *IEEE Transactions on Vehicular Technology* 65 (9) (2016) 7476–7487. doi:10.1109/TVT.2015.2485304

[26] P. Li, S. Guo, I. Stojmenovic, A Truthful Double Auction for Device-to-Device Communications in Cellular Networks, *IEEE Journal on Selected Areas in Communications* 34 (1) (2016) 71–81. doi:10.1109/JSAC.2015.2452587

[27] U. N. Kar, D. K. Sanyal, An Overview of Device-to-Device Communication in Cellular Networks, *ICT Express* 4 (4) (2018) 203–208. doi:10.1016/j.icte.2017.08.002. URL http://www.sciencedirect.com/science/article/pii/S2405959517301467

[28] C. Gao, Y. Li, D. Jin, Mobility Assisted Device-to-Device Communications Underlaying Cellular Networks, in: International Conference on Computing, Networking and Communications (ICNC), 2016, pp. 1–6. doi:10.1109/ICCNC.2016.7440571

[29] P. Gandotra, R. Jha, S. Jain, A Survey on Device-to-Device (D2D) Communication: Architecture and Security Issues, *Journal of Network and Computer Applications* 78 (2017) 9–29. doi:10.1016/j.jnca.2016.11.002

[30] J. Ye, Y. J. Zhang, A Guard Zone Based Scalable Mode Selection Scheme in D2D Underlaid Cellular Networks, in: IEEE International Conference on Communications (ICC), 2015, pp. 2110–2116. doi:10.1109/ICC.2015.7248637

[31] D. Marshall, S. Durrani, J. Guo, N. Yang, Performance Comparison of Device-to-Device Mode Selection Schemes, in: IEEE 26th Annual International Symposium on Personal, Indoor, and Mobile Radio Communications (PIMRC), 2015, pp. 1536–1541. doi:10.1109/PIMRC.2015.7343542

[32] F. Jameel, Z. Hamid, F. Jabeen, S. Zeadally, M. A. Javed, A Survey of Device-to-Device CommuniCations: Research Issues and Challenges, *IEEE Communications Surveys Tutorials* 20 (3) (2018) 2133–2168. doi:10.1109/COMST.2018.2828120

[33] Y. Pei, Y. Liang, Resource Allocation Ffor Device-to-Device Communications Overlaying Two-Way Cellular Networks, *IEEE Transactions on Wireless Communications* 12 (7) (2013) 3611–3621. doi:10.1109/TWC.2013.061713.121956

[34] S. Yu, W. Ejaz, L. Guan, A. Anpalagan, Resource Allocation Schemes in D2D Communications: Overview, Classification, and Challenges, *Wireless Personal Communications* 96 (2017) 303–322. doi:10.1007/s11277-017-4168-5

[35] P. K. Barik, A. D. Chaurasiya, R. Datta, C. Singhal, Trajectory Prediction of UAVs for Relay-Assisted D2D Communication Using Machine Learning, in: 2021 National Conference on Communications (NCC), 2021, pp. 1–6. doi:10.1109/NCC52529.2021.9530164

[36] L. Yang, W. Li, Y. Luo, Y. Duan, G. Fortino, A Social-D2D Architecture for People-Centric Industrial Internet of Things, in: 2017 IEEE 14th International Conference on Networking, Sensing and Control (ICNSC), 2017, pp. 744–749. doi:10.1109/ICNSC.2017.8000183

[37] Z. Zhang, L. Wang, D. Liu, Y. Zhang, Peer Discovery for D2D Communications Based on Social Attribute and Service Attribute, *Journal of Network and Computer Applications* 86 (2017) 82–91, special Issue on Pervasive Social Networking. doi:10.1016/j.jnca.2016.11.006

[38] Q. Du, H. Song, X. Zhu, Social-Feature Enabled Communications among Devices toward the Smart IoT Community, *IEEE Communications Magazine* 57 (1) (2019) 130–137. doi:10.1109/MCOM.2018.1700563

[39] F. H. Kumbhar, N. Saxena, A. Roy, Reliable Relay: Autonomous Social D2D Paradigm for 5G LoS Communications, *IEEE Communications Letters* 21 (7) (2017) 1593–1596. doi:10.1109/LCOMM.2017.2682091

[40] L. Militano, A. Orsino, G. Araniti, M. Nitti, L. Atzori, A. Iera, Trusted D2D-Based Data UploadIng in In-band Narrowband-IoT with Social Awareness, in: 2016 IEEE 27th Annual International Symposium on Personal, Indoor, and Mobile Radio Communications (PIMRC), 2016, pp. 1–6. doi:10.1109/PIMRC.2016.7794568

[41] L. Militano, A. Orsino, G. Araniti, M. Nitti, L. Atzori, A. Iera, Trust-Based and Social-Aware Coalition Formation Game for Multihop Data Uploading in 5G Systems, *Computer Networks* 111 (2016) 141–151.

[42] B. Zhang, Y. Li, D. Jin, P. Hui, Z. Han, Social-Aware Peer Discovery for D2D Communications Underlaying Cellular Networks, *IEEE Transactions on Wireless Communications* 14 (5) (2015) 2426–2439. doi:10.1109/TWC.2014.2386865

[43] Y. Meng, C. Jiang, H.-H. Chen, Y. Ren, Cooperative Device-to-Device Communications: Social Networking Perspectives, *IEEE Network* 31 (3) (2017) 38–44. doi:10.1109/MNET.2017.1600081NM

[44] Y. Cao, T. Jiang, X. Chen, J. Zhang, Social-Aware Video Multicast Based on Device-to-Device Communications, *IEEE Transactions on Mobile Computing* 15 (6) (2016) 1528–1539. doi:10.1109/TMC.2015.2461214

[45] A. M. Ortiz, D. Hussein, S. Park, S. N. Han, N. Crespi, The Cluster between Internet of Things and Social Networks: Review and Research Challenges, *IEEE Internet of Things Journal* 1 (3) (2014) 206–215. doi:10.1109/JIOT.2014.2318835

[46] B. Bai, L. Wang, Z. Han, W. Chen, T. Svensson, Caching based Socially-Aware D2D Communications in Wireless Content Delivery Networks: A Hypergraph Framework, *IEEE Wireless Communications* 23 (4) (2016) 74–81. doi:10.1109/MWC.2016.7553029

[47] M. Zorzi, A. Gluhak, S. Lange, A. Bassi, From Today's INTRAnet of Things to a Future INTERnet of Things: A Wireless- and Mobility-Related View, *IEEE Wireless Communications* 17 (6) (2010) 44–51. doi:10.1109/MWC.2010.5675777

[48] M. Kranz, P. Holleis, A. Schmidt, Embedded Interaction: Interacting with the Internet of Things, *IEEE Internet Computing* 14 (2) (2010) 46–53. doi:10.1109/MIC.2009.141

[49] L. Atzori, A. Iera, G. Morabito, SIoT: Giving a Social Structure to the Internet of Things, *IEEE Communications Letters* 15 (11) (2011) 1193–1195. doi:10.1109/LCOMM.2011.090911.111340

[50] G. Cndido, F. Jammes, J. B. de Oliveira, A. W. Colombo, SOA at Device Level in the Industrial Domain: Assessment of OPC UA and DPWS Specifications, in: 2010 8th IEEE International Conference on Industrial Informatics, 2010, pp. 598–603. doi:10.1109/INDIN.2010.5549676

[51] R. Zgheib, E. Conchon, R. Bastide, *Semantic Middleware Architectures for IoT Healthcare Applications*, Springer International Publishing, Cham, 2019, pp. 263–294.

[52] K. M. Heidemann, J. Probst, Online Social Networks: A Survey of a Global Phenomenon, *Computer Networks* 56 (2012) 3866–3878. doi:10.1016/j.comnet.2012.08.009

[53] P. Gomes, E. Cavalcante, T. Batista et al., A Semantic-Based Discovery Service for the Internet of Things, *Journal of Internet Services and Applications* 10 (11). doi:10.1186/s13174- 019-0109-8

[54] D. Guinard, V. Trifa, S. Karnouskos, P. Spiess, D. Savio, Interacting with the SOA-Based Internet of Things: Discovery, Query, Selection, and On-Demand Provisioning of Web Services, *IEEE Transactions on Services Computing* 3 (3) (2010) 223–235. doi:10.1109/TSC.2010.3

[55] S. Evdokimov, B. Fabian, S. Kunz, N. Schoenemann, Comparison of Discovery Service Architectures for the Internet of Things, in: IEEE International Conference on Sensor Networks, Ubiquitous, and Trustworthy Computing, 2010, pp. 237–244. doi:10.1109/SUTC.2010.22

Real-Time Face Mask Detection and Alert System Using IoT and Machine Learning

8

Manu Y M[1], Mohan Kumar K S[2], and Prasanna Kumar M J[1]

[1]*Department of Computer Science and Engineering, BGS Institute of Technology, Adichunchanagiri University, B.G. Nagara, Mandya, India*

[2]*Department of Electronics and Communication Engineering, BGS Institute of Technology, Adichunchanagiri University, B.G. Nagara, Mandya, India*

Contents

DOI: 10.1201/9781003282990-8

8.1 INTRODUCTION

The wearing of facial covers has exploded due to the worldwide COVID-19 plague. Before COVID-19, people used to wear covers to protect their health from air contamination. While others are hesitant with respect to their looks, they protect themselves from others for the most part by concealing their appearances. Authorities found that wearing facial covers deters COVID-19 transmission. Covid (known as Covid) is the latest pandemic ailment that hit the human achievement recently. In 2020, the catalyst spreading of COVID-19 obliged the World Health Organization to report COVID-19 as an overall pandemic. More than 5,000,000 cases of COVID-19 emerged in less than a half-year across 188 countries. The sickness spreads through close contact and in amassed, crowded regions. The Covid plague has incited an awesome degree of normally shrewd cooperation. Man-made intellectual ability (AI) considering machine learning and deep learning can help battle COVID-19 in various ways. PC-based information lets auditors and clinicians survey gigantic amounts of data to gauge the spread of COVID-19, to serve as an early notification structure for likely pandemics, and to coordinate slight social classes. The methodology of clinical benefits needs subsidizing for emerging issues; for instance, man-made insightful capacity, IoT, immense data, and AI to oversee and expect new issues. To all the near 100% sickness rates and to follow contaminations as soon as possible, the AI's power is being exploited to address the COVID-19 pandemic. People are obliged to wear facial covers in the open in various countries. These endless controls were enacted in response to the enthusiastic improvement in cases and deaths in various districts. Regardless, the most prominent method for managing huge social gatherings is causing conflict. The checking structure joins the ID of any person who isn't wearing a facial covering.

Here we present a cover face disclosure model that depends on learning. The proposed model can be united with observation cameras to forestall the COVID-19 transmission. It monitors the area of individuals, verifies who are wearing facial covers or not, and sends arranged messages. The model is mixed between critical learning and standard AI frameworks with OpenCV, tensor stream, and keras. We track down the most appropriate assessment that achieved the greatest precision the fastest during the time spent arranging, disclosing, and confirming faces.

8.2 RELATED WORK

It considered whole faces rather than explicit highlights. The face picture was addressed in a low aspect subspace framed by the PCA of the picture dataset. Eigenvectors of the covariance framework shape the eigenfaces of the picture set. The eigenvalues of this preparing set and loads were determined separately. The test pictures go across the comparative technique, and afterward, the distance between preparing pictures and testing pictures was determined. Two calculations were proposed for face acknowledgment: geometric component based and template matching based. The outcomes were acquired on front-facing faces. LDA based element extraction for face acknowledgment was proposed by Etemadi and Chalupa. In this technique, Eigen esteem examination was executed on partition framework other than on covariance lattice. The presentation and computational parts of PCA were introduced by Moon and Phillips. They proposed another calculation in view of PCA. The parts of proposed calculation are light standardization, low pass channel, first low request Eigen vector evacuation, and point and mahalaNobis similitude measure coordinating. They presented a nonexclusive secluded PCA calculation.

8.2.1 Aim

Our point is to break the steel of the COVID-19 disease starting with one individual and then the next to diminish this pandemic and shield individuals from contamination. When this programmed fine innovation is executed, there will no question of individuals defying the guidelines of wearing masks. It is one of the factors that are extremely simple to recollect, all things considered. By and large, people can recollect and perceive an individual in light of his face. Notwithstanding, a face is an intricate factor when seen according to the point of view of PC vision. Human appearances have changed highlights and attributes of every individual so that facial acknowledgment is an excellent tool to apply in different regions, including diversion, savvy cards, data security, and so on. It applies the human face acknowledgment framework utilizing the eigenface approach. Eigenface is one of the facial acknowledgment techniques in view of the principal component analysis (PCA) calculation. PCA involved a numerical methodology to determine a bunch of highlights for facial acknowledgment. The facial acknowledgment stage starts with the face location process utilizing a course classifier strategy, face preprocess, gather and train the face recognized, and lastly, the face acknowledgment.

8.2.2 Open CV

OpenCV (open source computer vision library) is an open source PC vision and AI programming library. OpenCV was tried to give an average structure to PC vision applications and to accelerate the utilization of machine insight in the business things.

Being a BSD-upheld thing, OpenCV chips away at it for relationship to utilize and change the code.

The library has more than 2,500 updated appraisals, joining a total methodology of both masterpiece and state-of-the-art PC vision and AI computations. These appraisals can be used to see faces, see objects, request human practices in accounts, track camera improvements, track moving things, dispose of 3D models of articles, produce 3D point clouds from sound framework cameras, secure pictures together to convey a colossal standard image of an entire scene, notice similar pictures from an image database, kill red eyes from pictures taken using streak, follow eye degrees of progress, see view and spread out markers to overlay it with broadened reality, etc. OpenCV has more than 47,000 people from client regions surveyed, with the number of downloads beating 18 million. The library is used ordinarily in affiliations, research social affairs, and by managerial bodies. Close by grounded affiliations like Google, Yahoo, Microsoft, Intel, IBM, Sony, Honda, and Toyota that use the library, there are different new affiliations like Applied Minds, Video Surf, and Zeitera that use OpenCV. OpenCV's conveyed uses length the reach from sewing street view pictures together, seeing breaks in understanding video in Israel, seeing mine stuff in China, helping robots investigate and get objects at Willow Garage, area of pool smothering out catastrophes in Europe, running instinctual craftsmanship in Spain and New York, really taking a gander at runways for trash in Turkey, concentrating on defects on things in progress lines from one side of the world to the next on to fast face ID in Japan.

8.2.3 Tensor Flow

Tensor Flow is a free and open-source programming library for dataflow and differentiable programming across a level of tasks. It is an expert number-related library and is similarly used for AI applications like psyche affiliations. It is used for both assessment and creation at Google; Tensor Flow is Google Brain's second-age structure. Structure 1.0.0 was done February 11, While the reference execution runs on single machines, Tensor Flow can run on various CPUs and GPUs (with optional CUDA and SYCL upgrades for all-around significant figuring on depictions-managing units).

Tensor Flow is available on 64-cycle Linux, MacOS, Windows, and more modest stages including Android and iOS. Its adaptable arranging mulls over the unmistakable sending of computations across a mix of stages (CPUs, GPUs, TPUs), and from workspaces to lots of waiters to limited and edge devices.

8.2.4 Keras

Keras is an API prepared for people, not machines. Keras follows best practices for diminishing mental weight: it offers solid and direct APIs, it limits how much client rehearsal is expected for common use cases, and it gives clear and fundamental Bumble messages. In like manner, it has wide documentation and originator guides. Keras contains different executions of typically used frontal cortex network building squares, for instance, layers, objectives, establishment limits, analyzers, and an enormous assembly of contraptions to make working with picture and text data more direct to further develop the coding to make basic psyche connection code. The code is used on GitHub, and neighborhood social affairs join the GitHub issues page and a Slack channel. Keras is a moderate Python library for expansive searching that can run on top of Theano or Tensor Flow. It was made to make completing basic learning models as speedy and fundamental as rational for innovative work. It runs on Python 2.7 or 3.5 and can execute superbly on GPUs and CPUs given the essential plans. It is conveyed under the liberal MIT license.

Keras was made and promoted by François Chollet, a Google engineer using four key convictions:

- **Mentality:** A model ought to be noticeable as a procedure or a chart alone. All of the concerns of a basic learning model are discrete parts that can be participated in conflicting ways.
- **Balance:** The library gives scarcely with the eventual outcome of achieving a miserable outcome.
- **Extensibility:** New parts are purposely easy to add and use inside the frame-work, speculated that for examiners should starter and explore remarkable contemplations.
- **Python:** No fascinating model records with custom report plans. Everything is nearby Python. Keras is made plans for control and confinement allowing you to quickly portray basic learning models and run them on top of a Theano or Tensor Flow backend.

A writing study or audit that consolidates both synopsis and union of explicit theoretical classifications. The writing overview gives a decision regarding how one can examination and comprehend that holes exist and how an issue has been investigated to date.

In [1], system is proposed that included histogram procedures to see faces, by using Viola Jones strategy with PC vision to recognize faces by taking features of eyes, noses, and mouths. For matching factors for affirmation, a histogram of individual components is enlisted. Closeby features of the histogram are explored from database picture for face affirmation considering part. The results show that the proposed technique achieves precision of 97% for the affirmation of appearances. Here face acknowledgment pro-cedures perceive the face, their facial part, isolated components, with their singular identity still unknown. The computation given worked for face affirmation with progress speed of 97%. Skin-concealing disclosures can recognize all face pictures yet also contain the neck and dress whose tone resembles the skin. So the error rate is high. So the result isn't extraordinary. It is furthermore possible to chip away at the precision of the matching procedure by hybridizing the component base and design-based approaches.

In [2], novel decolorization procedure is proposed to change over covering pic-tures into grayscale. The proposed strategy, called CorrC2G, checks the three in general direct-weighting cutoff points of the masks to dull change by affiliation. These cutoff points are reviewed obviously from the associations between each channel of the RGB picture and a qualification picture.

In [3] is the most vital piece of the body, believe it or not, that makes it a gigantic variable. In this assessment, we use facial structures consolidated in Ry-UJI robot. The robot is seen by an evident voice request looking for someone, and when a specific face has been found, face demand is done. This article will apply the human face demand structure using the eigenface approach. Eigenface is one of the facial authentication methods thinking about the principal component analysis (PCA) computation. PCA involved a mathematical method for managing reason a huge load of parts for face confirmation. The face demand stage begins with face district.

The [4] rule propels in object revelation were accomplished considering enhancements in object portrayals and AI models. An unmistakable layout of a top-level region framework is the deformable part-based model (DPM). It grows fastidiously organized portrayals and kinematically pushed part disintegrations of things, conveyed as a graphical model. Utilizing discriminative learning of graphical models considers fabricating high-accuracy part-based models for gathering article classes. Truly arranged portrayals associated with shallow discriminatively coordinated models have been among the best performing guidelines for the associated issue of thing portrayal, additionally to some degree as of late; deep neural networks (DNNs) have emerged as a solid AI model.

In [5] that DNN-based relapse is fit for learning highlights, which are great for arrangement, yet additionally capture solid mathematical data. We utilize the overall design presented for characterization by [10] and supplant the last layer with a relapse layer. The fairly amazing yet strong knowledge is that networks that somewhat encode interpretation invariance can catch object areas also. Second, we present a multi-scale box followed by a refinement step to create the exact location. Thusly, we can apply a DNN, which predicts a low-goal veil, restricted by the result layer size, to pixel-wise accuracy for a minimal price; the organization is accessed multiple times for every information picture.

In [6] differentiation to the customary techniques intended for normal pictures that mean to protect contrast between various classes in the changed-over dark picture, the proposed transformation strategy diminishes however much as could be expected the difference (for example power change) inside the text class. It depends on gaining a direct channel from a predefined dataset of text and foundation pixels that: I) when applied to foundation pixels, limits the result reaction; and ii) when applied to message pixels, amplifies the result reaction, while limiting the power difference inside the message class. Our proposed technique (called here LC2G for learning-based color-to-gray) is imagined to be utilized as pre-handling for report picture binarization. A dataset of 46 (46) chronicled archive pictures is made and used to assess abstractly and unbiasedly the proposed technique. The technique shows radically its adequacy and effect on the presentation of cutting-edge binarization strategies. Four other electronic picture datasets are made to assess the adaptability of the proposed method.

Currently, covered face acknowledgment is more significant [7]. Historically, fear-based oppressors and hoodlums covered their faces with veils for masks. Other than this use, sunglasses, caps, shading trim, and so on likewise carry on like veils. Utilizing various sorts of veils or impediments, the critical highlights to distinguish an individual are diminishing. Lower quantities of face highlights in the covered face cause challenges other than ordinary face acknowledgment methods; consequently, the precision pace of acknowledgment is diminishing. That is the reason veiled faces are a major concern in the field of face acknowledgment.

8.3 IMPLEMENTATION

Currently, there is no innovation to identify whether an individual is wearing a cover. Furthermore, individuals are taking benefit of this limitation and will go without cover, which places others at risk, and they might face difficulty by the day's end. This is additionally one reason for this pandemic to spread to this level.

This application distinguishes regardless of whether the individual is wearing cover continuously via video transfer. Whenever the individual isn't wearing a cover, then the essence of that specific individual will be identified, and the caught picture will be coordinated with the picture stored in the information base. Also, sends an admonition message to the distinguished individual (Figure 8.1).

Approach
    1. Deep learning train model.
    2. Apply cover indicator over pictures/live video transfer.

8.3.1 Methodology

Face recognition: The disadvantage of facial covering discovery is all with respect to location. Be that as it may, before facial covering recognition, we could reliably see a face. This can be fundamentally a division issue and in reasonable framework, most track down this errand. After all the specific identification, upheld choice separated from these facial milestones is scarcely a minor advance (Figure 8.2).

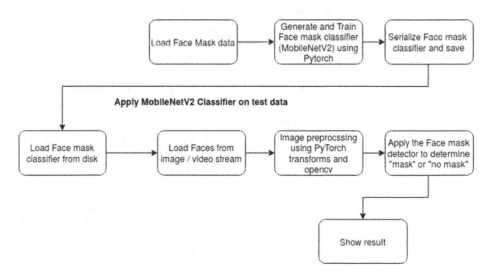

FIGURE 8.1 Proposed system architecture.

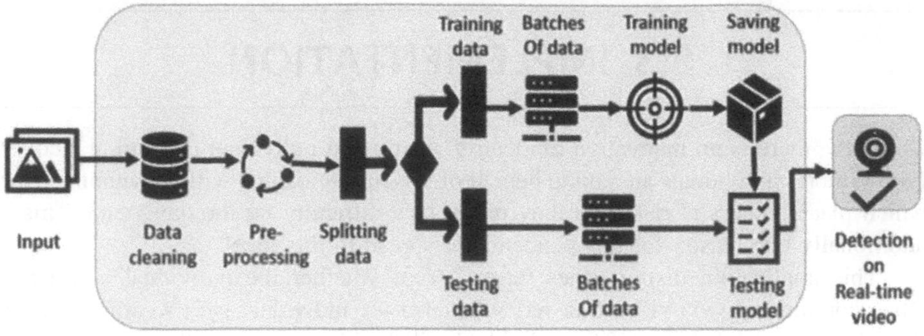

FIGURE 8.2 Flow diagram.

8.3.2 Algorithms Used

- Preparing stage for head and shoulder recognition
- Decide head and shoulder
- Facial covering detection algorithm
- Preparing for presence of human composition
- Distinguishing proof of the covered face

8.3.2.1 Face mask detection

A fitting and powerful facial covering acknowledgment estimation overhauls the introduction of facial covering area systems. It is performed in view of face cover detection algorithms. This estimation focuses more on speed and trustworthiness. This identifier uses Haar-like components and a course classifier. The course object identifier is pre-arranged to recognize appearances, noses, and changed articles.

8.3.2.2 Pre-handling

The recognized face is removed and presented to preprocessing. This pre-taking care of step incorporates altering and changing over concealing picture into grayscale and resize the image into 64 × 64 pixels. The guideline inspiration driving why grayscale depictions are as often as possible used is for removing descriptors as opposed to dealing with concealing pictures directly; grayscale enhances the estimation and diminishes computational requirements (Figure 8.3).

8.3.2.2.1 MobileNetV2

MobileNetV2 is a deep neural network that has been sent for the order issue. Pre-prepared loads of ImageNet were stacked from Tensor Flow. Then, at that point, the base layers are frozen to keep away from hindrance of currently educated highlights. Then, at that point, new teachable layers are added, and these layers are prepared on the gathered dataset so it can decide the highlights to characterize a face wearing a cover from a face

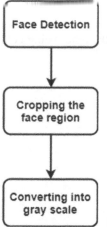

FIGURE 8.3 Pre-processing.

not wearing a veil. Then, at that point, the model is adjusted, and afterward, the loads are saved. Utilizing pre-prepared models maintains a strategic distance from superfluous computational expenses and helps in exploiting currently one-sided loads without losing currently scholarly elements (Figure 8.4).

This layer is the focal square of the convolutional neural network. The term convolution proposes a mathematical mix of two abilities to get beyond what many would

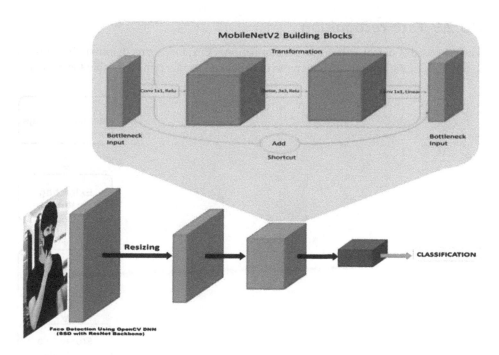

FIGURE 8.4 Building blocks of MobileNetV2.

consider possible. It manages a sliding window part, which helps in clearing out features from an image. This accomplices in age feature maps. The convolution of two utilitarian developments, one being the information picture network An and the other being convolutional piece B, gives us the outcome C as:

$$C(T) = (A * B)(x) = \int \infty - \infty A(T) \times B(T - x) \, dT$$

ALGORITHM 1: Pre-processing and Training on Dataset

INPUT: Images along with their pixels values
OUTPUT: Trained Model

STEP 1: Load Images and their pixel values.
STEP 2: Process the images, i.e., resizing, normalization, and conversion to a 1D array.
STEP 3: Load the Filenames and their respective labels.
STEP 4: Perform Data augmentation and then split data into training and testing batches.
STEP 5: Load MobilenetV2 model from Keras. Train it on training batches and compile it using Adam optimizer.
STEP6: Save the model for future use.

8.3.2.2.2 Dataset development
This dataset is used at the time of recognizing the individuals present in the classroom. The accuracy of this algorithm depends on the way we train the system; see Figure 8.5.

8.3.2.3 Face recognition

The proposed system uses head parts examination (PCA) for face recognition. Resulting to perceiving the faces from the data picture, the component is removed using the principle

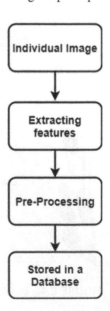

FIGURE 8.5 Database development.

component analysis strategy. This procedure is used to decrease the dimensionality of data space to the similar component space. For customized affirmation, we need to scour the informational collection. Different picture tests were taken for each person, and their components are removed and taken care of in the database as a train picture. For a data picture, face area and component extraction is performed, and features of each face class of arranged picture is contemplated and taken care of in the informational collection.

8.3.2.4 Post-processing

The post-processing method involves sending message to the particular person who is not wearing a mask. To establish this process, it requires information of that person, and it is stored inside the database. The grayscale image extracts from dataset and compares that person with stored data using a machine-learning model. And send warning message to that person.

ALGORITHM 2: Deployment of Face Mask Detector

INPUT: Choice of deployment and Files(optional).
OUTPUT: Images classified into the mask and no mask or Classification in Real-time.

STEP 1: Load saved classifier from disk. Also, load face detector from OpenCV.
STEP 2: If the choice is classification on image:

        Load Image(s)
STEP 2.1: Apply face detection model to Detect faces in an image
STEP 2.2: If Faces are detected:

        Crop face to bounding box coordinates from face detection model
Get predictions from the face classifier model.
Show predictions and save resultant image.
    Else:

        Show no output
STEP 3: If the choice is classification in real-time:
Load real-time feed from OpenCV
Read the feed frame by frame.
STEP 3.1: Apply face detection model to Detect faces in Frames read in real-time
STEP 3.2: If Faces are detected:

        Crop face to bounding box coordinates from face detection model
Get predictions from the face classifier model.
Show output in a real-time feed
    Else:

        Show normal feed
STEP 4: End stream when q is pressed

8.3.2.4.1 Camera placement at public places
The camera would be placed in public places like markets, sidewalks, public malls, etc. It is important to place the camera to detect faces with masks or without masks. Faces will be detected in different light. It will help to detect their face whether they are in a mask or not. Cameras will work 24 × 7 and take continuous live stream; this is completely based on live stream only See Figures 8.6 and 8.7.

8.3.2.4.2 Dataset collection
Dataset assortment is a course of gathering required information from every one of the applicable sources on a case-by-case basis for the examination issue, test the theory, and assess the results.

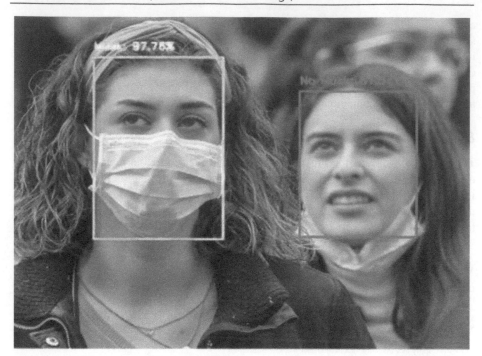

FIGURE 8.6   At public place.

FIGURE 8.7   At public mall.

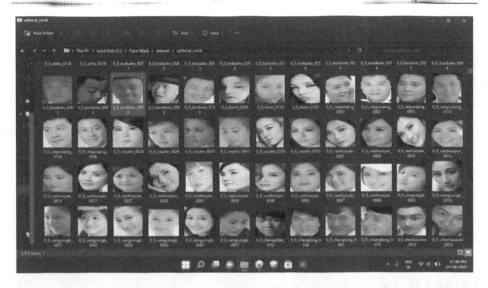

FIGURE 8.8 Dataset collected without mask.

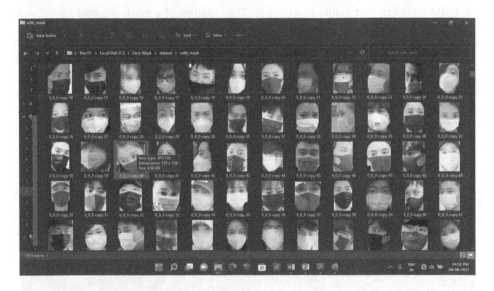

FIGURE 8.9 Dataset collected with mask.

In our proposed framework, we have collected a dataset from Google to train a model and extracted it into our chapter. The dataset will be stored inside a folder and extracted from a program. Each dataset is going to store with different ID and names; see Figures 8.8, 8.9, and 8.10.

8.3.2.4.3 Training and creating a face mask detector model
The first step is to create a training model from the datasets that are collected to build a perfect face mask detector. The next step is to create the main program to use

FIGURE 8.10   Dataset used for face recognition.

the build model in that main program file. The creation of a mask detector model will help in the main program file for detecting the face mask whenever a person's face is encountered in the main real-time video-stream frame. The training will take more time to complete, which makes the model work accurately. It will read all image from the directory that is specified, and the images are resize to fit only the face image within it. While creating a face mask detector model, it will undergo several training and testing processes; after creating the model, it will list the accuracy and loss of the face mask detector model; see Figure 8.11.

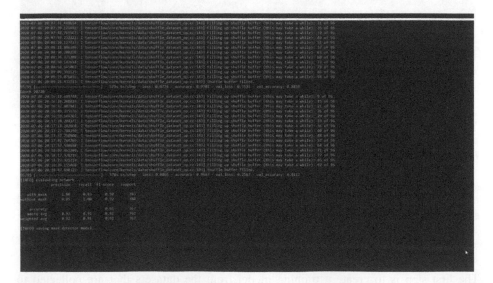

FIGURE 8.11   Creating the mask detector model.

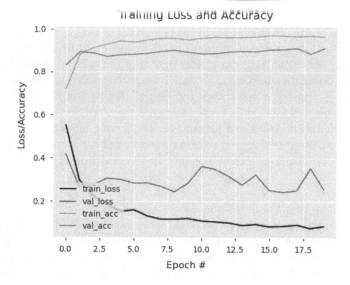

FIGURE 8.12   Training loss and accuracy.

The face mask detector model is plotted using graphical representation; see Figure 8.12.

8.3.2.5 Creating database for users

The details of the user, like name, age, email, phone number, address, are needed for the chapter. For that purpose, we need a database to store the user data. So we will create a database that holds individuals' details. These details will help the chapter to get the detected person's details to send the alert message to that person; see Figure 8.13.

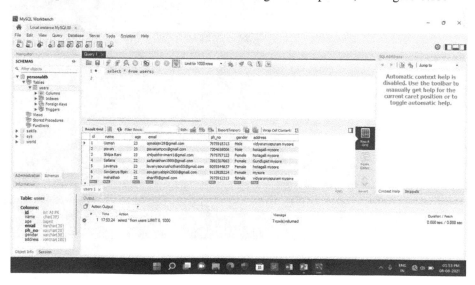

FIGURE 8.13   Database for storing details.

8.3.2.5.1 Face mask detection and recognition of face

The main aim of this chapter is to create face mask detection and face recognition without mask and alert the person not wearing a mask by SMS and email. Know the first step is to detect the face mask, like detecting the person, inside the real-time video-stream frame the chapter has to detect the person wearing a mask or not. And if the person is wearing a mask, then the face of that person has to be surrounded with green frame and labeled as mask and percentage; not wearing a mask means a red fame labeled as no mask and percentage. The person not wearing a mask has to be identified or recognized by not wearing a mask, and the name of that recognized person has to be displayed below the face in live video stream; see Figures 8.14 and 8.15.

8.3.2.5.2 Sending email to those who do not wear face masks

It is also one of the main parts that will help to spread COVID-19 awareness and alert people that if they don't wear mask, then a serious action will be taken against them. Whenever the people step out of their house, they have to wear a mask to protect them from COVID-19. A message is sent to the email address of the person to them; see Figure 8.16.

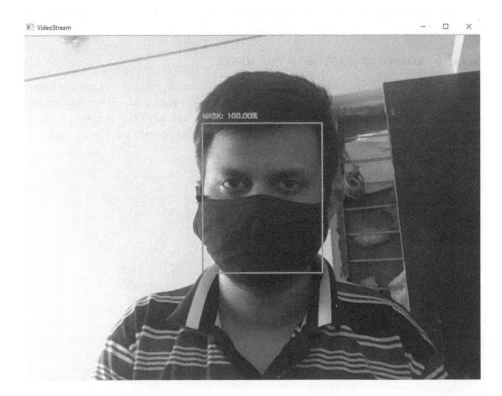

FIGURE 8.14   Face mask detected.

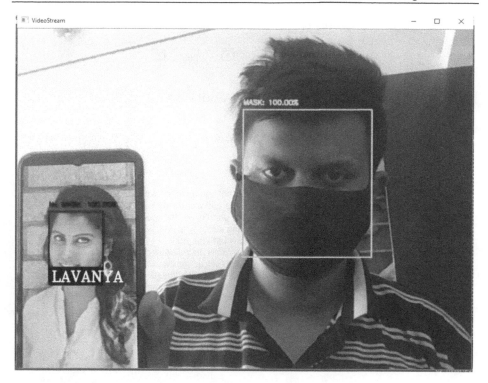

FIGURE 8.15   Face mask and without face mask.

8.3.2.5.3 Sending SMS to phone number
The SMS is sent to the phone number of the persons who are not wearing masks. In this chapter, we are using Twilio service for sending messages; see Table 8.1.

8.4 EXPERIMENT RESULTS AND ANALYSIS

This chapter mainly has three modules: detection of human face masks, recognition of the detected faces, and sending SMS and emails to people detected without face masks. For our experiments, for training, we have collected separate datasets from Google that show people with and without masks. We have 1915 images with masks and 1918 images without masks for training the mask detector model.

8.4.1 Mask Detection Result

The detection results were found to be better when the lighting came from the same side as the camera. The detection rates were also found to be better. The average detection rate is **98.40%**; see Table 8.2, Figures 8.17, 8.18, and 8.19.

Not Wearing Mask Alert Inbox ☆

Real Time Mask Yesterday
to me ∨

As our system has detected that you have not weared a mask Since COVID-19 has spread worldwide and played havoc with the lives of people, we, therefore, had devised the mask-wearing strategy to deal with the danger in an effective way but your non-compliance with the instructions is an indicator of the fact that you are not taking the instructions seriously and putting others in danger along with yourself which is not acceptable at all here. so wear a mask and Stay safe

FIGURE 8.16 Email message.

8.5 CONCLUSION

Improvements are occurring with emerging models, so we have novel facial covering finders that could really inform the public about the clinical status. The technique for OpenCV basic frontal cortex affiliations used in this model allowed us to accommodate results. Sales of pictures were done unequivocally using the MobilenetV2 picture

TABLE 8.1 Test cases

TEST ID	TEST CASE	EXPECTED OUTPUT	ACTUAL OUTPUT	PASS/FAIL
1	Training mask detector	Model has to be build	Model build	Pass
2	Mask detection	The face mask has to be detected	Face mask will be detected	Pass
3	Face recognition	Face has to be recognized	Face will recognize	Pass
4	Email sending	Email has to be Send	Email send	Pass
5	Sms sending	Sms must be send	Sms send	Pass
6	Exit	Q pressed then close camera and execution	camera closed and execution stop	Pass

TABLE 8.2   Accuracy and loss

	PRECISION	RECALL	F1-SCORE	SUPPORT
With Mask	0.98	1.00	0.98	382
Without Mask	1.00	0.98	0.98	383
Accuracy			0.98	766
Macro Avg	0.98	0.98	0.98	766
Weighted Avg	0.98	0.98	0.98	766

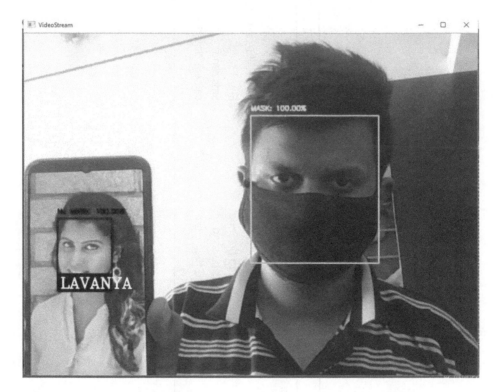

FIGURE 8.17   Multiple face detection with mask and without mask.

classifier, which is one of the unique aspects of the proposed approach. The arranging fuses Mobile Net as the spine; it will be used for high and low estimation conditions. To kill every one of the more extraordinary parts, we sort out a useful strategy for embracing loads from an indistinguishable endeavor facial covering assertion, which is ready on a marvelously immense dataset.

We used OpenCV, Tensor stream, Keras, and DNN to see if people were wearing facial covers. If the individual was not wearing a cover, then the face will be seen and the obvious individual will receive an organized message as SMS and email. The models were tried with pictures and steady video moves. The accuracy of the model is achieved and, the smoothing out of the model is a consistent cycle. We are building an on a very

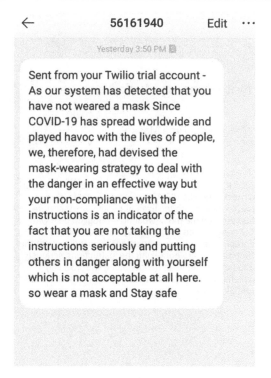

← 　　　56161940　　　Edit ⋯

Yesterday 3:50 PM

Sent from your Twilio trial account -
As our system has detected that you
have not weared a mask Since
COVID-19 has spread worldwide and
played havoc with the lives of people,
we, therefore, had devised the
mask-wearing strategy to deal with
the danger in an effective way but
your non-compliance with the
instructions is an indicator of the
fact that you are not taking the
instructions seriously and putting
others in danger along with yourself
which is not acceptable at all here.
so wear a mask and Stay safe

FIGURE 8.18 SMS received.

basic level definite course of action by tuning from a distance. This specific model could be used as a use case for edge appraisal. Moreover, the proposed framework achieves high-level results on a public facial covering dataset. By the advancement of facial covering area, we can see that the individual is wearing a facial covering and grant their entry. This ability would be of astounding help to the general populace.

8.6 FUTURE ENHANCEMENTS

Later, on the off chance that some generally excellent precise calculation provides additional exactness from an existing one, then it very well may be utilized. The future work is to further develop the acknowledgment pace of calculations when there are inadvertent changes in an individual, like shaving their head, utilizing a scarf, growing facial hair, etc. The framework created a distinguishing feature. It perceives the face up to 15 degree points, considering the left course as 0 degrees, which must be worked on further. Walk acknowledgment can be combined with face acknowledgment frameworks to accomplish better execution of the framework. The idea of SURF highlights can be executed to build the discovery rate. The framework will be conveyed as an

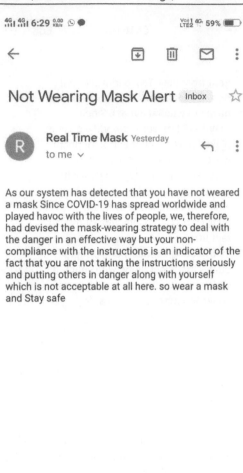

FIGURE 8.19 Email received.

independent tool, which could be utilized by others. This will currently be finished utilizing the MATLAB App developer. Some security elements can be added to encode information, like SMS and email accreditations [8–10].

REFERENCES

[1] Deep Spiking Neural Network for Video-Based Disguise Face Recognition Based on Dynamic Facial Movements, By Daqi Liu, Nicola Bellotto, Member, IEEE, and Shigang Yue Senior Member.

[2] Enhanced Human Face Recognition Using LBPH Descriptor, Multi-KNN, and Back-Propagation Neural Network, By, Mohammad A. Abuznied1 and Ausif Mahmood.

[3] CorrC2G: Color to Gray Conversion by Correlation, By Hossein Ziaei Nafchi, Atena Shahkolaei, Rachid Hedjam.

[4] Influence of Color-to-gray Conversion on the Performance of Document Image Binarization: Toward a Novel Optimization Problem, Rachid Hedjam, Hossein Ziaei Nafchi, Margaret Kalacska and Mohamed Cheriet.

[5] Gowtham M., M. K. Banga, and Mallanagouda Patil, "Secure Internet of Things: Assessing Challenges and Scopes for NextGen Communication" in 2nd IEEE International Conference on Intelligent computing, Instrumentation and Control Technologies (ICICICT-2019) at Vimal Jyothi Engineering College, Kerala.

[6] Deep Learning Based Face Liveness Detection in Videos, Yaman AKBULUT, Abdulkadir SENGÜR, Ümit BUDAK, Sami EKICI.

[7] Face Recognition on Surgically Altered Faces Usig Principal Component Analysis, By Radhakrishnan. B, Dr. L. Padmasuresh.

[8] An Advancement towards Efficient Face Recognition Using Live Video Feed, By Jalendu Dhamija, Tanupriya Choudhary, Praveen Kumar, Yogesh Singh Rathore.

[9] Video Face Recognition Using Siamese Networks with Block-Sparsity Matching, By Fania Mokhayeri, Student Member, IEEE, and Eric Granger.

[10] http://mathworks.com https://www.wikipedia.org https://towardsdatascience.com https://youtube.com

Social Content Distribution Architecture of SIoT

9

Applications, Challenges, Security, and Privacy Paradigm

Venkadeshan Ramalingam[1] and
Senthil Ramadoss[2]

[1]*Information Technology Department, University of
Technology and Applied Sciences-Shinas, Sultanate of Oman*
[2]*Engineering Department, University of Technology and
Applied Sciences-Shinas, Sultanate of Oman*

Contents

DOI: 10.1201/9781003282990-9

9.1 INTRODUCTION

The smart environment is a trendy paradigm based on the Internet of Things (IoT) platform. The Internet of Things (IoT) is a recent technology that aims to completely reshape today's wireless communications by enabling the various gadgets around us, including sensor devices, actuators and controllers, ID tags, smartphones, and smart objects; thus, we can cooperate and collaborate to attain common goals and enhance end-users' daily lives. IoT-related devices collect sensitive information and respond to input changes in near real-time. IoT contributions solve optimization, technology, and device challenges that help people in their daily activities. IoT devices provide solutions that enable the elderly or people with disabilities to live in a more independent and individual world. Thus, it increases autonomy and empowers you to make decisions about your own routine. It also positively affects the quality of your daily life.

Social networking services (SNSs), on the other hand, are defined in the literature as huge networks of individuals in which interactions between community members are modeled and documented. People are the nodes of a social network, and the edges between them reflect relationships. The intersection of IoT and SNS has been highlighted in recent literature as a way for individuals to connect to the omnipresent world of computers. Information from the Internet of Things (IoT) and social networks is used to connect people and things in this architecture [1]. In this way, the Internet of Things and social media may be combined with the purpose of integrating the physical and social worlds in cyberspace. The emerging paradigm, known as the Social Internet of Things (SIoT), could enable network services and new IoT applications in a more efficient and effective manner [2], but solutions to increase service intelligence and resource visibility are needed for the evaluation of object reputation, service discovery, crowdsourcing, and service structure.

To better serve end users, SIoT has exploited everything that is globally linked to form social networks based on shared interests and motivations [3]. The value of SIoT is found in the efficient and safe interaction of multiple entities to meet the end needs of users for certain basic factors, such as dependability, security, time, cost-effectiveness, and availability. In fact, in the ubiquitous computing environment, user confidence and adoption of these services is regarded as a fundamental value when various BT situations offer local or global information services. As a result, the next wave of SIoT will be shaped by the intimate contact between people and things.

As a result, the best service to provide to users is optimized, resulting in improved QoE. The move from these pairs of devices-to-devices and human-to-devices was born out of the notion of trust in the social community. It means that end-users are no more merely customers of the services but rather the participants in the development of applications. In terms of advantages, context, and communication, this travel brings new obstacles. Meanwhile, one of SN's key objectives is to achieve collaboration. Individuals' and communities' online presences are no longer dormant since a plethora of social and contextual data is exchanged and archived. They collaborate to provide data and materials that are relevant to everyday living.

Users and devices in general are the primary players in the development and consumption of services under the SIoT paradigm. People and communities are the centers of the wheel, which collects social data and shares it with shared devices in the real world, ultimately delivering a set of services and improving cooperation for communities and individuals. Because the concept of ubiquitous computing [4] is to deliver computing power whenever, wherever for the benefit of humanity and society [5], it cannot be fully realized without a thorough grasp of society's needs and challenges. This objective will be achieved by combining the social information and relationships that are accessible in online social networking with the world of tangible objects.

Therefore, the main directions of this chapter are to:

- Acquire a better understanding of the major features of SIoT and create a taxonomy.
- Demonstrate a thorough understanding of the fundamental principles and ideas of SIoT to examine and investigate the basic structure of SIoT and address knowledge and awareness gaps.
- Provide a comprehensive narrative of all facets of the SIoT trust relationship, including important functions, assessment factors, and modeling instruments for each SIoT component.
- Exhibit security and privacy challenges to evaluate SIoT samples of the studied literature.
- Research and analyze multiple documents to provide meaningful statistical and descriptive information.
- Ensure key SIoT goals for smart object networks.

Many review papers do not provide a comprehensive focus on SIoT for a detailed discussion of all aspects of SIoT.

- Due to a lack of a complete understanding of SIoT systems, they can be thoroughly examined and compared in every way, yielding reliable data and findings.
- In the SIoT, the absence of appropriate knowledge about an object's structure and communication may be a useful guide for researching and identifying its features and issues.
- Summarizing results and estimates results in less accurate results by exploiting scarcity and underutilization of resources.

- Lack of clarity on structural problems, particularly in the perspective of existing and future problems, with details such as platforms, data sets, entity relationships, human roles, components, and solutions that can solve or predict problems.

The following is the chapter's structure: In section 2, *"The Social Internet of Things (SIoT)"* gives a quick overview of the topic and highlights recent research. The *"SIoT Smart Framework"* section outlines the SIoT's primary structure, as well as taxonomy and analytic comparisons of framework. The section *"Security and Privacy Difficulties in SIoT Applications"* discusses the many security measures and privacy challenges encountered throughout the development of the application. Then in section 5, we expound on the many trust attributes, trust relationships, and trust-related threats that disrupt SIoT operation. As a result, in section 6, we examine the features of valuable knowledge while discussing the SIoT's trust evaluation process.

9.2 THE SOCIAL INTERNET OF THINGS (SIOT)

From the literature, SIoT is a recently described articulation that results from combining social networks (SNs) and the Internet of Things (IoT). The basic behavior is the communication between smart things over the internet as a common network and its characteristics, such as exchanging information, its relationships, are independent of human intervention [1,6]. Furthermore, things may create social ties with one another on their own, and the communication between them might be basic or sophisticated. It presents a wide range of technologies in a wide range of industries, all of which are based on the internet's new intelligent objects. It seeks to address the difficulties of the IoT, such as security, trust, scalability, and resource discovery, by borrowing creativity from social computing. The SIoT is an enhancement of the IoT, which includes a lot of potential in wide range of applications. Despite its lack of intelligence and inability to match the rising application performance expectations from various industries, the social object's relationship seems to be a viable alternative in the deployment of the Social Internet of Things. The extension of social networking in the IoT concept can yield a variety of advantages [7]:

- Similar to human social networks, the SIoT architecture may be changed as essential to enable network mobility, thus enabling rapid objects and services discovery while also assuring scalability.
- The measurement of trustworthiness may be determined by considering the scale of engagement amongst friends.
- A social network analysis model might be adapted to focus IoT challenges (innately related to huge number of objects interconnected in a network).

However, SIoT accede to physical characteristics from the various computational and networking contexts, such as the volume and diversity of appropriate information that

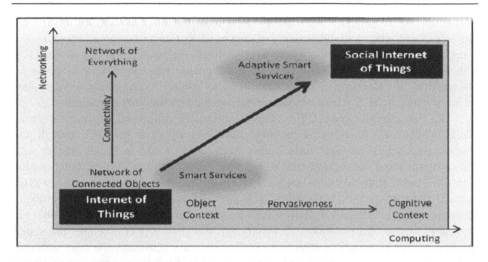

FIGURE 9.1   Evolution of SIoT.

Source: "Reprinted with the permission from Dina Hussein Ali et al., *A social Internet of Things application architecture: applying semantic web technologies for achieving interoperability and automation between the cyber, physical and social worlds* (Ubiquitous Computing. Institut National des Telecommunications, 2015)".

could be maintained for increasing the SIoT adaptive service provisioning [8]. The development of SIoT applications is seen in Figure 9.1. The figure shows that the evolution from IoT to SIoT can be derived from an increase in connectivity on the one hand, which is introduced by the interactions of individuals and communities within the IoT service loop, and an increase in pervasiveness on the other hand, which is introduced by cognitive context (i.e., the integration of objective and subjective context).

In comparison to the more generic smart services promised by IoT, SIoT might be defined by increased flexibility and matching to customer preferences and needs [9].

9.3 SIOT SMART FRAMEWORK

SIoT is based on the evolving notion of social objects [10], where the smart devices are connected to the internet and communicate with people and other social objects through commands and controls. Instead of engaging with one item at a time, the goal is to create a new user experience that leverages mashup capabilities across devices, services, and web applications, which we call "smart services." By leveraging the search mechanisms of social objects as the scope of revelation to manageable network relationships and interactions that resemble social network services, the SIoT creates social structures between objects and people to improve network navigability (SNS). Humans and their interests, wants, and goals are seen as integral parts of cyber-physical-social systems (CPSS), rather than as peripheral elements. In this sense, the reasoning and intelligence of human social features, such as behaviors, choices, emotives, and other individual aspects implanted in human societies, serve as the foundation for attaining integration across the virtual, physical, and social worlds [11]. The Social Internet of Things (SIoT), a paradigmatic type of CPSS that gives an observation for addressing diversification in CPSS while also promoting sociality, has recently evolved. SNS provides social advantages under the SIoT paradigm.

The rich profiling system, for example, maintains contextual data on numerous social factors, such as relationships, trust, and hobbies [12]. In the SIoT, though, the idea of sociality is extended further than individuals to take in social objects with the computing and networking capabilities required to become sensible components. The SIoT smart framework, as depicted in Figure 9.2, uses social structures to offer and utilize smart services, with an intellect system in charge of controlling these social structures. This intelligence system is based on the internet and may be accessible via several platforms and networks. To supply and consume services, people and social objects engage in proactive interactions. This diagram illustrates the core sociality features that describe social way of behaving inside the SIoT framework along with the larger CPSS domain.

To begin, personality is the most crucial attribute of social things that allows them to perform their personal social functions, which includes initiating encounters, communicating, sharing, giving, or canceling resource access based on desires. Second, proactivity means to entities that participate in goal-oriented behavior, such as offering or accepting services to meet out their own needs. In this perception, social things can have objectives that other objects might prepare for, draw the inference, or openly request. Third, the edge property enables social things to adhere to the modest-world phenomenon, which claims that people are all connected across the local network and exchanges are based on short chains of acquaintances. Finally, the trust-worthiness permits social things to offer and utilize data, as well as respond to, build, and retain social relations based on a predefined or attained level of trustworthiness.

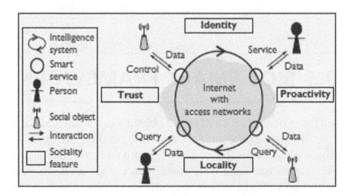

FIGURE 9.2   SIoT framework.

Source: "Reprinted with permission from Dina Hussein et al., *Dynamic Social Structure of Things: A Contextual Approach in CPSS* (IEEE Internet Computing 2015), DOI: 10.1109/MIC.2015.54".

9.3.1 Smart Things to Social Things

Even though the SIoT concept of integrating social aspects with the IoT is still new and under research, some meaningful contributions have already been achieved by providing keys for fetching users via social network services (SNS), as well as using embedded sensors and distributed devices as a technique to improve the applications and services. The IoT paradigm could be supplemented with Twitter communication capabilities in [13], for example, to provide status updates and information on current tasks and activities.

Similarly, [3] shows a WSN-based approach that uses Twitter to share and trade the physical sensed data and resources. According to [14], the IoT framework is a social paradigm for federating pervasive IoT architecture. Further options include extending the IoT with social networks application programming interfaces (APIs). [15] suggests an example that the platform lets individuals to contribute their web-enabled smart devices through which others can share and contribute the information.

9.3.2 SIoT Paradigm

The term SIoT paradigm is a social ecological environment that permits people to connect with smart devices in a social parameters. Web technologies may be used to provide applications and services on top of this foundation. Some essential building pieces need be given to create this framework. The essential parts that make up SIoT are summarized in this section: social roles, socialized objects, everything as a service, and intelligence.

- *Social role:* It is derived from users' SN in [16], and the justification for bringing it into the world of IoT is to ensure network mobility and fast discovery of services. The purpose of available social networks and their application's interfaces to retain a societal model and interactions with smart things promotes the social role in [17]. Furthermore, the recommended social structure enables for the sharing of smart items while depending on the community's confidence. The SN accounts of users can aid service management for SIoT in [9], for example, by utilizing geo-location information and/or publishing the device updates and status. [4] mentions the social role when it comes to using SNs as a control interface for smart things.
- *Intelligence:* According to [17], intelligence is an important element of the SIoT paradigm since it is in control for initiating, terminating, and updating the objects' interactions in SIoT. However, it is not merely the scope of intellect; in [18], intelligence is defined as the ability to allow vibrant things-to-things service discovery in which smart devices may automatically comprehend each other's services. Intelligence is envisioned as a bridge incorporating numerous techniques such as ontologies, methodologies for evaluating user-provided material, and recommendation systems, according to the work given in [19]. To summarize, intelligence appears to be

restricted in the literature to self-governing control systems that promote the usage of services.

- *Socialized objects:* Early contribution in SIoT, such as [14–16], established the concept, which is likely the most essential architectural elements because it describes how numerous smart devices and sensors will initiate the communication with users via the source of internet. This work also includes the study of the characteristics of social devices, concentrate on the idea of facilitating smart objects to "talk" with other objects, communicate the experiences about certain circumstances, and seek assistance. The authors [6] introduced the notion of creating the relationship between SNs and social objects; in [20], social gadgets connect with humans through an SN background using web protocols.
- *Everything as a service:* The concept of converting social things and SN functions into services and making them readily discoverable and interconnected with other services has been advocated in the background studies to take advantage of the merging the social and device responsibilities encouraged by SIoT. As a result, users may share smart object services with peer users or other devices [2]. This sort of sharing comprises making usage of one's social media to find and nurture services. By connecting smart devices with the services they provide, [12] conveys the concept of turning "everything" into a service as a bigger vision. The social role may help users find new services to utilize or integrate with existing services, allowing them to do more with less.

9.4 SECURITY AND PRIVACY CHALLENGES IN SIOT APPLICATIONS

In general, security refers to a means of defending data from a computer system assault. The importance of data determines how security approaches change from one application to the next. The following components may make up a network's overall security framework:

1. Confidentiality
2. Integrity
3. Authentications
4. Non-repudiation
5. Availability
6. Privacy

SIoT, on the other hand, has shown an ability to face the identical difficulties as cloud computing. The authors of Farris et al. [20] created SIoT design and refined it by leveraging cloud-processing concepts to reduce or eliminate interruption time. The following are the SIoT's most pressing security and privacy issues:

- *Heterogeneity:* The network of SIoT is composed of millions of smart objects in conjunction with several parameters like protocols, and standards, that must all be recoverable [19]. These discrepancies have allowed the development of a heterogeneous system of objects that directly impact their communication and consistency with one another, resulting in increased complexity [21], and the heterogeneousness nature of objects led directly to several important challenges such as interoperability and compatibility, which require results.

- *Mobility and dynamicity:* In a dynamic environment, smart objects regularly change locations, resulting in challenges such as a absence of adequate object search for choosing and offering services [4]. Another essential topic is the dynamic performance of things and their environs, which results in difference in the state of objects. As an outcome, the objects' network state changes. Some solutions to these problems have been presented, such as:

  Create objects communities: Communities of objects may be established for the aim of resolving mobility based on distinct qualities such as mobility, social behavioral patterns, social resemblence [15], and mutual motivations to interact [22]. When an object moves, the structure of the community alters as well. Consequently, we may use Euclidean, adjacent matrix, or GPS functions to detect the present position of items to compute their distance, or we can use the SWIM27 model to describe their mobility [3], to build SIoT objects based on the location traces [22].

  Dynamic behavior of objects: To prevent the network topology from changing, objects must establish certain fundamental guidelines and procedures by their owners to handle these updates. Yet, adaptation is another challenge that results from this dynamic nature since an object must respond to these rapid changes [2].

- *Tracking objects:* Tracking objects, interactions, and activities is one of the most important concerns in SIoT and large-scale networks that has received little attention [5]. We can offer some suggestions for resolving this issue, such as:

  - *Using a graph model:* Based on the social behaviors of following objects, we may offer a network model for smart object interactions.

  - *Determine rules:* To create, update, forecast, or remove the edges between two items, certain rules must be defined. Each item may be thought of as a primary node. Their edges are formed by their relationship with one another. Their actions give it more weight based on the kind and characteristic of a set of objects' relationship, such as a shared interest, delivering a certain service/services, being in the same place, and so on.

  - *Using objects movement patterns:* For tracking item movements with the support of GPS and three-dimensional location techniques, a resource discovery based on preference and movement similarity (RDPM) was described [11].

- *Security, trust, and privacy:* Since the SIoT [23] has such a large linked ecosystem of devices, adaptable services, and users, security is critical to safely sharing information. In contrast to most of the research done in this subject, it remains one of the major difficulties that must be addressed for the system's survival in spite of multiple threats to have security, dependability, availability, and resiliency in interactions [24]. As a result, there are a few options for dealing with this issue, such as:

- *Access control method:* We require a security mechanism to avoid unwanted data access.
- *Effective encryption system:* We can also encrypt data with a reliable encryption technique or employ cost-efficient and self-synchronizing patterns to protect actual characteristics from attacks.
- *Trust management framework:* We construct new apps for establishing trust between devices and users using the SIoT trustworthiness management framework.
- *Model for secure data exchange:* Regulations may also be used to generate privacy-preserving consumer and object communities, which results in a vibrant and secure data sharing paradigm with greater privacy and data security.
- *Node behavior predictions: U*se the approaches similar to machine learning [25] and decision trees [24] to predict node behavior.
- *Resource-constrained devices:* Despite the fact that the SIoT is a resource-constrained system and this problem has a serious influence on the network's life and information exchange, there is still no optimum solution to deal with the current issues by considering resource constraints at all stages of design to achieve a meaningful interaction [10]. We really need further investigations and evaluations to build an efficient resource management system [26] on the SIoT to get the most out of it.
  - *Effective management of resources:* Because of the dynamic behavior of social objects, that results to significantly much more computational energy and strength in this system, we need to have an outstanding resource management system to address it.
- *Effortless service discovery and search:* Because of the increasing quantity of items in SIoT, picking friendships, looking for services, and building proper connections between objects has become more difficult. This problem raises the overhead of the SIoT method at all levels. Effective service search and discovery is one of the key issues to lowering the system overhead, providing more efficient service provision [14], quicker object transactions, and greater network navigability and scalability.

9.5 MANAGEMENT OF TRUST IN THE SOCIAL INTERNET OF THINGS (SIOT)

The challenge of this new paradigm is trust on the user's sensitive data, on the other hand, stay apprehensive and hesitant. They are afraid that their personal information will be shared and that their privacy will be abused. Without trustworthy solutions to safeguard users' secure means of communication and trustworthy interactions, the SIoT paradigm will not achieve sufficient traction to be deemed a well-established technology, and most of its promise will be compromised. As a result, trust management has emerged as a crucial concern in SIoT [24] to provide accurate trustworthy analysis of data, certified services, and improved user protection. It aids users in addressing and conquering their suspicions and anxieties, as well as increasing IoT service and app uptake and consumption.

A stage of trustworthiness must be developed to use the degree of contact among social objects, and network models can be customized to handle SIoT [23]. A trust relationship entails at a minimum two parties: a trustor and a trustee who are mutually trusting one another for mutual gain, as well as the objectives in which the relationship of trust exists, much like the trust relationship's goals, the trust context (e.g., location, time, activity, their operational mode, devices being used, etc.), and the trust threat.

It identifies some information that might be applied to define the context or status of the parties involved [27]. Trustworthy management is crucial in networking systems like SIoT.

9.5.1 Trust Properties

The trust properties have been calculated in a variety of ways, based on the properties that were considered, as below:

- Direct trust: According to this attribute [7], the trust between the trustor and the trustee is founded on firsthand interactions, experiences, or observations that reflect this attribute.
- Trust can be indirect: In this situation, the trustor and trustee had never met or worked together before. The trust here is based on other nodes' suggestions and views [28]. We're talking about transferable trusts.
- Trust can be local: It fluctuates from one object to the next, suggesting that an object "I" can trust an object "J" while another object "K" can distrust the same object "J".
- Trust must be asymmetric, means the two objects connected through a link might got several stages of trustworthiness. The truth that object "A" has trust on object "B" does not mean that object "B" be supposed to believe on object "A" [8].
- Trust can be global: The fact that each object in the network has a unique trust value that is known by all other objects is referred to as global trust, also known as reputation.
- Trust must be subjective: The trust value is fundamentally a subjective assessment based on several factors, a few of which may be additionally important when compared with others [23]. Trust could be an objective in certain situations, for example when it is act as a deterministic factor on a device's QoS characteristics.
- Trust can be context-dependent, meaning that a object "I's" trust in a object "J" differs from one scenario to the next.

- Trust may be a compound property: It consists of a variety of diverse traits, such as consistency, honesty, candor, safety, competency, and appropriateness, all of which must be believed in context [25].
- Previous experiences can impact current levels of trust: This feature suggests that past experiences can influence current levels of trust.
- Trust should be dynamic: It changes over time in a non-monotonic way. It can be changed or revoked at any moment, and it must be flexible enough to react to changing circumstances in the environment where the trust decision was made [5].

9.5.2 Trust-Related Attacks

A malware node seeks to disrupt the IoT's core functionalities (for example, service composition). It can also carry out the trust-related attacks listed below [12]:

- Self-promotional assaults (SPA): They might exaggerate their reputation (by making positive endorsements for itself) to be chosen as a service provider, but later cease to offer services or provide services that are defective.
- Bad-mouthing attacks (BMA): These attacks have the potential to devastate the reputations of well-behaved objects (by making negative remarks against them) and diminish the chances of better objects being chosen as service suppliers.
- Ballot stuffing assaults (BSA): This can assist poor objects in improving their reputation (by providing positive suggestions) and so increase their chances of getting carefully chosen as service providers.
- Whitewashing attacks (WA): a mischievous object might vanish and reappearance in the program to erase its negative status.
- Discriminatory attacks (DA): In social IoT systems, a malicious node may discriminate against non-friends or nodes with weak social links due to human nature or a predilection toward friends (without many mutual friends).
- Opportunistic service attacks (OSA): A malicious object may offer excellent service to get a valuable status on the cheap, particularly if it perceives its reputation is sliding due to bad performance. If it has a good reputation, it may be able to work with another malicious objects to carry out bad-mouthing and ballot stuffing assaults.

9.5.3 Requirements and Limits for Trust Management in SIoT

SIoT environments are distinct from social networks, which have a huge variety of criteria and restrictions, for instance:

- A big number of objects and gadgets are engaged.
- Storage capacity is restricted for entities and devices.

- Entities and gadgets have limited compute resources.
- A huge number of social objects join and leave networks at any given instant, resulting in high dynamism.
- Energy utilization, which is one of the most significant challenges for businesses and battery-powered devices.
- The criticality and sensitivity of the services and apps that are employed because they interact with the actual world.
- Power efficiency, which supports tiny objects limits by creating trust management algorithms and processes quicker and a smaller amount of energy-consuming.

As a result, trust management methods must account for and assure the SIoT network's scalability, flexibility, survivability, power efficiency, and robustness.

9.6 TRUST EVALUATION MECHANISM IN THE SOCIAL-INTERNET-OF-THINGS (SIOT)

In the emerging Internet of Things era, the trust factor has been acknowledged as an essential component in ensuring secure, dependable, and smooth connections and essential services. Nevertheless, many problems persist due to the vagueness of the idea of trust as well as the different types of trust models used in various settings. With the support of the Internet of Things (IoT), we are nearing a new idea in a cyber-real-social system (CPSS), which links cyber-social webs with the actual world [12]. Thanks to billions of detecting and triggering devices, the Internet of Things (IoT) is anticipated to monitor many facets of human existence from anywhere on world. Data collected from observations is collated, computed, and examined to offer relevant intelligence on occurrences and events related to a variety of real-world experiences. Using different categories of information from the cyberspace and social domains, a collection of services might uncover latent operational competences and build an endwise feedback amongst people's requirements and social object reactions.

In this way, trust is crucial factor in supporting both individuals and services in overcoming risk and uncertainty when making decisions [2]. In our opinion, one of the most important characteristics of a trustee's credibility is dependability (in the case where the trustee act as a machine). The important difference among trust and reliability is the enrollment of societal relationships (both human and technological), which is regulated in the form of social capital elements (Figure 9.3a). Individuals and social networks can utilize social capital to examine various aspects of themselves and their behaviors, networks, patterns, and norms that have emerged over time as a result of social interactions, as well as to quantify trust. In this sense, trust refers to a wide concept that includes dependability.

When it comes to the SIoT, trust should be seen from the standpoint of a trustor in relation to a society. Social connections, an individual's subjective perception, and the

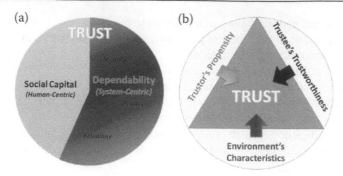

FIGURE 9.3 (a) Trust relationship between social capital and dependability; (b) three characteristics of trust.

Source: "Reprinted with permission from Nguyen Binh Truong et al., *Toward a Trust Evaluation Mechanism in the Social Internet of Things* (Sensors 2017), no. 17, 1346; DOI: 10.3390/s17061346".

surroundings should not be overlooked [29]. We have previously said that, in addition to a trustee's trustworthiness, environmental elements such as vulnerabilities, threats, and dangers play a role in trustworthiness evaluation (Figure 9.3b). It is clear since trust only develops in high-risk situations where the trustor is vulnerable. As the three primary characteristics of trustworthiness, trust attributes (TAs) are typically divided into three categories: ability, benevolence, and integrity [27].

- *Ability:* It's a trustworthiness metric that measures a trustee's ability to meet a trust's objectives. For achieving a trust aim, an object may have great benevolence and truthfulness, but the outcomes may not be adequate if it is not competent. Other ideas utilized as trust attributes in a lot of trust-associated work include competency, expertise, and integrity.
- *Benevolence:* It's a trust metric that assesses a trustee's willingness to perform well or avoid causing damage to the trustor. It also guarantees that the trustee has been operated in the best interests of the trustor. This idiom includes certain trust related attributes, such as trustworthiness, significance, and self-assertion.
- *Integrity:* It is a trustworthiness measurement that reveals the trustee remains to a set of criteria that allows the trustor to consider the trustee is not destructive and will not fail to deliver on its promises. Justice and morality are two examples of where these ideals might originate from. Some of the TAs in this term include truthfulness, comprehensiveness, and reliability [30].

Table 9.1 lists several trust attributes keywords that are grouped into three types. A few of the TAs in Table 9.1 are widely utilized in trust background studies varying from social learning to recent information technologies, while others are less widely utilized and only exist in limited situations [12]. Despite the fact that every one of the three components, ability, benevolence, and integrity, reflects certain distinct characteristics

TABLE 9.1 Three levels of trustworthiness keywords

ABILITY TAS	BENEVOLENCE TAS	INTEGRITY TAS
Competence, ability, capability, expertness, credibility, predictability, timeliness, robustness, safety, stability, scalability, reliability, dependability	Good intention, goodness, certainty, cooperation, cooperativeness, loyalty, openness, caring, receptivity, assurance	Honesty, morality, completeness, consistency, accuracy, certainty, availability, responsiveness, faith, discreetness, fairness, promise, fulfilment, persistence, responsibility, tactfulness, sincerity, value, congeniality, accessibility

Source: "Nguyen Binh Truong et al., "Toward a Trust Evaluation Mechanism in the Social Internet of Things", *Sensors* (2017), no. 17, 1346; DOI: 10.3390/s17061346".

of trust factors, most of the categories are not clearly differentiated, and how they are understood clearly relies on the context and trust goals. In certain instances, and for some goals, specific TAs are the same, while in others they are unique.

9.7 CONCLUSION

For beginners interested in SIoT research, this chapter provides a detailed, systematic explanation of SIoT framework, trust management, relationships, applications, and privacy and security problems in SIoT implementation. SIoT is a new paradigm, yet in its early stages, that attempts to tackle reliability, scalability, and recognition of data and knowledge by pulling inspiration from SNs and offering a stage for improved human-to-thing interactions. This developing area is expected to have many studies and highly technical research in the future.

REFERENCES

[1] A. Pandharipande, 1 June 1, 2021. Social Sensing in IoT Applications: A Review. *IEEE Sensors Journal*, vol. 21, no. 11, 12523–12530. 10.1109/JSEN.2021.3049714

[2] D. Dhivya, and R. Venkadeshan, 2016. "Bayesian Spam Filtering in Online Social Networks."

[3] W. Abdelghani, C. A. Zayani, I. Amous, and S. Florence, 2016. Trust Management in Social Internet of Things: A Survey. In Y. Dwivedi et al. (eds.) *Social Media: The Good, the Bad, and the Ugly. I3E 2016*. Lecture Notes in Computer Science, 9844, pp. 430–441.

[4] H. Huang, D. Zhang, F. Xiao, K. Wang, J. Gu, and R. Wang, 2020. Privacy-Preserving Approach PBCN in Social Network with Differential Privacy. *IEEE Transactions on Network and Service Management*, vol. 17, no. 2, 931–945.

[5] H. Shao et al., Jul. 2020. Truth discovery with multi-modal data in social sensing. *IEEE Transactions on Computers*, vol. 70, no. 9, 1325–1337.

[6] D. Wu, B. Liu, Q. Yang, and R. Wang, 2020. Social-Aware Cooperative Caching Mechanism in Mobile Social Networks. *Journal of Network and Computer Applications*, vol. 149, 102457.

[7] D. Hussein, et al., 2015. Dynamic Social Structure of Things: A Contextual Approach in CPSS. *IEEE Internet Computing*, vol. 19, no. 3, 12–20. 10.1109/MIC.2015.27

[8] G. Beigi, and H. Liu, Mar. 2020. A Survey on Privacy in Social Media: Identification Mitigation and Applications. *ACM/IMS Transactions on Data Science*, vol. 1, no. 1, 1–38.

[9] D. Dhivya, and R. Venkadeshan, 2016. Averting Intruder Attack on Social Network by Data Sanitization. *International Journal of Computer Science and Engineering*, vol. 4, no. 2, 1410–1414.

[10] S. Rho, and Y. Chen, 2018. Social Internet of Things: Applications, Architectures and Protocols. *Future Generation Computer Systems*, vol. 82, 667–668. 10.1016/j.future. 2018.01.035

[11] H. Vahdat-Nejad et al., 2019. Social Internet of Things and New Generation Computing-A Survey. book chapter entitled *Toward Social Internet of Things (SIoT): Enabling Technologies, Architectures and Applications*, Springer. https://link.springer.com/chapter/10.1007/978-3-030-24513-9_8

[12] H. Lee, and J. Kwon, 2015. Survey and Analysis of Information Sharing in Social IoT. In *Proc. 8th International Conference on Disaster Recovery and Business Continuity (DRBC)*, Jeju Island, South Korea 15–18. 10.1109/DRBC.2015.13

[13] I. Chen, F. Bao, and J. Guo, 2015. Trust-Based Service Management for Social Internet of Things Systems. *IEEE Transactions on Dependable and Secure Computing*, 13, 684–696.

[14] O. Ben Abderrahim, M. H. Elhedhili, and L. Saidane, 2017. CTMS-SIOT: A Context-Based Trust Management System for the Social Internet of Things. In *Proc. 13th International Wireless Communications and Mobile Computing Conference (IWCMC)*, pp. 1903–1908. 10.1109/IWCMC.2017.7986574

[15] N. B. Truong et al., 2017. Toward a Trust Evaluation Mechanism in the Social Internet of Things. *Sensors*, vol. 17, 1346. 10.3390/s17061346

[16] M. Z. Hasan, and F. Al-Turjman, 2019. SWARM-Based Data Delivery in Social Internet of Things. *Future Generation Computer Systems*, vol. 92, 821–836. 10.1016/j.future.2017. 10.032

[17] M. Rad et al., 2020. Social Internet of Things: Vision, Challenges, and Trends. *Human-Centric* Computing *and Information Sciences*, vol. 10, 52. 10.1186/s13673-020-00254-6

[18] R. Bi, Q. Chen, L. Chen, J. Xiong, and D. Wu, 2020. A Privacy-Preserving Personalized Service Framework through Bayesian Game in Social IoT. *Wireless Communications and Mobile Computing*, vol. 2020, 8891889. 10.1155/2020/8891889

[19] D. Hussein, P. Soochang, and N. Crespi, 2015. A Cognitive Context-Aware Approach for Adaptive Services Provisioning in Social Internet of Things. In *IEEE ICCE Conference Proceeding*.

[20] K. H. Rahouma et al., 2020. Challenges and Solutions of Using the Social Internet of Things in Healthcare and Medical Solutions—A Survey. *Toward Social Internet of Things (SIoT): Enabling Technologies, Architectures and Applications*, Studies in Computational, Springer Nature Switzerland Intelligence 846. 10.1007/978-3-030-24513-9_2

[21] K. Rabadiya, A. Makwana, and S. Jardosh, 2017. Revolution in Networks of Smart Objects: Social Internet of Things. In *Soft Computing and its Engineering Applications*. Changa, India.

[22] S. Rho, and Y. Chen, 2018. Social Internet of Things: Applications, Architectures, and Protocols. *Future Generation Computer Systems*, vol. 82, 667–668.

[23] A. M. Ortiz et al., 2014. The Cluster between Internet of Things and Social Networks: Review and Research Challenges. *IEEE Internet of Things J.*, vol. 1, no. 3, 206–215.

[24] L. Atzori et al., 2012. The Social Internet of Things (SIoT)—When Social Networks Meet the Internet of Things: Concept, Architecture and Network Characterization. *Computer Networks*, 56, 3594–3608.

[25] S. P. George et al., 2017. Social Internet of Vehicles. *International Research Journal of Engineering and Technology (IRJET)*, vol. 4, no. 4, 712–717.

[26] R. Venkadeshan, and M. Jegatha, 2018. TMV: Trust-Matrix-Value Based Neighbor Peer Selection for Secure Query Forwarding in P2P Networks. In Smart Trends in Information Technology and Computer Communications. SmartCom 2017. Communications in Computer and Information Science, vol. 876. Springer, Singapore. 10.1007/978-981-13-1423-0_10

[27] R. Venkadeshan, and M. Jegatha, 2021. A Survey on Internet of Things (IoT): Communication Model, Open Challenges, Security and Privacy Issues. In M. Tuba, S. Akashe, and A. Joshi (eds.) *ICT Systems and Sustainability. Advances in Intelligent Systems and Computing*, vol. 1270. Springer, Singapore. 10.1007/978-981-15-8289-9_48

[28] H. Xiao, N. Sidhu, and B. Christianson, 2015. Guarantor and Reputation Based Trust Model for Social Internet of Things. In *International Wireless Communications and Mobile Computing Conference (IWCMS), IEEE*, 600–605. 10.1109/IWCMC.2015.7289151

[29] S. Shahab et al., 2022. SIoT (Social Internet of Things): A Review. *ICT Analysis and Applications*. 10.1007/978-981-16-5655-2_28

[30] M. S. Roopa, S. Pattar, R. Buyya et al., 2019. Social Internet of Things (SIoT): Foundations, Thrust Areas, Systematic Review and Future Directions. *Computer Communications*, vol. 139, 32–57.

Efficient and Secured IoT-Based Agriculture Wireless Sensor Network Using Swarm Optimization

10

Venkatesh Shankar and Shrinivas A Sirdeshpande

Department of Computer Science and Engineering, KLS Vishwanathrao Institute of Technology, Haliyak, Karnataka, India

Contents

10.1	Introduction	180
	10.1.1 Most Important IoT Structure Blocks and Layers	181
	10.1.1.1 Profits and Trials of IIoT	184
10.2	Literature Survey	186
10.3	Secured and Efficient Swarm Based Method	191
10.4	Results and Discussions	193
10.5	Conclusion	195
References		196

DOI: 10.1201/9781003282990-10

10.1 INTRODUCTION

With the development of wi-fi sensor communities, [1–3] has been used in a green approaches to adorn community performances in numerous domain names. Because of their potential and clear arrangement format, remarkable sensors should be used in environmental problems [4–7]. Furthermore, the sensor knobs operate independently and assemble the system using an ad-hoc technique. Nodes in a cutting-edge form of organization do not have a strong network topology and will be part of a more suitable neighbor for records communication based on a few parameters. With the help of certain entry and cluster skulls, the sensor nodes enjoy searching records earlier in the direction of Base Station. All cluster skulls have the responsibility of consolidating the information gathered. Moreover, the cluster skulls preserve the obtained information in the memory, look at the works, and run a mechanism. Clients can access the compacted BS through the internet or precise net primarily based complete packages to retrieve the desired information [8–11]. At the time of data communication, organized sensors might be motionless or portable. The fixed sensors are called nonadaptive, and their built transmitting tables are fixed. At the same time, routing tables of sensors update frequently since any alternate acquires the system topology.

The fixed routing methods are better secured as related to dynamic routing, but the reactions, probably grounded by static methods, are inappropriate for large area networks [12,13]. In recent years, the era of the Internet of Things is compounded through different arenas to advance communication in phrases throughput source consumption and capacity dissemination [14–16]. In the Internet of Things, numerous physical tools are associated with reworking the records as the internet is used. Moreover, the methods of sensor networks deliver the inspiration meant for Internet of Things structures and provisions in looking at and accelerating the environments of network surroundings. The below Figure 10.1 exemplifies the state of keen farming cultivation using sensors.

Figure 10.1 In the planned structure, wireless farming, cultivation sensors are distributed inside the cultivation terrestrial for extracting particular statistics related to

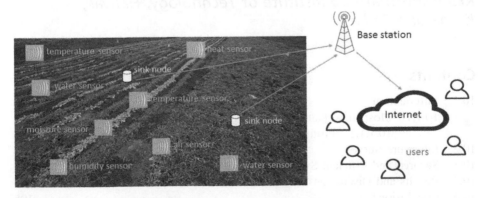

FIGURE 10.1 Agriculture monitoring using WSN.

earth or soil configuration, corresponding moisture, hotness, wetness tiers, and aquatic finders. This proceeding is steadily communicated to cluster skulls, which are working as reminiscence barriers or storage areas to store facts within the BS route. Next to the reaction of information with the aid of the BS, the BS can securely delivery-update statistics to customers for an inexperienced preference in a short amount of time. The proposed framework invests resources on experienced and dependable routing to automate agricultural productions while reducing farmer strain. Agricultural sensors' monitoring data is intelligently and safely routed through the BS channel, which increases agricultural land monitoring and productivity. The suggested framework's simulated experiments outperformed results in the same amount of time when compared to giving answers that were mostly focused on certain network parameters.

10.1.1 Most Important IoT Structure Blocks and Layers

Earlier, it's important to note that no single, globally acknowledged IoT design exists. Depending on the business requirement, the complexity and quantity of construction stages vary. Cisco, IBM, and Intel, for example, suggested a reference model at the 2014 IoT World Forum; this model includes up to seven layers. The engineering will "assist with educating CIOs, IT divisions, and designers on sending of IoT projects, and speed up IoT reception," according to a Cisco-authorized public statement (Figure 10.2).

An extensive range of "topics" or endpoint devices characteristically link a few of the bodily and digital worlds in the early ranges of any IoT machine. They are available in a wide variety of shapes and sizes, from tiny silicon chips to massive vehicles. Based on their capabilities, IoT gadgets may be divided into the subsequent primary classes.

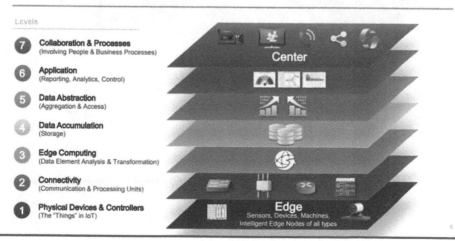

FIGURE 10.2 IoT reference model.

Examples include probes, gauges, metres, and different sensors. They collect physical statistics like temperature and humidity, convert it to electrical impulses, and send it to the IoT sensors for the Internet of Things; they are frequently small and coffee-energy.

Actuators convert electrical impulses from the IoT device into bodily moves. Actuators are required with the aid of motor controllers, lasers, and robot hands. Sensor-prepared machines and gadgets are used. The 2d degree leads factors of all communications for some of the IoT infrastructure's gadgets, networks, and cloud services. Connectivity among the physical layer and the cloud may be done in approaches: immediately through the TCP or UDP/IP stack, or in a roundabout way through gateway hardware or software program program modules that cope with protocol translation in addition to encryption and decryption of IoT information.

Different networking technologies are used to speak among gadgets and cloud offerings or gateways. Ethernet connects IoT gadgets, which are permanently hooked up, include protection and video cameras, commercial equipment, and sport consoles, as shown in Figure 10.3.

Wi-fi, the maximum extensively used wi-fi networking protocol, is good for providing in-depth IoT answers that want to be recharged and operated in a compact area. Smart domestic gadgets that might be linked to the electrical grid are a terrific illustration of the way they can be used.

NFC (near field communication) is an area that permits two devices to share statistics throughout a distance of 4 inches (10 cm) or much less. Wearables typically

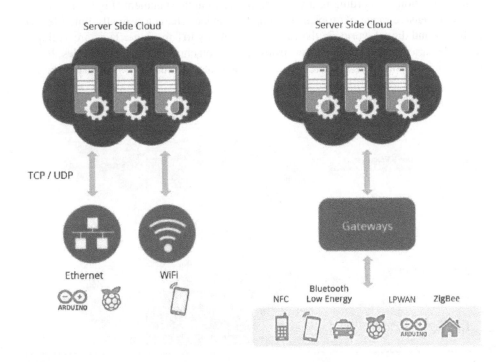

FIGURE 10.3 IoT reference model.

use Bluetooth for short-range conversation. The Bluetooth low-energy (BLE) model became the popular solution to meet the wishes of low-power IoT gadgets.

LPWAN (low-electricity wide-vicinity network) was created mainly for IoT gadgets. It has a long-range wi-fi communication variety, minimal strength consumption, and battery lifestyles of 10 years or greater. By presenting records in small portions on a ordinary basis, the generation satisfies the desires of smart cities, smart buildings, and clever agriculture (field monitoring). ZigBee is a low-energy wireless community that enables the transmission of small records packets throughout quick distances. ZigBee can accommodate up to 65 nodes, its maximum function. It became used ordinarily for domestic automation, but it could also be utilized for low-electricity gadgets in commercial, scientific, and clinical environments. Cellular networks offer dependable information transmission and almost global insurance. Two cell requirements were designed especially for this motive.

The studies have come to be completed in additives to obtain facts about the studied problem memory variety. The first part focused on research based almost entirely on published materials, such as magazine articles, website data, and books. This study aided in comprehending the concept of the Internet of Things and how it is being safeguarded in the enterprise world (Industrial Internet of Things). The second section of the study looked into the technology acceptance model (TAM) and how it could be used to identify the drawbacks of incorporating Industrial Internet of Things concepts into Fiji's manufacturing industries. This study was carried out using surveys that were created after reviewing the variables investigated in the technology acceptance model. Two surveys were created, both of which focused on people collaborating through their devices. The first sample consisted of 50 participants, all of whom were managers from the information technology and operations departments of Fiji's manufacturing sector. The second survey was designed in the direction of a larger well-known character base, which comprised records-era police and one-of-a-kind buyers of the included technology. This pattern was centred on a hard and quick group of 100 persons.

We looked at five IoT (Industrial Internet of Things) applications (IIoT). From business automation to predictive preservation, smart logistics management, extra-excessive exceptional product quality, and smart stock control, there's a lot to consider. To begin, enterprise automation is the use of coordinated systems such as computer systems or mechanical devices, as well as records systems, to control various techniques and systems in a manufacturing organisation for potential workers. In addition to mechanisation, success hinges on the expansion of business opportunities. Regular automation, programmable automation, and flexible automation are three smooth commands that can be applied to these architectures.

"Industrial automation encompasses a wide range of amazing manipulative structures, such as motion control, safety structures, and digital control. Commercial automation can also be defined in a large number of super domains that perform precise procedures" (Breivold & Sandström, 2015).

- Predictive maintenance is a technique that uses smart metered connections to ensure cost-effective monetary savings for routine or time-based certainly preventive maintenance. Procedures are designed to be a beneficial resource in completing the kingdom of in-provider tools in a way that predicts how long preservation will take. Predictive preservation is continuing to advance, thanks to advancements in big data analytics and cloud computing. Predictive safety is built on meticulous records, and the Internet of Things (IoT) provides a wonderful method for reading data and connecting it.

- Smart logistics management is the result of smart products and services, essentially having the right product at the right time in the right place in the perfect circumstance. They are imperceptible, tranquil, and, as a result, obvious on top of things, freeing personnel from logistics control. "A smart technique to successfully combine planning and scheduling, ICT infrastructure, human beings, and government policymaking" (2012, Kawa).
- The coordination of those four critical areas is called smart logistics. ICT infrastructure provides the right assets at the right time for more quick and specific information, allowing for better planning and scheduling. As we move closer to augmented intelligence, people and robots will collaborate for the greater good.

10.1.1.1 Profits and Trials of IIoT

- Facility management is the interconnection of all systems in communication with one other and with personnel via interface while also maintaining hardware's relevance. These physical structures are able to control and be a part of themselves on a regular basis inside the factual community, grade by grade. "This is more than just adding a robot or processing a highly automated conveyor belt. In a converted environment, these biological structures may be able to act as self-contained systems" (Hartmann & Halecker, 2015). Sensors can also be used to present display alarm vibrations, temperature changes, and high-quality dynamics that could be future causes for a great deal fewer operational problems.
- Real-time records are mobile data that is compared to cloud-based, honestly true, or decentralised data. A cloud is a large data centre located somewhere in the world that may be accessed as needed. Real facts, on the other hand, are communicated at the same time since operations are taking place in those industries where records are critical to success. Integration with IIoT allows businesses to collect data from their properties and make informed decisions in real time. The most significant employer concern is security, which can be significantly reduced when IIoT is identified through using industries. Potential problems are identified ahead of time, reducing the risks made by humans and allowing serious threats to be avoided. Enhanced company security is enabled by unskilled techniques and a long way beyond real-time troubleshooting essential to a far less unsafe experience for employees.

Finally, smart metres that exhibit consumption of organisational commercial enterprise assets such as fuels, time, water, strength, and so on permit an environmental footprint. The metres are most likely used to determine resource utilisation, and changes may be made as a result. IIoT adoption can significantly reduce any environmental impact, from accelerated everyday state-of-the-art, ubiquitous ordinary performance to reduced safety threat and travel time. Using a great deal less energy, avoiding oil spills and one-of-a-kind injuries, and emitting hundreds of loads less carbon are all significant enough to be covered by IIoT. Furthermore, the IIoT provides for more precise monitoring of power and usable resource utilisation.

The most significant project of IIoT devices is security risks, as personal information can be conveyed through robotically exchanged data. "Protecting privacy in the IoT environment becomes more difficult than in typical ICT environments due to the fact that the style of attack vectors on IoT entities appears to be very large. 2014 (Xu, He, and Li). Adoption of the IIoT can result in increased security.

In the absence of a well-coordinated and encrypted community, risks and tense situations arise. Data from commercial enterprise employers can be tracked, monitored, and connected using the IIoT. "Reasonable efforts in era, law, and law are required to protect you from unauthorised access to or disclosure of private information" 2014 (Xu, He, and Li). "As a result, the software programme application form of an IoT solution wants to protect the interconnected devices from intrusions and interference from new assault vectors (i.e., coming from the communication channels) from entering into the tool that allows you to make certain safe operations" (Breivold & Sandström, 2015). The absence of IIoT requirements is the second task. It is necessary for industrial industries to succeed in standardization in phrases of capability, interoperability, and reliability. "IoT's technical needs must be established to outline the specification for statistics exchange, processing, and communications amongst topics in order to deliver excessive first-rate services to give up clients," says the author (Xu, He, & Li, 2014). Overall, standardisation will have a significant impact on IIoT technologies and advancements. The cost of imposing IIoT is an important duty for the company that should not be overlooked. If an in-depth proposal isn't constantly prepared, the return on investment isn't very promising in terms of pricing. The benefits of integrating with existing infrastructure or migrating to modern technology should be explained with as much detail as possible. If this type of step is done inside the gift, a lot of potential future problems and difficult situations can be avoided. The last task recognized is the abilities set, surely having the approval with investment from higher authorities. Lastly, the environmental footprint, enabled through manner of smart meters that show consumption of commercial enterprise and business enterprise agency property, which includes fuels, time, water, electricity, and so forth. Resource usage might be identified through the meters and modifications that might be made. From extended common fashionable normal overall performance to lessened protection chance and decreased journey, IIoT adoption can substantially reduce the environmental effect. Using loads considerably lower in electricity, avoiding oil spills and precise accidents, and emitting masses, considerably less carbon are sufficient to be aware about IIoT. IIoT furthermore permits for clearer tracking of energy and useful resource usage.

The largest undertaking of IIoT gadgets are safety vulnerabilities as personal information can be communicated with the robotically shared facts. "Protecting privateness within the IoT environment will become greater immoderate than the conventional ICT surroundings because of the truth the form of attack vectors onIoT entities is seemingly loads big" (Xu, He, & Li, 2014). Adoption of IIoT can bring about extra protection vulnerabilities and traumatic conditions inside the absence of a nicely consistent and encrypted community. IIoT permits monitoring and connectivity of business enterprise company information. "Reasonable efforts in generation, regulation, and law are had to prevent unauthorized get right of get right of entry to to to to or disclosure of the privateness facts" (Xu, He, & Li, 2014). "Therefore, the software program software shape of an IoT solution desires to guard the interconnected gadgets from intrusions and interference from new assault vectors (i.e., coming from the communication channels) from stepping into the tool that lets in you to make certain snug operations" (Breivold & Sandström, 2015). Second assignment is the absence of IIoT requirements. For the success of producing industries, it requires standardization in terms of functionality, interoperability, and reliability. "In order to offer immoderate remarkable offerings to surrender clients, IoT's technical necessities need to be designed to define the specification for information trade, processing, and communications among subjects" (Xu, He, & Li, 2014). All in all, IIoT technology and enhancements will spread substantially from standardization. A critical assignment for the business organization is the charge of enforcing IIoT which can't be underestimated. Return of funding isn't always very promising in phrases of rate if an in-depth idea is not prepared. Advantages of integration with the present day or circulate to the modern-day infrastructure need to be listed with all the statistics viable. A lot of viable future issues and annoying situations can be averted if this step is taken within the gift. Last mission diagnosed is abilities set; having the approval with investment from better manipulatives isn't always enough. We need to preserve in thoughts who's going to make it appear and take the mission to completion, to layout, growth, positioned into effect, success, and hold the modern-day shape. This is where an information set project is to be had. To have the right capability organized for the appropriate merger from the current form to the contemporary-day one with IIoT. "Analyzing or mining huge portions of information generated from every IoT programs and modern-day-day IT structures to derive treasured records calls for sturdy huge facts analytics abilties, which can be difficult for loads prevent customers" (Xu, He, & Li, 2014). Managing isn't always enough. We need to maintain in thoughts who's going to make it real and take it to completion, to format, growth, positioned into effect, succeed, and maintain the contemporary form. This is where the information set venture is to be had. To have the right capability organized for an appropriate merger from present day to the modern-day with IIoT.

10.2 LITERATURE SURVEY

Due to their low fee, clean association, and charge-powerful environment, the length of networks with sensors has been finished today throughout sudden fields [17,18]. In a WSN, a huge amount of sensor nodes are dispersed around the world as a way to reap the favored statistics. For post-evaluation, all of the statistics are accumulated and forwarded toward BS thru a single or multi-hop observed records transmission paradigm. Agriculture now plays a crucial characteristic in any of America's development and financial gains. As a result, the rural sphere ought to be exploited with current generations; in addition to Internet primarily based on WSN, to lessen time and human efforts and to enhance agricultural throughput [19]. Different kinds of sensors are utilized in agriculture to assess soil, weather, moisture, and temperature conditions. Many studies inside the agricultural enterprise have used WSN to increase its ordinary performance and lessen the farmer's load [20,21]. However, in terms of reminiscence, processing, transmission, and electrical power, the prepared sensors require constrained regulations. Furthermore, due to the unreliable, unregulated, and unfastened-region conversation foundation of WSN-based programs, information security is an crucial research problem.

Many researchers have proposed one-of-a-type clustering algorithms in sensor networks [22,23], with the purpose of growing community sturdiness and statistics transmission performance [24,25]. Now, such structures, networks, and cluster heads are deployed during various locations, with one cluster head accumulating and advancing sensory input within the BS direction. In addition, most sensor nodes went into sleep mode to enhance the community's lifespan. Low-energy adaptive cluster hierarchy was used with the aim of introducing the concept of a cluster-based totally general technique and improving strength performance over conventional tactics. The cluster head's feature is randomly turned around, which lets in the LEACH protocol to keep the strength intake of some sensor nodes. [26], as an instance, The analytic hierarchy technique (AHP) was modified into proposed via the authors as a way to centralize the cluster head choosing mechanism technique. For the choice of cluster heads, residual strength, mobility, and distance in the route of the cluster centroid are all considered essential criteria. In assessment to distinct answers, the proposed answer substantially improved network sturdiness. The authors provided an energy-efficient properly sufficient technique for determining the top-notch cluster heads. In addition to the BS, the determined cluster heads are in the path of the cluster member. The proposed approach reduces the communique distance between nodes and will increase community longevity. Though, in an insecure and unconstrained place setting, the recommended answer is not accurate, as it's miles susceptible too.

Authors [27] used a fuzzy surrounding to assign the organization head in wi-fi sensor networks. The proposed approach is based totally on the exception of a couple of function selections making method and cluster heads the usage of residual electricity, distance to BS, and the sort of associates factors. Under a homogeneous historical past, the virtual system lifespan is longer than the hierarchical agglomerative clustering set of regulations. Cluster creation, cluster bean selection, chain improvement, and statistics programme degrees are all part of the improved cable grounded actually clustering hierarchical routing, a difficult and fast of commands based totally on LEACH. The suggested protocol's organisation head preference and movement are inefficient and bring about extended electric consumption. Based on version significances, the future set of recommendations reduces the connection among strength intake and weight distribution among sensor nodes. For cell sensor networks, the authors of [28] advocated an optimized area, primarily based on a 100% energy-green routing method. The recommended solution's critical reason is to enhance network typical overall performance in terms of cluster formation and cluster head choice using tremendous distance, density, mobility, and energy parameters. The predicted rationalization balanced power intake and network lifetime; however, the reality that the proposed approach lacks an evaluation of wireless linkages. Furthermore, safety measurements are not considered, resulting in commonplace linkages and strong routing.

The time period "Internet of Things" was adopted by people of the RFID agency to explain the functionality for finding out records by using a tagged tool for browsing a web URL or database to gain entry to that corresponding to a selected RFID or near field communication [29] technology. The test paper "Research and application at the clever residence primarily based mostly on hassle technology and Internet of Things" mentions RFID, sensor technology, nanotechnology, and intelligence embedded generation as examples of important IoT generation. RFID is the inspiration and networking coronary coronary heart of the Internet of Things [30]. Consumers were able to hyperlink actual devices to the net through the Internet of Things (IoT).

This emerged through diverse tagging technology, which incorporates NFC, RFID, and 2D barcode, which allowed bodily devices to be identified and said over the net [31]. The Internet of Things (IoT), which mixes sensor technology and radio frequency technology, is a ubiquitous community that connects internet content cloth material devices and is constructed on the internet's omnipresent hardware belongings. With the use of computer fields, communique networks, and international roaming technology, it's also a modern-day tool inside the IT enterprise. It consists of many new Internet of Things helping technologies for data series generation, a protracted communication era, far off information transmission technology, sea measures information intelligence analyses and manipulate generation, and so forth [32], in addition to present-day PC and communication technology for outdoor use.

The Internet of Things (IIoT) is the very last consequences of cleverly combining multiple gift generation. Several technologies, in addition to their packages and reference to crucial technology, are quickly reviewed in this segment. A) Cloud Computing— Cloud computation offers computing to clients on call. Platforms, infrastructure, and software utility software can all be supplied as a service.

Sensors can preserve community statistics because of their restricted memory and processing electricity. IoT apps also can use the cloud to reveal and study all of the devices. Artificial intelligence is also supported for desire-making, obviating the want for human touch. B) Big Data—Big data is the time period used to symbolize a huge amount of facts on which normal data processing software programs aren't able to carry out records-related operations. Some particular techniques, like Hiveql and Hadoop, are used to manipulate the massive amount facts.

Big records might be very useful in lots of areas, like social networking, research fields, in governments, and so forth. In IIoT technology, a huge amount of gathered facts is supported via cloud computing. At the same time as combining this with large data, it gives a superb benefit to retrieve and keep beneficial facts. C) Ubiquitous Computing—The primary cause of the ever-present computing is to include invisibly embedded technology within the surroundings. Mark Weiser (father of ubiquitous computing) defines ubiquitous computing as "the bodily global that is richly and invisibly interwoven with sensors, actuator, indicates and computational factors, embedded seamlessly in the normal items of our lives, and linked via a non-prevent network. The reason of IoT is to revel in the environment with out the intervention of human and ubiquitous computing is a way to gain this motive." D) Smart Devices—A clever device is a virtual device that could function to some extent autonomously and usually is related to precise devices or networks with the assist of various protocols like wi-fi, 4G, and Bluetooth and loads of others. Some examples of those varieties of gadgets are smartphones, pills, clever band, and watches. IoT era uses masses of those gadgets to accumulate and study records. E) Sensors and Actuators—A sensor is a device that converts one form of sign to a few different forms, which may be measured. Types of sensors are temperature, proximity, imaginative and prescient, gyroscope, compass, acceleration/tilt and so forth. The actuator is a hardware tool that converts the command into bodily trade; this alteration is typically mechanical (e.g. position or pace). F) Artificial Intelligence (AI)—Human or animal-like intelligence proven through gadget is known as artificial intelligence. In IIoT, it's miles examined via the usage of smart gadgets (e.g. sensors and hundreds of others). Due to this intelligence, today's machines can get signs and symptoms earlier than any undesirable scenario takes place, or they'll take critical moves based totally on their programs in brilliant varieties of industries. G) RFID (Radio Frequency Identification)—RFID technology is used to expose gadgets.

This tool has special enhancements: RFID reader and RFID tag. RFID reader begins with an evolved conversation using a tag with the useful resource of sending a question to RFID tag to end up privy to it. RFID tag is a small chip with an antenna and related to a particular ID. This tag can be associated with any object needing to be tracked. Various forms of RFID tags are available. One is passive RFID tags, which don't have any battery. It takes strength from the question signal transmitted through the reader in the same time as any other one is active; RFID includes a battery. It can speak by transmitting its ID. It is extensively speaking in the company's hold to music gadgets. H) GPS (global positioning system) Technology—GPS is a network of satellites that have advanced through the U.S. authorities for the military, but now everyone with a GPS tool can acquire signs from the satellites. GPS makes use of a manner known as trilateration at the identical time as it has data; as a minimum, three satellites are needed to pinpoint the region. This generation is done in logistic departments of industries. I) Advanced Robotic and Automation Technology—A robot can be described as an automated, controllable, reprogrammable, multipurpose sensible system that may be programmed to do such duties the ones that consume time or manpower. Automation uses several tools for going for walks which embody machines, mills, ovens, boilers, warm temperature exchangers, strategies in industries and so on. J) Wireless Sensor Networks (WSN)—Wireless sensors are used for sensing and controlling environmental parameters. Each sensor consists of the sensor interface, small memory and processing gadgets, transceivers, converters for analogue to virtual and vice versa. These sensors can revel in and communicate with specific sensors.

Inside the environment we may use many sensors. Many such sensors integrate to shape a wireless sensor network. K) Wireless Fidelity (Wi-Fi)—Wireless Fidelity (Wi-Fi) is a shape of networking generation that lets in wi-fi communications among computer systems and smart devices. Vic Hayes is known as the father of wireless fidelity. Many devices now have built in wi-fi and may be related to the internet through the WLAN. Wi-fi usually uses 2.Four and 5.Eight GHz radio bands. Wi-fi is extra vulnerable to assault than a stressed-out community. L) Bluetooth—Bluetooth technology is short-variety radio era that does not want cabling to replace statistics. In 1994, Ericson Mobile Communication enterprise started out an assignment named "Bluetooth." It is the top one used to create personal area networks (PAN) for information sharing with the resource of connecting 2-eight devices at a time. The IEEE standardized Bluetooth as IEEE 802.15.1, but now it does no longer maintain at this level anymore. M) ZigBee—ZigBee modified into advanced to enhance the talents of wi-fi sensor networks and created through the ZigBee Alliance. Features of this protocol are low information rate, shorter distance, scalability, flexibility, and reliability. Its walking variety is spherical 100 meters with 250kbps pace. This protocol is typically executed in domestic automation, medical, agricultural, and industries. N) Barcode—Barcode is tool readable, optical, numbers and letters encoded through using an aggregate of numerous width bars and gaps. Barcode is device-readable labels related to the bodily product and embodies facts, such as a product-like product description, price, unit of length and so forth. There are mainly styles of barcode available 1D and 2D. The 1D barcode consists of a lot less data than the 2D barcode. V. APPLICATION OF IoT IN INDUSTRIES—IoT technology is now being completed in industries on a large scale. In this section, a few essential packages of IoT generation are stated briefly. A) Smart Factories—IIoT enabled tool can experience the surroundings and transmit records to managers or engineers, which permit them to remotely manipulate their production unit devices and take benefits of device automation.

IIoT gadgets also can transmit records concerning production, losses, and inventory to their managers concerning well-timed essential actions. B) Maintenance Management—IIoT sensor allows state of affairs-based protection via tracking essential machines and alerting managers after they deviate from set parameters like temperature or vibration levels. This capability reduces breakdown time, fees, and operational growth of the plant. C) Process Management—IIoT in manufacturing industries allows tracking of refining device of raw fabric to packaging of the final product.

This nearly real-time monitoring allows manufacturing managers to regulate plant parameters so production objectives can be met with quality and price. D) Inventory Management—IIoT permits tracking of every deliver chain sports from cloth arrival to cloth dispatch; any deviation from the plan can be captured through managers in actual time, a splendid enhancement. IoT device RFID and barcodes are carried out in stores for fabric manipulation, which reduces a massive quantity of time and power consumed with this useful aid. E) Quality Control—Uses of IIoT inside the production line can enhance the the very last product to show an approach and tool on real-time and maintain plant parameters like temperature, pH, acidity, impurity, densities and so forth. In a preference that results in an amazing product. They can also show show 0.33 celebration raw material and may capture customer evaluations on every last product, which may be later analyzed for problems. F) Safety and Security—IIoT devices can serve as paintings in unstable surroundings, such as in an acid plant or in restricted places, as an end result reducing or eliminating human existence intervention. IIoT gadgets themselves can take without delay actions based totally on their vicinity of software program application. For instance: Stopping furnace if the temperature is going beyond the preferred limit, honking a siren if the boiler is going to blow up or a stack is going to fall, and loads of others. Overall, employee safety can be improved through the use of large information and IoT era tools. G) Logistic Management—IIoT can provide almost actual-time monitoring information of unprocessed fabric, the very last product, plant tool, and their spare factors. This information will help managers to anticipate problems and their resolutions in time. GPS-enabled automobile tracking devices can help producers to anticipate raw fabric availability and final product's shipping in time.

10.3 SECURED AND EFFICIENT SWARM BASED METHOD

Numerous scholars ensure the technology in sensor networks in many fields involving environmental statistics. Networks with sensors have similarly finished a critical function inside the statement and manipulate of farming plots in positions of blossoms, microclimate, aquatic operation, and so forth. But, the rural land nevertheless has a few disturbing situations, together with energy efficiency, statistics routing, and protection; these are due to the constrained battery control of devices and exposed communication standard. The number one purpose of the proposed manner is to increase a power-green with secured based wireless system context for the tracking and manufacturing of cultivated plot. Proposed method, swarm-based band heads are decided on primarily through the superior choice function. Additionally, the SNR moreover included inside the choice to compute the power of wireless signals and growth the achievement relation of sensors packets.

Wireless sensor networks are particularly sensitive to denial of service attacks (DoS), such as jamming attacks. Because of the network's services, DoS attacks have a high chance of succeeding in wireless sensor networks. Network performance would suffer as a result of the difficulty in identifying a denial of service attack in this case. Data integrity and confidentiality attacks, such as denial of service (DOS) attacks, power consumption-related attacks, such as denial of sleep attacks, and service availability-related attacks, such as flooding and jamming attacks, are all threats to wireless sensor networks. One of the most common types of DOS attacks on wireless sensor networks is jamming. When an attacker sends a high-power signal to produce interference and prevent legal packets from being received correctly, this action is referred to as jamming. A jamming assault on a wireless network entails sending a high-power signal through the network to tamper with legal messages. A jamming attack's main purpose is to disrupt signal transmission during user communication. The jamming gadget deliberately emits electromagnetic radiation. It's one of the most dangerous hostile threats, and it slows down network performance. By continuously broadcasting jamming signals, attackers would be able to disrupt the users' communication.

Here planned work gives reliable, secured, and energy techniques for the development of huge-sized agricultural land. Additionally, the algorithm gathers the information about security between farmed devices to cluster heads and from cluster heads to the main station based on master keys at the same time as the use of the linear congruential generator; this needs the slightest memory in addition to the processing period. Hence, here are our proposed work assurances the secured and energy efficiency in agriculture fields.

Procedure

 i. Number of nodes N farming sensors remain isolated in land.

 ii. Sensor nodes, base station remain secure once the nodes deployment FINISH.

 iii. Communication associates are symmetric.

 iv. Agriculture nodes are assorted in positions of vitality possessions.

 v. Base station with maximum controlling node through infinite assets.

This detail discusses the counseled energy arrangement, similar to proper and inexperienced hyperlink routing, which incorporates vital levels. For the choice of extremely good cluster heads, the primary degree is on a multi-requirements selection characteristics. After that, the nodes with the bottom strength intake are formed into outstanding clusters. The proposed electricity and hyperlink green routing's second diploma is to decorate the routing channel for an prolonged time frame, preventing the wireless link from misbehaving acts from cluster heads to the BS. As tested in equation 10.1, our counseled framework makes use of the node power ey, the signal-to-noise ratio, SNRi, BS, and the distance to BS to BS as a multi-requirements choice-making feature f(n) for cluster head desire. The cause of the usage of SNR in the proposed framework is to decide the signal's power and increase the transport ordinary performance successfully. The received signal strength indicator (RSSI) to historical noise ratio is defined as SNR. Because RSSIi suggests the received sign energy indicator and Bni denotes the recorded noise for hyperlink I, the fee of SNRi can be calculated using RSSIi/Bni. The link with the lowest SNRi is picked because the maximum suitable for transmitting records.

$$f(n) = ey + (1/di, BS) + (1/SNRi) \tag{10.1}$$

$$Yn + 1 = (\alpha Yn + \beta)\bmod m \tag{10.2}$$

$$Ej(mi) = mi \oplus Yi \tag{10.3}$$

$$Dj(mi) = Ej(mi) \oplus Yi \tag{10.4}$$

In this studies, statistics from agricultural gadgets are transferred the use of a device this is primarily based mostly on a network close to the institution leaders and, in the long run, the lowest station. The BS creates thriller keys in this framework via the usage of the recurrence of the linear congenital equation; it's furnished with the useful resource of Equation (10.2).

Where Yi are the generated thriller random values for sensor node ni, m is the modulus parameter, which need to be greater than 0, is the multiplier parameter, which ought to be more than zero and considerably less than the modulus m, is the increment parameter, which ought to be more than zero and considerably less than the modulus m, and Y0 is the seed fee, which needs to also be more than zero and drastically less than the modulus m. As a result, the use of equation 10.2, all sensor nodes are given thriller keys. Following that, even as the sensor node ni sends records mi to the cluster head CHj, it is encrypted the usage of Equation 10.3 and 10.4.

10.4 RESULTS AND DISCUSSIONS

Here considering some simulation parameters used for result analysis of the proposed method compared to appropriate results with PSO, the experiment done using network simulator and that gives best results for routing in networks. Simulation parameters are mentioned in the below Table 10.1. Assess the results with 20 rounds; the number of sensor nodes in agri field with unnamed nodes is set to 100 and 15. Agrarian sensors means hotness sensors, light sensors, mud wetness, position and airflow sensors, unidentified nodes are distributed arbitrarily. The performance is evaluated depending on link throughput, energy consumption, and routing overheads.

In Figure 10.3, the proposed device is as compared to a present method in terms of network throughput and the extensive form of rounds. The outcomes display that the brand-new swarm approach outperforms the existing outcomes in terms of community throughput. Furthermore, the recommended swarm method's improved device ordinary performance, in addition to offer findings, is due to the allocation of data encryption mystery keys based on the linear congenital generator, ensuring in green community throughput with regular network connectivity. Figure 10.4 suggests the common overall performance assessment of the proposed framework in evaluation to other replies during many simulation cycles. The simulation consequences display that the advised framework complements the strength consumption ratio via 11% and 21%

TABLE 10.1 Simulation constraints

WEBCAM	DEFAULT IP
Simulation area	200 m × 200 m
Deployment	Random
Sensor nodes	100
Malicious nodes	15
Packet size, k	64 bits
Payload size	256 bytes
Transmission range	20 m

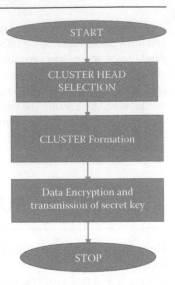

FIGURE 10.4   Secure network method.

while in comparison to diverse strategies. This is because of the proposed framework's moderate weight distribution of electricity intake among sensor nodes. The routing overheads between the proposed framework and competing answers are depicted in Figure 10.5 for numerous simulation rounds. In assessment to the existing strategies, the experimental findings show that the proposed framework reduces routing overheads. The proposed framework gives smart cluster head preference with minimal processing overheads on sensor nodes, primarily based on a mixture of things as shown in Figure 10.6 and Figure 10.7.

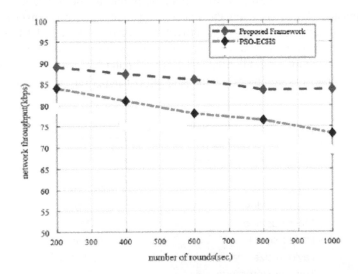

FIGURE 10.5   Simulation rounds on network throughput.

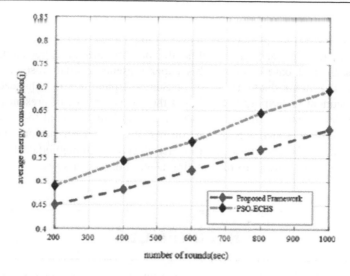

FIGURE 10.6 Rounds on energy consumption.

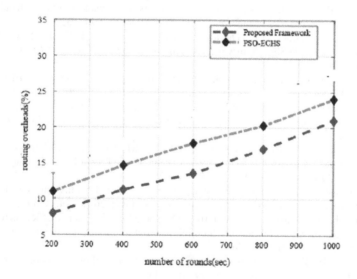

FIGURE 10.7 Rounds on routing overhead.

10.5 CONCLUSION

This chapter has presented an efficient and secured IoT-based agriculture wireless sensor network using the swarm method. The goal of the proposed method is to assign the additional appropriate cluster nuts depending on multiple criteria choices. The choice depends on residual vitality, distance to base station, and signal-to-noise influences. Moreover, the planned method is to implement a single hop pattern aimed at data communication and then decline the probabilities of congestions between farming sensors and base stations. This paper presents a smart resolution of data transmission and then reductions in part of energy depletion with enhanced data distribution enactment in farming fields. Using the distinct record of present results, the proposed method exploits a mechanism that is established on signal-to-noise issues to control the asset of signals. It attains further steady system performance among farming sensors and base stations. Additionally, the proposed method deals secure data communication from sensors to base station centred on secret keys.

REFERENCES

[1] Dvir, A., Ta, V.T., Erlich, S., Buttyan, L. STWSN: A novel secure distributed transport protocol for wireless sensor networks. *Int. J. Commun. Syst.* 2018, 31, e3827.
[2] Mehra, P.S., Doja, M.N., Alam, B. Fuzzy based enhanced cluster head selection (FBECS) for WSN. *J. King Saud Univ.-Sci.* 2018, 32, 390–401.
[3] Tripathi, A., Gupta, H.P., Dutta, T., Mishra, R., Shukla, K.K., Jit, S. Coverage and connectivity in WSNs: A survey, research issues and challenges. *IEEE Access* 2018, 6, 26971–26992.
[4] Shahzad, M.K., Cho, T.H. An energy-aware routing and filtering node (ERF) selection in CCEF to extend network lifetime in WSN. *IETE J. Res.* 2017, 63, 368–380.
[5] Zhang, D.G., Zheng, K., Zhang, T., Wang, X. A novel multicast routing method with minimum transmission for WSN of cloud computing service. *Soft Comput.* 2015, 19, 1817–1827.
[6] Awan, K.A., Din, I.U., Almogren, A., Guizani, M., Khan, S. StabTrust—A stable and centralized trust-based clustering mechanism for IoT enabled vehicular ad-hoc networks. *IEEE Access* 2020, 8, 21159–21177.
[7] Venkatesh Shankar. Contemporary Secured Target Locality in Wireless Sensor Networks Global Transitions Proceedings, November 2021, vol. 2, no. 2, 194–198.
[8] Hamzah, A., Shurman, M., Al-Jarrah, O., Taqieddin, E. Energy-efficient fuzzy-logic-based clustering technique for hierarchical routing protocols in wireless sensor networks. *Sensors* 2019, 19, 561.
[9] Kang, S.H. Energy optimization in cluster-based routing protocols for large-area wireless sensor networks. *Symmetry* 2019, 11, 37.
[10] Elshrkawey, M., Elsherif, S.M., Wahed, M.E. An enhancement approach for reducing the energy consumption in wireless sensor networks. *J. King Saud Univ.-Comput. Inf. Sci.* 2018, 30, 259–267.
[11] Awan, K.A., Din, I.U., Zareei, M., Talha, M., Guizani, M., Jadoon, S.U. Holitrust-a holistic cross-domain trust management mechanism for service-centric Internet of Things. *IEEE Access* 2019, 7, 52191–52201.
[12] Abuarqoub, A., Hammoudeh, M., Adebisi, B., Jabbar, S., Bounceur, A., Al-Bashar, H. Dynamic clustering and management of mobile wireless sensor networks. *Comput. Netw.* 2017, 117, 62–75.
[13] Lin, C.C., Tseng, P.T., Wu, T.Y., Deng, D.J. Social-aware dynamic router node placement in wireless mesh networks. *Wirel. Netw.* 2016, 22, 1235–1250.

[14] Khattak, H.A., Amoon, Z., Din, U.I., Khan, M.K. Cross-layer design and optimization techniques in wireless multimedia sensor networks for smart cities. *Comput. Sci. Inf. Syst.* 2019, 16, 1–17.

[15] Din, I.U., Guizani, M., Hassan, S., Kim, B.S., Khan, M.K., Atiquzzaman, M., Ahmed, S.H. The Internet of Things: A review of enabled technologies and future challenges. *IEEE Access* 2018, 7, 7606–7640.

[16] Awan, K.A., Din, I.U., Almogren, A., Guizani, M., Altameem, A., Jadoon, S.U. Robust trust–a pro-privacy robust distributed trust management mechanism for Internet of Things. *IEEE Access* 2019, 7, 62095–62106.

[17] Alaparthy, V.T. Morgera, S.D. Multi-level intrusion detection system for wireless sensor networks based on immune theory. *IEEE Access* 2018, 6, 47364–47373.

[18] Rawat, P., Singh, K.D., Chaouchi, H., Bonnin, J.M. Wireless sensor networks: A survey on recent developments and potential synergies. *J. Supercomput.* 2014, 68, 1–48.

[19] Bandur, Bandur, M., Jovic, S. An analysis of energy efficiency in wireless sensor networks (WSNs) applied in smart agriculture. *Comput. Electron. Agric.* 2019, 156, 500–507.

[20] Zia, H., Harris, N.R., Merrett, G.V., Rivers, M., Coles, N. The impact of agricultural activities on water quality: A case for collaborative catchment-scale management using integrated wireless sensor networks. *Computer Electron. Agric.* 2013, 96, 126–138.

[21] Yu, Y., Liu, J. An energy-aware routing protocol with small overhead for wireless sensor networks. In Proceedings of the International Conference on Data Mining and Big Data, Shanghai, China, 17–22 June 2018.

[22] Ullah, U., Khan, A., Zareei, M., Ali, I., Khattak, H.A., Din, I.U. Energy-effective cooperative and reliable delivery routing protocols for underwater wireless sensor networks. *Energies* 2019, 12, 2630.

[23] Haseeb, K., Islam, N., Almogren, A., Din, I.U. Intrusion prevention framework for secure routing in WSN-based mobile Internet of Things. *IEEE Access* 2019, 7, 185496–185505.

[24] Darabkh, K.A., Albtoush, W.Y., Jafar, I.F. Improved clustering algorithms for target tracking in wireless sensor networks. *J. Supercomput.* 2017, 73, 1952–1977.

[25] Enam, R.N., Qureshi, R., Misbahuddin, S. A uniform clustering mechanism for wireless sensor networks. *Int. J. Distrib. Sens. Netw.* 2014, 2014, 1–14.

[26] Zhu, C., Wu, S., Han, G., Shu, L., Wu, H. A tree-cluster-based data-gathering algorithm for industrial WSNs with a mobile sink. *IEEE Access* 2015, 3, 381–396.

[27] Azad, P., Sharma, V. Cluster head selection in wireless sensor networks under fuzzy environment. *ISRN Sens. Netw.* 2013.

[28] Srivastava, J.R., Sudarshan, T.S.B. A genetic fuzzy system based optimized zone based energy efficient routing protocol for mobile sensor networks (OZEEP). *Appl. Soft Comput.* 2015, 37, 863–886.

[29] Zeng, X., et al. IOTSim: A simulator for analyzing IoT applications. *J Syst Architect.* 2017, 72, 93–107.

[30] Fantacci, R., Pecorella, T., Viti, R., Carlini, C. A network architecture solutions for efficient IoT WSN backhauling: Challenges and opportunities. *IEEE Wirel. Commun.* 2014, 21(4), 113–119.

[31] Kim, M., Ahn, H., Kim, K.P. Process-aware Internet of Things: A conceptual extension of the Internet of Things framework and architecture. *KSII Trans. Internet Inf. Syst.* 2016, 10(8), 4008–4022.

[32] Hsieh, H.-C., Chang, K.-D., Wang, L.-F., Chen, J.-L., Chao, H.-C. ScriptIoT: A script framework for and Internet of Things applications. *IEEE Internet Things J.* 2015, 3(4), 628–636.

Review on Autonomous Vehicle and Virtual Controlled Delivery Truck System Using IoT

11

Gowtham M, Ajay A V, and Srinidhi H R

Department of Computer Science and Engineering, The National Institute of Engineering, Mysuru, Karnataka, India

Contents

DOI: 10.1201/9781003282990-11

11.1 INTRODUCTION

New movements in correspondence and mechanical advancement have influenced our bit-by-bit way of life, of which transportation is no remarkable case. These advancements have prompted the possibility of self-driving automobile (AV) advancement, which aims to reduce crashes, drive use, pollution, and blockage while also developing vehicle openness. The possibility of driverless vehicles has been around for a long time, but the cutoff price has discouraged any ambitious creation [1]. In the long run, there has been a speedy development in the innovative work that attempts to pass on the opportunity of the AV to affirmation. For instance, the strategy of the vehicle was passed on to AV.

Because of the rapid advancement of correspondence and the need to consider developing individuals in nations, nations have hypothetically completed AVS as a fundamental business point of view [2]. Considering the push toward memorable thoughts and advances like easygoing affiliations, PDAs, and the like, a few researchers have vehemently advised that the transportation area is rapidly developing [3–5]. A model is Uber, which is clearing metropolitan organisations to the degree that taxicab affiliations are attempting to hold professional and to stay veritable. Manyika et al. [6] recall automobile mechanisation for an outline of the key 10 hazardous movements of what may be not too far off (Table 11.1).

From the AV point of view, "related" and "huge data." Accordingly, the enunciations "related" or "related vehicle" propose the headways that guarantee correspondence between each contributing topic master and assistants, including walkers, prepared experts, and vehicles, comparably as a framework. Figure 11.2 depicts a speculative portrayal of a connected design. The connected area will require a huge extent of information from a variety of sources.

TABLE 11.1 Estimated measurement of self-directed vehicles (2020) [7]

AUTOMOBILE	BMW 5 SERIES	MERCEDES BENZ INTELLECTUAL DRIVE RESEARCH VEHICLE	NISSAN LEAF EV	GOOGLE PRIUS AND LEXUS	UNIVERSAL MOTORS CADILLAC SRX
MAIN EXPERTISE	• Video camera path lane markings and reads road symbols • Radar sensors detect things ahead • Side laser scanners • Ultrasonic sensors • Variance GPS • Exact guide	• Stereo camera • Supplementary cameras read road symbols and spot traffic lights • Short- and long range radar • Infrared camera • Ultrasonic sensors	• Front and side radar • Camera • Front, rear, and side laser scanners • Four wide-angle cameras display the driver the car's surroundings	• LIDAR on the roof senses things around the car in 3-D • Camera helps detect things • Anterior and side radar • Inertial measuring unit tracks position • Wheel encoder tracks drive • Exact guide	• Numerous laser sensors • Radar • Variance GPS • Cameras • Very accurate map

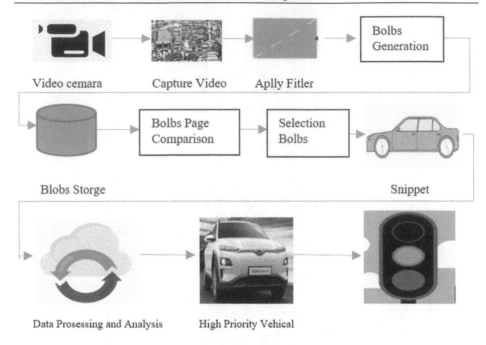

FIGURE 11.1   A portrayal of associated vehicles and framework.

AV advancement should be considered at the intersection of various controls, for example, transportation science, electric planning, statistics advancement, programming and device planning, law, morals, and theory. In this article, we look at AV from a transportation standpoint. We want to learn more about the general effects of AV for researchers, technique creators, organizers, and experts interested in transportation.

We create specifically by referring to circulate engineering such as security, gas utilization, street comparing and preventing fundamentals, land use, and inquiring for anticipating. We also deal with different associated issues, for example, community security, law and rule, as well as high-quality concerns.

The truth of the issue is to work through the probabilities and issues that may arise from the show and utilisation of AVS. First, we will ruminate AV inside the present transportation structures and civilization, correspondingly portraying some related phrasings. We can then work to uncover the bearing of AVS for the fast and delayed period of the future, subject to past audits. To do that, we have zeroed in on more than 118 references perceived with AV advancement, which have been spread typically in the first 5 years to introduce an enormous and enabled story.

Surprisingly, modern designers would not dissect the methods by which AVS novelty out and pick their guides in the street affiliations (vehicle organizing). Doubtlessly, it's mentioned that AVS isn't various to different automobiles in vehicle planning. As checked already, associated car development is a vital piece of a functioning AV plot. Such (advancing) correspondence data can also be laboured with effort among the AVS directionality limits, resulting in more useful and intelligent way locating (or traffic flow).

Dependable records (counting tour time and activities) can be dealt with and isolated most of the way to research and paintings with (or brief) [8,9] AVS toward the exceptional route.

11.2 RELATED WORK

11.2.1 History on Autonomous Vehicle

When compared to those from lower-income families, the AV is associated with a number of positive social aspirations, such as a more secure vehicle framework and an empowering touch of flexibility for the mobility impaired. According to research, the immediate social value that will be created will be somewhere between 0.2 and 1.9 trillion dollars per year by 2025 [6]. Such certain effects are essential impetuses after the rise of AV headway, making it a helpful, cash-related model. Thusly, "huge data" is a term castoff to feature the rank of dealing with a particularly phenomenal extent of data for which uncommon plans, including programming and staff, will be required.

At any rate, human drivers are now required in level 3 vehicles, which can move security key capacities to the vehicle under certain traffic or natural conditions. The vehicle surmises that the driver is now present and will intercede if necessary, yet isn't relied upon to screen the condition, which it has accomplished for the past levels.

Level 4 is simply what is inferred by "totally self-administering." Level 4 vehicles are "expected to play out all their essential driving limits and screen road conditions for the entire outing." However, again, this is confined to the operational arrangement space (ODD) of the vehicle, which implies it doesn't cover each driving circumstance.

This level suggests a totally self-administering system wherein it is typical for the vehicle's introduction to ascend to that of a human driver in each driving circumstance—including ludicrous conditions like back roads that are presumably not going to bc investigated by driverless vehicles soon.

Even today, there are numerous difficulties in completing decision vehicles making the rounds. In any case, so is the affirmation of our analysts, modelers, and issue solvers from various controls. The total effort of the businesses will make the autonomous vehicle making the rounds a reality one day, and the benefits will be enormous. Not only will it save fuel and support compelling transportation and shared organizations, but it will also help in saving various lives that are reliably lost in road disasters.

11.2.2 Benefits and Disadvantages

Disregarding how transportation is a way to build up the accomplishment of social orders, it is definitely encoutnered negative externalities like contamination, mishaps, and human incidents. There are limitless assessments investigating these prices concerning human-driven vehicles [10,11]. These prices fluctuate from direct prices like the price of oil, vehicle upkeep, vehicle decisions, and community vehicle labels. The externality cost is a perplexing cost imposed on society in light of everything; it raises prices for things like gridlock, natural disasters, and environmental pollution, as well as security. In general, AV advancement is everything viewed as clearly an extremely important level die down (if not mishap) massive measures of these current negative externalities. When all is said and done, these external prices can be essentially as high as the cost of fuel, which is a constraint on civilization, including for low-wage individuals who are only required to drive open vehicles [3]. AVS can also provide extra advantages, like developing straightforwardness and versatility and incredibly improving locale use. Despite the fact that there could be essential weaknesses related to AVS, it is generally recognised that these weights are, for the most part, outperformed by the benefits. In the course of the locale, we build up the pros and cons of AVS.

11.2.2.1 Prosperity and mishaps

The statistics for street scenes in the United States in 2010 are stunning: 32,999 completed, three.9 million mischief, and 24 million engines damaged, with the obvious and hypothetical costs totaling $277 billion [12]. This cost burden has a wide-ranging impact, affecting performance, clinical price, veritable and court charges, operating environment issues, disaster affiliation charges, the hinder bother, safety affiliation prices, and asset harm. A decrease in the number of incidents in the United States [13] is fundamentally due to the assurance of new actions, for example, airbags, robotized finishing devices, electronic security controls, head-confirmation aspect air packs, and forward-affecting advice [4,5]. Those are highlights, a good way to make AV headway. Many appraisals estimate that the lower setbacks may be as high as 33% if all motors appear to be outfitted with adaptable headlights, forward influence signals, way flight reprimands, and frail aspect help [6,14,15], which are credited to level zero or stage 1 automobile computerization. Human mistakes are censured for in excess of a large number of accidents [12]. Thusly, AVS should have the decision to thwart an obvious range of those incidents, in this route killing by using a long way to most visitors' delays [3].

11.2.2.2 Clog

The portions of statistics for road difficulties inside the U.S. in 2010 is super: 32,999 executed, three.9 million harm, and 24 million automobiles harm, the plain and speculative prices of which complete $277 billion [8]. This price bother has a miles reaching sway, affecting viability, medical prices, valid and court expenses, work environment mishaps, disaster association expenses, the plug up burden, confirmation association price, and property harm. A slipping model in the measure of setbacks within the U.S. [9] is on an exceptionally vital level obliged to the assurance of new movements, as an instance, airbags, robotized stopping gadgets, digital safety control, head-confirmation side air packs, and forward have an effect on courses [15–20]. These are highlights in an effort to be included in AV advancement. two or 3 critiques take a look at the discount of accidents may be in any case excessive as 33% if all automobiles seem, by using all accounts, to be supplied with adaptable headlights, ahead affect indicators, manner flight advices, and feeble side assist [1,21,22] that are credited to level zero or degree one vehicle computerization. Human blunder is chided for in excess of plenty of incidents [10]. Thusly, AVS ought to have the choice to hinder an unmistakable wide variety of these setbacks, sooner or later killing a large part of most site visitors' delays [3].

11.2.2.3 Taxi and automobile ownership

AV advances can be useful for driverless taxicabs or equal vehicle sharing plans in which the price of repaying drivers' period and restrictions is eliminated. As requirements are, driverless taxis are estimated to get more moderate, which in the long run may debilitate automobile possession.

The danger of driverless taxis is similar to that of automobile distribution; it's a flourishing path of movement. AVS can hold vehicle and experience-sharing plans as they could take into account diverse humans on request [1]. Appropriately, families can also find driverless cabs extra obliging and more reasonable to choose than having an automobile. Except if confirmed to be distinctively in line with automobile sharing, driverless taxicabs ought not to be a more desired option. Given the way that the driverless taxi forestalls the need for every year's fixed expenses and maintenance, usually related to vehicle sharing and leaving, it might deliver altogether more primary consolation. In truth, automobile sharing has really been located to reduce VKT within the United States market [15]. Considering the whole lot, surely alluded to, extra affordable rides would be joined by way of new requests, especially from finished for (less-pay) people who can also now have the alternative to bear to 1 or the opposite drive or to take a taxi. Some other assessment of us through family information shows a critical reduction in automobile proprietorship and a shift to vehicle sharing [6]. This lower ownership may be essentially as high as 43%—from 2.1 to at least 1.2 automobiles in keeping with circle of relatives. Of direction, it's normal that this shift would increase particular vehicle use something like 75%, from 11,661 to 20,406 miles for each car every year. (This development in mileage does not eliminate the miles made for the duration of each "get again to-home" experience.)

Considering the whole lot, AVS can reduce distinct expenses associated with personal modes as they're absolutely going to have an effect on more tours, carrying out headway in VKT. AVS could also begin a rise in driverless cabs, for which a definitive impact on VKT is now overcast. AV and electric automobiles' concerns, backed by better fuel expenses, have been the fundamental drivers behind the development of electrical vehicle (EV) headway. The EV reports some functioning obstacles along with a distance-setting out restriction bound to the scale and energy of the batteries. The battery limits the EV to short-run travel and may make the course toward locating charging places relentless [14]. On this first rate situation, we possibly have found out ordinary and normal collaboration among shared AV maritime powers and EV progression: an armada of AVS can remedy the reasonable uttermost scopes of EVs, which includes tour range uneasiness, authorization to charging framework, and energizing time the heap [12,14].

Their financial assessment proposes that the combined rate of charging basis, vehicle capital, sponsorship, electricity, safety, and enlistment for an armada of AVS is going from $0.42 to $0.49 in line with the included mile ventured. As necessities be, shared AV association may be provided in keeping with the mile value of private car proprietorship for low-mileage households. Modernized electric-powered motors will no doubt be absolutely critical with back-and-forth improvement truly chosing vehicle-sharing institutions prove to be all-round extra sensible than on-request driving force-labored transportation associations.

11.2.2.4 Streets' capacity

AV drives provide finely tuned velocity booms, obstructing movements dependably at the same time as interminably and vigorously seeing the fusing site visitor's climate. Subsequently, AVS can move at better quotes while preserving extra-restricted distances (reducing tiers of development). Semiautonomous vehicles with adaptive cruise control (ACC) have attainably demonstrated an especially promising cutoff [23,24]. Lower phases of improvement via a line of AVS may be a bad arrangement, and along these lines, we are plausibly going to look at a platooning of AVS. Consequently, the output of the roads (or cutoff) will be limited in general—a few assessments have concentrated by utilising as many different events [25]. In specific appraisals, how AVS are linked has been mistreated in signal manipulate, which has accomplished on a completely simple level much less deferral at signals or proportionately higher road limit [2–4].

11.2.2.5 Clog comparing

As investigated in advance, the example setting headways of AVS should give a good run of visitors' movement and bring down the advancement price, which thusly may additionally affect the greater improvement. Such a hobby may be viewed as both a chance and a danger. The chance increases that the improved sales might also pulverize gridlock. The extra interest is the aftereffect of more challenges (AVS) embedded into the vehicle structure. Such trepidations are getting guaranteed. For instance, examiners at Delft School in the Netherlands have requested that the Dutch government take measures (e.g., travel mandate the heads) to control the improvement of advancement and the following externalities of the move nearer to AV propels [11]. On the off chance that one desires to keep up requests at tantamount levels as before the rise of AVS, then there is a valid chance to misuse the actuated interest through blockage evaluating. The evaluation can be set to the level at which the provoked interest disseminates. Plug up evaluating is as of now a functioning space of appraisal [8]. The enormous degree of correspondence types of progress among AVS can monstrously smooth out such surveying plans as, for example, distance-based charging and dynamic regarding plans.

11.2.2.6 Land use

AVS may have a longer impact on the land-use plan. The appraisal of land expands respectably with its space to the focal city, where open positions exist in different associations like banking, cash-related business territories, and different other help regions. Closeness is shown up by transportation. The incident involving vehicles at the start of the 20th century has surpassed the commonplace. The relationship between AVS and land use is both bewildered and somehow jumbling. In one circumstance, the introduction of AVS could revive a model toward liberally more dispersed and low-thickness land-use plans, including cosmopolitan regions. As requirements be, AVS may achieve the further progress of normal areas and may even collide further with ex-urban zones. In this dumbfounding circumstance, the AV movement debilitates the certifiable requirement for parking places. Significant parking places in the point of convergence of metropolitan districts can be opened up for other uses. Hence, AVS could wind up reinforcing metropolitan progression in a focal locale, adding to the thickness of CBDs. Note that stopping work environments swarm a huge piece of room in CBDs. Shoup [9] reviewed that the absolute area zeroed in on parking spot is on common vague from around 31% of region zones.

In the graph, the drawn-out assumption with the designation of level 4 AVS is that one would probably see denser metropolitan environments, more plans, and fewer parking places. Simultaneously, AVS could incite altogether more prominent dispersing of low-thickness progress in metropolitan edges zones given the constraint of proprietors to look into different exercises while vehicles pilot themselves [3].

11.2.2.7 Farming countries

Young nations battle with a deficit of transportation structures like streets, expansions, and public vehicles, which is thwarting their money-related new turn of events. Confirmation of AVS by these non-mechanical countries may save them the expenses related to broadening their capital-guaranteed establishment. A comparable point of view was seen when cultivating nations ricocheted over to telephone advancement, which exonerated them from costly landline foundation [3,15].

11.2.2.8 Climate (Energy and Delivery)

Anderson et al. [3] have raised 3 segments where the influence of AVS on the climate could be both ups and downs:

- Gas capacity of AVS,
- Carbon-pressure and life-cycle arrivals of the oil primarily based outstanding used to manipulate AVS, and
- Overall exchange in VKT is coming to fruition due to using AVS.

We've sincerely tested VKT. Within the going with phase, we are able to clarify the gasoline use and capacity of AVS. The rise of AVS and progress in vehicle planning and motor capacity have, from a standard point, diminished gas use. In one evaluation for pioneer vehicles, fuel utilisation changed into an almost isolated stand, isolated from the figures apparent 30 years earlier [6]. The challenge of AV improvement, even at degrees 1, 2, and 3, will incite out utilising and progress, besides being alluded to as "eco-utilizing." Some urgent improvements result in eco-utilising experience control and simple and stable speed development and deceleration. Eco-driving seems to improve effectiveness by using 4% to 10% [26]. More merry measures have imagined a development in eco-invitingness of up to 39.0% [12]. We've similarly evaluated that AVS might also actuate a higher tour restriction and a diminishing in gas wastage throughout seasons of gridlock.

AVS also supplies cars with fuel for their trips and sports activities, which may additionally reduce dormant time, enhancing each site visitor's power-cycle efficiencies [3]. What's more, a unit of emphatically dispersed AVS that forestalls or upsets much less regularly will resemble a train. The end result is based on any charge for better convincing rates (improving mileage) and improving tour time [22,23]. From completely substitute attitude, the complete level of prospering of AVS may also prompt lightweight motors from automobile makers.

Virtually, thriving endeavours are being made in the direction of calamity revulsion and faraway from extra organized style crashworthiness cars. Appropriately, mild motors are promising symptoms of the AV movement, which, as such, phenomenally adds to much less gasoline use. For general motors, up to 20% of the burden is credited to progress-associated capabilities [14]. As an orchestrating general rule, a 10% decline in weight can actuate a 6-to 7% decline in gas use [3]).

Going to electric-fueled vehicles (from fossil-based engines) in due course passes on advanced eco-neighbourliness. It's been shown that the plentifulness of the qualification in fossil-based vehicles versus electric vehicles is 1–3 [3]. Solicitation gauging truly examined, the ramifications and utilizations of AV headway are overpowered by shortcomings. One key worry of automobile producers, rule-prepared specialists, and extremely instructive researchers is to parent the future hobby of AVS. With the aid of Bansal and Kockelman [9], the entire outline of Bansal and Kockelman [9]. These presumptions depended upon the extrapolation of models that were given from beyond automobile headways, simply professional hypotheses, and proportions of supply-aspect additives, with for all intents and purposes, no accentuation of the fundamental questions at the back of these assessments.

As checked ahead, [13] anticipates 50% of the general car marketplace being credited to AVS through 2040. As shown by one test [69], the reduction of the pie of stages 2 and 3 robotized automobiles will add up to some USD 87 billion. These examinations or suppositions change us inside and out. One of the kinds of exams takes an outright more confident view on the matter [see the verbal exchange given with the aid of Bansal and Kockelman [9]].

Given the propelling profits in AV headway through the goliath car makers, the vehicle marketplace should first accept the tremendous AVS. How massive this circulation might be is hard to assume; by the way, it's apparently going to be sufficiently exceptional to warrant the entire factor of convergence of these related to the getting taken care of stage. Inside the leader place, we blanketed topics straightforwardly diagnosed with the transportation techniques. The AV, regardless, has clear repercussions. In Appendix 2, we study some of the greater blessings and harms of AVS, together with system morals, community security, and legal guidelines and rules.

11.3 DESCRIPTION OF THE USE INSTANCES

The inspirations and fashionable questions basic to the usage instances are fanned out above, and the attributes considered for their portrayal are clarified. The combo of those attributes, or possibly their characteristics, activates a really enormous quantity of utilization instances, which cannot be depicted in detail.

The four use instances depicted within the going with serve, as alluded to above, as middle people for this huge variety of conceivable use cases. Different use instances aren't overlooked; our complement is 4:

- Interstate pilot the usage of driver for prolonged availability.
- Full automation is the use of motive force for extended availability.
- Automobile on call
- A virtual control method

11.3.1 Interstate Pilot

The driving robotic expects management over the driver's driving challenge in reality on roadway. The driving force finally ends up being an explorer all through the free excursion, can take his/her arms off of the steering/coordinating device, and may be searching for specific sporting events. When the vehicle has entered the thruway, he/she will, every time required, authorise the riding robotic. This happens most astutely when displaying the ideal goal.

The driving robot acknowledges authority over course, bearing, and regulator until the exit from or end of the turnpike is reached. During one's own self-choice excursion, no special care is needed from the inhabitant; the definition of absolutely robotized driving applies. Due to coordinate view and restricted unimaginable things, this utilization case is considered as a hidden situation, regardless of whether the high vehicle speed empowers achieving the danger immaterial state.

11.3.2 Full Automation Using Driver for Extended Availability

In the event that the driver needs to do so in this manner, he/she gives up the driving job to the driving robot in allowed regions. The driver winds up being only an explorer during the autonomous excursion, can take his/her hands off of the steering mechanism, and can seek out different exercises.

In the event that the driver needs, he/she can surrender the driving undertaking to the driving robot, at whatever point the to and fro development see is unfurnished to do around there. Fundamentally the whole traffic flow district in the allowed nation is stated for the vehicle; in any case, such endorsing is penniless upon limitations. In the event that, for example, the traffic stream is rerouted, another stopping development opens, or equivalent changes are made to the construction, by then, the various regions can't be examined as self-governing until extra safeguards are taken. It additionally produces an impression of being sensible in the current situation where street areas are denied help never-endingly or quickly, for example, streets with a high number of people strolling across. Here, once more, the abdication between driver and driving robot ought to be overseen in a good way.

This utilization instance may come basically near the flow dreams for autonomous driving as it relates unequivocally with the momentum explorer vehicle use, and the driving undertaking is totally allotted to the driving robot while the standard fundamental client driver truly participates in the trip.

11.3.3 Vehicle on Demand

The driving robot drives the vehicle self-rulingly in all conditions with residents, with load, and without load. The driving robot makes the vehicle open at any alluded to space. Wayfarers use the progression time absolutely uninhibitedly for unexpected activities and, conversely, for playing out the driving endeavor. The motel is engineered to be absolutely self-governing from any prerequisites of a driver's workplace, utilising all methods. Weight can be passed on with the aide of the driving robot interminably for 24 hours reliably, as long as it's anything but constrained by the energy resource for driving. The driving robot gets the alluded-to centre from tenants or outside sections (customers, ace neighbourhood, so on), to which the vehicle proceeds straightforwardly. Individuals don't have any decision to expect command over the driving job. Humans can fundamentally show even-handedness or set up an ensured exit with the objective that he/she can leave the vehicle safely as quickly as possible, which could truly be seen as normal. With this driving robot, a wealth of dissimilar methods are implausible.

A mix of taxi affiliation and vehicle distribution, self-administering load vehicles or even use models that goes past the unadulterated transportation jobs. One model could be a vehicle for communal affiliations that uses material from the alliance straight to configuration courses, equal persons, or interfaces to further affiliations that have not yet been thought of.

11.3.4 Virtual Controlling Method

The Web of Things has gigantic applications that can be used for the prosperity of humanity. In light of new age advancement and resources, we now have the option to make things, which was at one time an abnormal inventive psyche. Days have come where one can sit at home and deal with their work with no inconveniences or stresses with the exception of just by using their phone. They can convey the product beginning with one spot, then onto the next by sitting in their home safely, no matter how far the goal is. The visuals of the road can be seen with the objective that the driver can screen the vehicle from home. Close to the camera, ultrasonic sensors are related in front and back of the truck with the objective of assessing the distance between the vehicles. An Android application is made, which is used to control the improvements of the truck and also shows the distance between the vehicles.

11.4 STRUCTURE OVERVIEW

This part shows the gear used in the proposed model. This hardware complements the Raspberry Pi 3, Pi Camera, L293d motor driver, ultrasonic sensors, and servo motors located near the vehicle's body.

11.4.1 Raspberry Pi

The Raspberry Pi is a simple, charge card-evaluated PC that interfaces with a PC show or TV, and uses a mainstream guide and mouse. The Raspberry Pi three model B was passed on in February 2016 with a 1.3 GHz 64 piece quad acknowledgment processor, on-board 802.11n c084d04ddacadd4b971ae3d98fecfb2a, Bluetooth and USB boot limits. On Pi Day 2018, the Raspberry Pi 3 model B+ was spurred with a speedier 1.3 GHz processor and a 3-examples faster. The Raspberry Pi 3 model B utilises a Broadcom BCM2837 SoC with a 1.3 GHz 64-piece quad-mindfulness ARM Cortex-A53 processor and 512 KiB of shared L2 storage. The models A+ and B+ are 1.44 GHz. It's anything but a successful little instrument that permits people, matters being what they might be, to break down enrolment and compose a couple of approaches to adapt to programmes in tongues like Scratch and Python. It might do all that you'd expect a PC should do, from investigating the web and playing overwhelming, incredible videos, to making bookkeeping pages, getting organised, and betting. The Raspberry Pi three, with a quad-acknowledgment ARM Cortex-A53 processor, is portrayed as having one-of-a-kind wireless exercises, the showing of a Raspberry Pi 1. The Pi three can boot from USB, for instance, from a gleam pressure. Considering remote VMware blocks in assorted models, the Pi 2B v1.2, 3A+, 3B, and 3B+ are the essential sheets that can do this. It might, in a similar way, be consumed with USB collecting, USB to MIDI converters, and contemplating the entire parcel, a couple of other contraptions/parts with USB limits, subordinate upon the provided.

FIGURE 11.2   Raspberry PI.

11.4.2 Camera

The Pi camera unit is a restricted-weight digital camera that maintains the Raspberry Pi. It banters with Pi about the usage of the MIPI camera reformist crossing point display. It is dependably used in photograph handling, AI or in notion endeavors. Within the wake of interfacing the stuff, we need to facilitate the Pi to draw a camera. Use the command "sudoraspi-config" to open the association window. With the aid of then beneath interfacing choices entice digital camera. Finally reboot the Pi and your camera module will be installed. Through then, you may make the Pi to take pix or record money owed the usage of clean python substance. The digicam module may be used to take high-quality video, as well as still photos. A. it is glaringly not hard to apply for enthusiasts, yet has abundance to convey to the desk pushed customers. There are loads of models online of people using it for recreation, mild new improvement, and other video crafts. You can actually, likewise, use the libraries bundled with the camera to add effects. In the same manner, Pi can, use common USB webcams, which can be used on a nearby laptop. On the Raspberry Pi B+, 2, and 3, the digicam port is between the sound port and the HDMI port. On the Raspberry Pi B, it has an ethernet port and an HDMI port. The association needs to be implanted with the right bearing: the blue essentials to defy the ethernet port, and the silver aspect is confronting the HDMI port. It is very lightweight and flexible, and has an objective of 2592 x 1944, which can keep 1080p, 720p, or 480p. The Raspberry Pi Board has a CSI (camera serial interface) to which we are able to attach the Pi camera module doubtlessly (Figure 11.3).

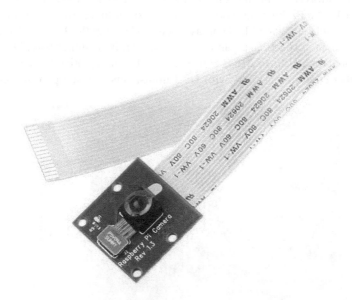

FIGURE 11.3　PI Camera.

11.4.3 L293D Motor Driver

The motor driver is a module for engines that licences you to govern the running tempo and heading of two engines at the same time. The L293D is a 16-pin motor motive force IC. This is required to present bidirectional drive streams at voltages ranging from 5 V to 36 V. This motor motive force is orchestrated and made dependent on the L293D IC. An engine driving force is an arranged circuit chip that is typically used to govern engines in self-supervising robots. Engine motive force passes, most likely as an interface between the Raspberry Pi and the engines. The maximum historically utilised engine driver ICs are from the L293 method. For instance, L293D, L293NE, and so forth, those ICs are required to control 2 DC engines at a comparable time. L293D encompasses two H-associates. The H-interface is the least inquiring of the circuits for controlling a modern-day survey engine. We will endorse the engine driver IC as L293D, so to speak. L293D has 16 pins. It has an agile voltage of 4.5V to 7V, a development period of 300ns, and is automatic. The thermal conclusion is open. L293D is used to force excessive musical development in cars using digital circuits, stepper engines, high-repeating design LEDs, and relay driving force (Figure 11.4).

11.4.4 Ultrasonic Sensor

Ultrasonic sensors work by releasing sound waves at a frequency that is arbitrarily high for individuals to hear. They by then trust that the sound will be reproduced back,

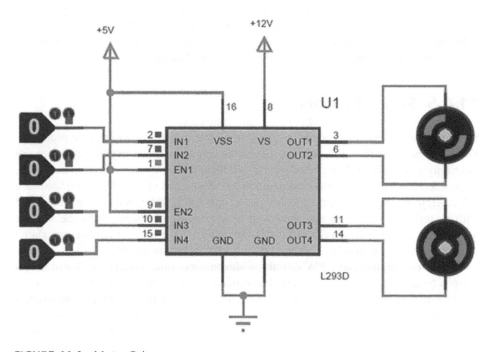

FIGURE 11.4 Motor Driver.

FIGURE 11.5 Ultrasonic sensor.

figuring partition reliant on the time required. This resembles how radar estimates the time it takes for a radio wave to return in the wake of hitting something (Figure 11.5).

Numerous sensors utilize every other sound author and beneficiary; it's in like manner workable to sign up for these into one accumulating system, having an ultrasonic portion shift from side to side among delivering and getting signals. The sort of sensor may be made in a smaller percentage than with separated components; that's beneficial for applications where size is including a few mysterious expenses. For the reason that ultrasonic waves can mirror the shape of a pitcher or a fluid floor and get returned to the sensor head, even direct goals may be perceived. Recognizing that verification is not affected by improvement or earth nearness spotting verification is regular for centers, as an instance, work plates or twigs. Ultrasonic sensors are except utilized in robotized obstruction vicinity frameworks, comparably as social affair headway. Alternatively with infrared sensors in close proximity perceiving packages, ultrasonic sensors are not as weak to the impedance of smoke, fuel, and different airborne debris. Ultrasonic sensors are comparatively applied as degree sensors to understand, screen, and manipulate fluid degrees in shut cubicles.

11.4.5 Servo Motors

Servo engines have been around for quite some time and are used in unique programs. They may be insignificant in size, but they sneak up on you all of a sudden and are very electricity-professional. These highlights award them the ability to work on inaccessible, well-ordered or radio-controlled toy automobiles, robots, and planes. The servo hardware is located just in the engine unit and has a positional shaft, which is commonly equipped with a stuff. The engine is managed with an electric sign which selects the volume of headway of the shaft. In the event that the engine being utilised is managed via its AC-energised motor, then it is referred to as an AC servo motor (Figure 11.6).

Servo engine plans with PWM (Pulse width balance) rule, induces its edge of turn is obliged by using the duration of applied heartbeat to its manage PIN. Essentially a servo engine is a contained DC engine that is limited through a variable resistor (potentiometer) to two or three gadgets. The servo engine can be deserted 0 to 180 degrees, but it may move as much as 210 degrees, dependent upon the amassing. This stage of flip can be obliged by using applying the electrical Pulse of bona fide width, to its manipulate pin.

FIGURE 11.6 Servo motor.

11.5 IMPLEMENTATION

This section shows the implementation of hardware and software for the proposed model. Figure 11.1 shows the hardware connections of the truck. The Raspberry Pi is connected to a camera module, ultrasonic sensors, and motor drivers for the working of the prototype. The vehicle is operated remotely and it is necessary for the user to know the surroundings so that he/she can drive the vehicle without any accidents, so the camera module streams live surroundings to the user. The video streaming by the camera can be seen from anywhere with the help of an application [27] (Figure 11.7).

Since it is a delivery vehicle, a door is attached to the body of the truck so that whenever the truck reaches the destination, the door can be unlocked by the user so that the goods can be unloaded. A servo motor is used to open and close the door of the truck. Ultrasonic sensors are connected to the front and rear of the vehicle so that the distance between the vehicles can be seen, which also helps the user to control the vehicle. The Raspberry Pi is connected to Google Firebase so that the data between the Pi and the controlling app is transmitted. The distance between the vehicles is sent to the real-time database from which the controlling app fetches that data and displays it in the app [25]. An efficient Python code is written on the Pi, which is responsible for all these actions, and it is executed as soon as the Pi is turned on. Hence, no extra service is needed to execute the code.

Figure 11.2 shows the android application to control the truck. The app is created using Java in the Android studio, which is used to control the movements of the truck and its door, and it also fetches the values from the real-time database which is sent by the ultrasonic sensors from the Pi. The app is also connected to the real-time database in which it sends the data for pi and it is used for movements like forward, reverse, left, and right. For delivering the product to the destination, the truck has been implemented by Dijkstra's Algorithm. So the truck can find the shortest path to the destination, and it mainly helps in time consumption; the product can be delivered within a shorter

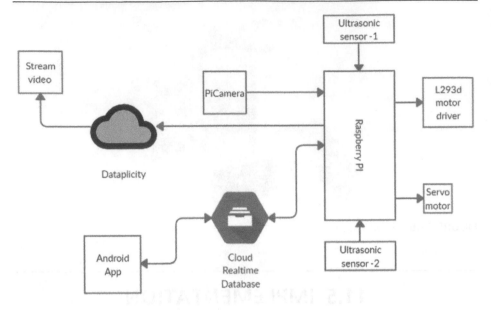

FIGURE 11.7 Block diagram of truck.

time. After reaching the destination, the product will be delivered to the customer only if they know the one-time password that is provided by the application. This technology has already been implemented in every country, so now we are implementing it in our country. When we consider the safety of the product, it has reached the customer's satisfaction. The product inside the truck will be transported to safety as it is constructed using very powerful instruments. Definitely, the truck will not meet with an accident because the sensors that are used on all four sides of the truck will maintain the required distance between the vehicles, and while moving, the truck will stop suddenly as it reaches the minimum distance between the vehicles. So the truck will indeed provide good service to the customers by providing the delivery on time. The text FWD_DIST in the figure represents the distance between the truck and the vehicle in front of it, whereas BD_DIST shows the distance between the truck and the vehicle behind it (Figure 11.8).

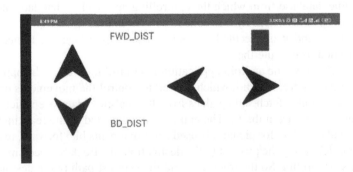

FIGURE 11.8 Android application to control truck.

TABLE 11.2   Test results

DISTANE (IN KMS)	TIME DELAY (IN SECS)		
	BREAK	FORWARD AND REVERSE	LEFT AND RIGHT
5	0.5	1	1
10	0.5	1	1
50	0.5	1	1
100	0.5	1	1

11.6 RESULT

The prototype of the RC truck has been implemented and tested at various locations with a distance of more than 100 km between the truck and the controller.

The output from the test was promising, although it has a delay of 1–2 seconds, which can be eliminated in future work. Table 11.2. shows the results of the tests conducted.

11.7 CONCLUSION

This work exhibits the prototype of a remote-controlled truck that can be controlled by a smart phone from anywhere. With a well-designed prototype of this truck, it can be used to deliver goods from one place to another with minimal human intervention. The same truck can be used for military purposes and much more.

While IoT devices can significantly increase cost-effectiveness for organizations, they also carry hazards. Since IoT gadgets are accompanied by the web, they can be hacked simply like some other web-installed appliances. To adequately confirm the system, it's essential to understand the security weaknesses of IoT gadgets.

Even when it comes to physical issues, if the truck stops working in between shipments, the door of the truck remains closed until it is unlocked by the controller. In other words, the goods inside the truck will be secured.

In future works, face recognition can be implemented, which can be used to unlock the doors along with that the delays can be eliminated. Along with that, integration of Blockchain with IoT can reduce the security bleach for IoT devices.

REFERENCES

[1] World Health Organization, 2022. https://www.who.int/news-room/fact-sheets/detail/road-traffic-injuries

[2] Herbst, J., 2006, *The History of Transportation* (Twenty-First Century Books, Minneapolis) Quitney Anderson, J. & Rainie, L. (2008): The Future of the Internet III. Pew Internet & American Life Project.

[3] Fleisch, E., 2010, What is the Internet of Things? An Economic Perspective. Auto-ID Labs White Paper WP-BIZAPP-053. Retrieved on 28th May 2010, from http://autoidlabs.org/uploads/media/AUTOIDLABS-WP-BIZAPP-53.pdf

[4] Bauer, M., Gluhak, A., Johansson, M., Montagut, F., Presser, M., Stirbu, V., Vercher, J., 2009, Towards an Architecture for a Real World Internet. In Tselentis, G. et al. (Eds.).

[5] Hernández-Muñoz, J. M., Bernat Vercher, J., Muñoz, L., Galache, J. A., Presser, M., Hernández Gómez, L. A., & Pettersson, J. Smart Cities at the Forefront of the Future Internet. In *The Future Internet*, Lecture Notes in Computer Science, Springer, Berlin, Heidelberg, 2011.

[6] Abramowicz, H., Baucke, S., Johnsson, M., Kind, M., Niebert, N., Ohlman, B., Quittek, J., Woesner, H., Wuenstel, K., A Future Internet Embracing the Wireless World. In Tselentis, G. et al. (Eds.) *Towards the Future Internet – A European Research Perspective*. IOS Press, Amsterdam, 2009.

[7] Bagloee, S. A., Tavana, M. *Autonomous Vehicles: Challenges, Opportunities, and Future Implications for Transportation Policies*, Springer, 284–303, 2016.

[8] D'Orey, P. M., Ferreira, M. IT'S for Sustainable Mobility: A Survey on Applications and Impact Assessment Tools. *IEEE Trans. Intell. Transp. Syst.* 2014, 15, 477–493.

[9] Ondruša, J., Kollab, E., Verta, P., Šari´c, Ž. How Do Autonomous Cars Work? *Transp. Res. Procedia* 2020, 44, 226–233.

[10] Vishwas, D. B., Gowtham, M., Gururaj, H. L., Goundar, S., Industrial Internet of Things 4.0: Foundations, Challenges, and Applications–A Review - Innovations in the Industrial Internet of Things (IIoT), 2021.

[11] Kaiwartya, O., Abdullah, A. H., Cao, Y., Altameem, A., Prasad, M., Lin, C.-T., Liu, X. Internet of Vehicles: Motivation, Layered Architecture, Network Model, Challenges, and Future Aspects. *IEEE Access* 2016, 4, 5356–5373.

[12] Gowtham, M., Pramod, H. B., Vishwas, D. B., Fathima, M., Availability Analysis of Individuals using IoT. In 1st International Conference on Advances, 2019.

[13] Levis, P., Madden, S., Polastre, J., Szewczyk, R., Whitehouse, K., Woo, A., Gay, D. et al. TinyOS: An operating system for sensor networks. In *Ambient Intelligence*, pp. 115–148. Springer Berlin Heidelberg, 2005.

[14] Horrocks, I., 2007, Semantic Web: The Story So Far. W4A2007 Keynote, May 07–08, 2007, Banff, Canada.

[15] Dunkels, A., Gronvall, B., Voigt, T. Contiki-A Lightweight and Flexible Operating System for Tiny Networked Sensors. In Local Computer Networks, 2004. 29th Annual IEEE International Conference, 2004, pp. 455–462. IEEE.

[16] Wu, F., Luo, H., Jia, H., Zhao, F., Xiao, Y., GAO, X. Predicting the Noise Covariance With a Multitask Learning Model for Kalman Filter-Based GNSS/INS Integrated Navigation. *IEEE Trans. Instrum. Meas.* 2021, 70, 1–13.

[17] Ngoc, T. T., Khenchaf, A., Comblet, F. Evaluating Process and Measurement Noise in Extended Kalman Filter for GNSS Position Accuracy. In Proceedings of the 13th European Conference Antennas Propagation, Krakow, Poland, 31 March–5 April 2019, pp. 1–5.

[18] Cui, B., Wei, X., Chen, X., Li, J., Li, L. On Sigma-Point Update of Cubature Kalman Filter for GNSS/INS under GNSS-Challenged Environment. *IEEE Trans. Veh. Technol.* 2019, 68, 8671–8682.

[19] Stengel, R. F. *Stochastic Optimal Control: Theory and Application*. John Wiley and Sons, New York, NY, USA, 1986.

[20] Xu, B., Zhang, P., Wen, H. Z., Wu, X. Stochastic Stability and Performance Analysis of Cubature Kalman Filter. *Neurocomputing* 2016, 186, 218–227.

[21] Kiran, V. V., Santhanalakshmi, S., Raspberry Pi Based Remote Controlled Car using Smartphone Accelerometer. In 2019 International Conference on Communication and Electronics Systems (ICCES), Coimbatore, India, 2019, pp. 1536–1542, 10.1109/ICCES45898.2019.9002079.

[22] Jing, Y., Zhang, L., Arce, I., Farajidavar, A., AndroRC: An Android Remote Control Car Unit for Search Missions. In IEEE Long Island Systems, Applications and Technology (LISAT) Conference 2014, Farmingdale, NY, 2014, pp. 1–5, 10.1109/LISAT.2014.6845227.

[23] Petit, J., Schaub, F., Feiri, M., Kargl, F. Pseudonym Schemes in Vehicular Networks: A Survey. *IEEE Commun. Surv. Tutor.* 2015, 17, 228–255.

[24] Qazi, S., Sabir, F., Khawaja, B. A., Atif, S. M., Mustaqim, M. Why is Internet of Autonomous Vehicles not as Plug and Play as We Think? Lessons to Be Learnt From Present Internet and Future Directions. *IEEE Access* 2020, 8, 133015–133033.

[25] Gowtham, M., Pramod, H. B., Banga, M. K., Patil, M. Intrusion Detection and Avoidance for Home and Smart City Automation in Internet of Things. *IoT: Security Privacy Paradigm.* 2020.

[26] Arena, F., Pau, G. An Overview of Vehicular Communications. *Future Internet* 2019, 11, 27.

[27] Fagnant, D. J., Kockelman, K., Preparing a Nation For autonomous Vehicles: Opportunities, Barriers and Policy Recommendations. *Transp. Res. Part A* 2015, 77, 167–181.

IoT-Enabled Smart Parking to Reduce Vehicle Flooding

12

Anusha K S, Andra Pujitha, Megha Annappa Naik, Nishkala I N, and Parivarthana S R

Department of Computer Science and Engineering, Vidyavardhaka College of Engineering, Mysuru, Karnataka, India

Contents

12.1 INTRODUCTION

The Internet of Things (IoT) is the internetworking of physical devices that embed the electronics in their architecture to interact and perceive one another's and the outside world's interactions [1]. IoT-based technology will bring fully advanced quality of service in the next years, radically changing how people actually live their everyday routines. Health, energy, potential treatments, farming, building automation, and smart buildings are just some of the fields where IoT has made a significant impact. IoT makes anything and everything sophisticated by enhancing aspects of human life

DOI: 10.1201/9781003282990-12

through the use of data collection, AI technologies, and communication systems [2]. In the Internet of Things, a person with a diabetes diagnostic device, an animal with monitoring devices, and so on can all be called "things."

Parking-seeking motorists are thought to be responsible for around 30% of metropolitan traffic congestion. Businesses, towns, and property vendors are always attempted to strike a balance between increased demand and parking requirements [3]. However, it has become evident that just adding more parking places would not solve the congestion problem. Smart parking systems are being used in new techniques to present a more balanced viewpoint of parking that better balances the relationship between producers and consumers. As part of an urban mobility strategic approach, smart parking is the application of modern technologies to the efficacy, supervision, and enforcement of parking spaces [4]. In 2016, the global market for smart parking systems was worth $93.5 million, with 46% of the market accounted for by the United States, indicating a large development opportunity for both domestic and international service providers [5]. The technologies that underlie smart parking services include vehicle sensors, remote accessibility, and data analytics. Technological improvements in aspects such as apps for customer service on smart parking has also been facilitated by cellphones, contactless banking, as well as in car navigation systems. "The smart parking concept is founded on the capacity to access, collect, assess, share information, and respond to information about parking usage [6]. Advanced technologies are progressively delivering this data in real time, allowing both urban planning and drivers to make the most of available parking space".

The rest of the paper is laid out as follows: Section 12.2 presents the related works on smart parking systems using IoT. Section 12.3 presents the proposed work. Section 12.4 conducts results and discussions.

12.2 RELATED WORKS

Seema Hanchate et al. [7] the proposed method is implemented with the help of a cloud-connected mobile application. The user will choose a time to allocate the space. If he/she does not occupy it later, the user will be notified. The app displays the number of parking spaces available as well as any that are vacant. The drawback is that after allocating, if another user requests the same spot, the system is unable to allot that spot, resulting in a waste of time, money, and space if the first customer cancels later.

Sayali Deshmukh et al. [1] here the analysis of smart-phone integrated sensors and Bluetooth connectivity, automatic identification of users' parking activities is realized. Once a parking spot has been identified, an adaptive technique allows the information to be circulated to the target situation over the internet via a remote server and device-to-device communication via wi-fi direct linkages.

Anam Fathima et al. [8] the user can be pre-registered in this smart parking system and an IP camera will capture the vehicle registration number, allowing them to go without interruption. According to the information provided, parking duration is estimated, as well as the location of their visit. The sum will be debited from the e-wallet of preregistered users, which will be visible to the user. For new customers, a similar pricing scheme will be used, but it will be in an offline mode.

Saarika P. S. et al. [9] the data is exchanged by the internet service between the cloud server and sensor security. By using internet, the availability of slot can be checked by the remote device. Parking slots which are free and filled can be checked by the sensors. When the parking spot is free, it will send information to the cloud to tell there is parking slot available, else it will indicate the slot is not available or filled. The car should wait until the slot becomes free if the parking slots are full. Here we have signboards that show distance, routes, weather, traffic congestion. The sensors used here can send the weather information to the cloud. Raspberry Pi the situation of traffic is monitored, and the information is displayed on the screen.

Mahendra B. M. et al. [10] the sensors which have input can be given to the embedded system. If there are any changes in the input, the embedded system will update the collected information from sensor to database sensor. The embedded system used here is Raspberry pi model 3b. All the information about the users who are registered, the duration of parking slot, and the parking lot status is maintained. The information about the parking lot availability is shared to all users. This server is updated with two terminals. Sensors and the embedded system are on one terminal, and users are on another terminal. This application is running on the user's mobile. By using this application, we can check the availability status and also book the lot; the system is connected with an Aadhar card. By using IR sensors that are connected to lot, we can collect the status of parking slot. This motor is used for main gate opening and closing. If the user enters ID and booking ID is valid, then the gate opens.

Mohammad saifullah Bin Mohd Salman et al. [11] the app designed will display the parking lot status, and this can be obtained from cloud. Through the cloud, the request is sent if the user reserves it by using the app. By using the scheduling method, the system can find the current location and assign with the location near to the user. After this, the user will get the details of the reserved parking lot. Here we are using an ultrasonic sensor to detect parking lot availability, and it can be sent to wirelessly with Zigbee.

12.3 METHODOLOGY

According to the majority of analysts, the demand for intelligent parking services will grow rapidly in the near future due to the growing automotive industry [12]. By using the smart parking system, the parking lots would be managed automatically by

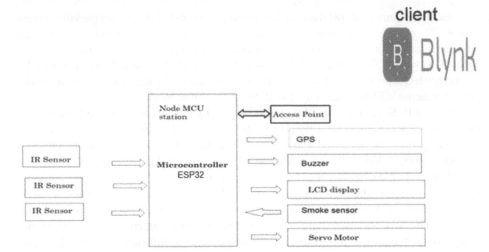

FIGURE 12.1   Block diagram of parking system.

collecting and delivering accurate data to customers and administrators. The product, as designed, is able to detect vacant spaces in parking areas so that it can guide the driver to the vacant spaces without requiring any human interaction.

The smart parking system uses hardware components like IR sensors, ESP32 microcontroller, RFID tag, LCD display, servo motor, smoke detector sensors, and water detector sensors.

The Figure 12.1 represents the block diagram of the parking system, the each component and their uses are as discussed.

   i. IR Sensors—Infrared sensors emit light to detect a moving object. Most of the objects emit some form of heat in the infrared spectrum [13]. Infrared sensors can detect these types of radiation, which are invisible to our eyes. This radiation is used to detect the vehicle in the parking slots.
   ii. ESP32 Microcontroller—With integrated wi-fi and dual-mode Bluetooth, ESP32 microcontrollers are extremely low-cost, low-power systems on chips. It features Tensilica Xtensa LX6 microprocessors featuring dual and single cores in addition to built-in antenna switches, a RF balun, a power amplifier, low-noise receive amplifier, filters, and power-management modules. It is the main microcontroller used in this project because of its functionalities.
   iii. LCD Display—Liquid Crystal Displays (LCD) are flat-panel displays that use liquid crystals as their primary source of illumination. This component is used to display the message to the user/client.
   iv. RFID Cards—Radio Frequency Identification is a non-contact wireless data transfer method that utilizes radio frequencies [14]. RFID tags can be attached to items to automatically and uniquely identify them. Security and verification of users can be ensured by using RFID tag.

v. Servo Motor—Servomotors are linear actuators or rotary actuators that enable fine control over velocity, acceleration, and position when turned. A motor and a sensor are coupled together to provide positional feedback. Gates of parking area is opened and closed using this servo motor.

vi. Smoke detector Sensors—Typically, a smoke detector alerts you to the presence of smoke, which indicates that there is a fire. In case of fire breakout in the parking area, it will buzz the alarm.

vii. GPS Module—Global Positioning System (GPS) is used to determine the exact location of objects around the world at any time [15]. Satellite data is directly transmitted by satellites through dedicated RF frequencies to GPS modules through miniature processors and antennas. GPS is installed at parking area to get the location of it.

The circuit diagram of the proposed system is as shown in the Figure 12.2. "It involves three IR sensors, one servo motors, and one 16x2 LCD. Here the ESP32 will control the complete process and also send the parking availability information, it can be monitored from anywhere in the world over the internet. Three IR sensors are used at entry and exit gates to detect the presence of a car and automatically open or close the gate. IR Sensor is used to detect any object by sending and receiving the IR. One servo will act as entry and exit gate and they rotate to open or close the gate. Finally, an IR sensor is used to detect if the parking slot is available or occupied and send the data to ESP32 accordingly."

Every component in the circuit is connected to an ESP32 microcontroller. ESP32 is a powerful 32-bit microcontroller. The circuit consists of a servo motor, which is

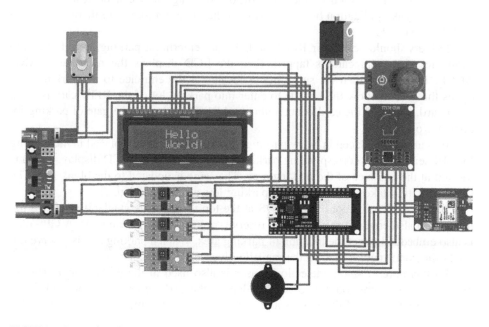

FIGURE 12.2   The circuit diagram.

connected to an LCD regulator knob that is used to adjust the brightness of the LCD. There is a GPS that gives an accurate location for users. By using a regulator connected to a microcontroller, another circuit is made to divide the power supplies into 3V and 5V. Three IR sensors were used, and they are connected to pin number 15,34,4 of the microcontroller. In IR sensors, the digital output is always high, if there is any object detected, it becomes low. We used a 16x2 (16 columns and 2 rows) LCD display, 4 digital pins, namely 14,27,26,25 from the LCD are connected to ESP32. Buzzer is used to make a beep sound when an incorrect tag is detected; it is connected to microcontroller pin number 5. Smoke sensor is connected to pin number 35 of the microcontroller, which is used to detect the smoke.

The software's used to carry out the implementation work is

    i. Arduino IDE—Code can be written and uploaded to the Arduino board with the Arduino software (IDE). Any Arduino board can be used with this software.
    ii. Blynk Application—Blok is a platform that allows Arduino, Raspberry Pi, and other devices to be controlled anywhere in the world over the internet. With this digital dashboard, we can use mouse to drag and drop widgets to create an interface for the project.

The flow description of the smart parking system is represented in the Figure 12.3. The process begins with the entry of the vehicle into the parking lot. LED display near the entrance gate displays the information about parking slots such as vacant slots and slot numbers. The availability of slots can also be checked through a mobile application called blynk. In addition, parking slots can be reserved using the same blynk application before arriving at that location to ensure there is space to park their vehicle.

Drivers should scan their RFID cards before entering a parking area if slots are available. If a valid card is tapped, then the LCD displays the message "CARD ACCEPTED," and then the servo motor located at the entrance to the parking area opens the gate to allow the vehicle to enter into parking lot. If the RFID card is not a valid card, that is, if the card is not authorized RFID card, then the gate of parking lot does not open.

IR sensors are placed in every parking lot. When vehicles are placed in the parking lots, IR sensor sends corresponding parking information for the LCD display, which is located at the entrance of the parking area. The same is updated to the blynk app. The same operation takes place when the parking lots are unoccupied.

Blynk application consist of LEDS at the top to show the availability of parking lots, and it also contains the buttons to reserve corresponding parking lots. A GPS map is also embedded to get the location of parking area. When a parking slot is reserved, it sends the confirmation mail to the mail ID given in the application.

Furthermore, a smoke detection sensor is also used in the parking area. Due to excessive heat, there could be a fire accident in the parking area. Sensors can detect smoke before the fire fully ignites and send an alert to the management through the blynk application.

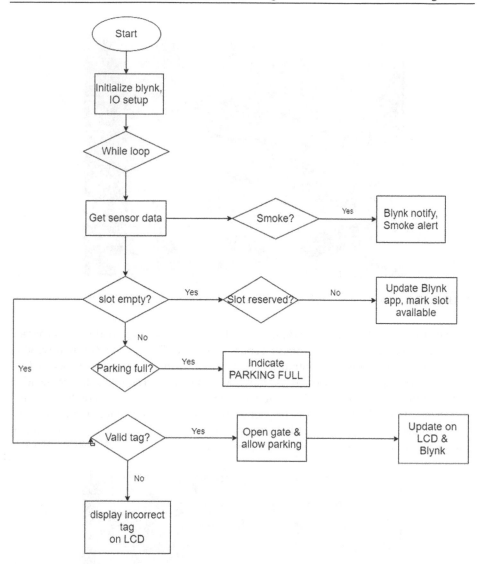

FIGURE 12.3   Flow diagram of the parking system.

12.4 RESULTS AND DISCUSSIONS

Hardware devices are connected to each other using jumper wires. Components like IR sensors, ESP32 microcontroller, GPS module, Buzzer, Smoke sensor, etc. are connected to give desired output, as in Figure 12.3.

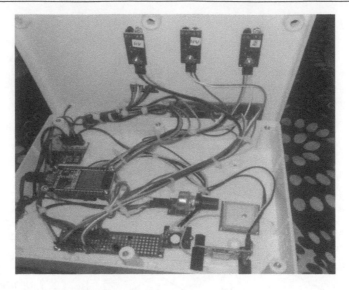

FIGURE 12.4 Components connection image.

The Figure 12.4 shows the parking area, which consists of three parking slots named slot 1, slot 2, and slot 3. At the entrance, it contains an LCD display with RFID card reader. It also has a servo motor at the entrance gate. The LCD displays the status of parking lots.

The blynk application view is as shown in Figure 12.5. The top of the application contains three LED displays, which show the status of the three corresponding parking slots. The LED is high when the respective parking slot is occupied. Otherwise, the LED remains low. Below the LED are two buttons for reservation. At the end, it contains a GPS map location of the parking area.

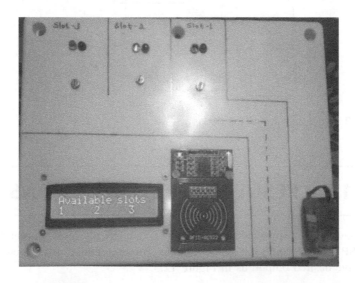

FIGURE 12.5 Parking slots.

FIGURE 12.6   Blynk application view.

The user needs to have an authorized RFID card, as shown in Figure 12.6, to enter into the parking area. When the user taps his card on the RFID card on the RFID reader, the LCD displays the details of the card; details include whether the card is accepted and the card number. If the card is accepted, then the servo motor opens the gate and allows the user to enter into the parking area (Figure 12.8).

When an unauthorized user tries to enter a parking area and taps the RFID card against the RFID reader, the LCD displays a message saying "INCORRECT TAG" and makes the buzzer beep, as shown in Figure 12.7.

From Figure 12.9, the observation can be made that a car was parked at the parking slot numbered 2. Thus, the corresponding information is also updated in the blynk app. We can notice that the LED named slot 2 is high, that is, it shows that slot 2 is already occupied.

When an unauthorized user tries to enter a parking area and taps the RFID card against the RFID reader, the LCD displays a message saying "INCORRECT TAG" and makes the buzzer beep, as shown in Figure 12.10.

The user can reserve a parking slot using the blynk app. In the above figure, it is shown that when the user reserves the slot 1, he gets the confirmation emailed to his mail ID. Figure 12.11 shows the reservation and the confirmation mail.

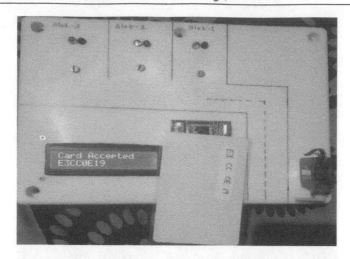

FIGURE 12.7 Authorized user entry.

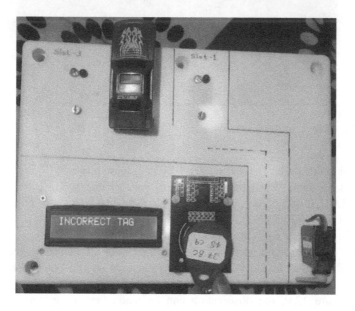

FIGURE 12.8 Unauthorized user.

When all the slots are full, the LCD at the entrance shows the message "PARKING FULL." The same is also updated in the blynk application; all the three LEDs in the blynk app are high, indicating that the parking slots are full, as shown in above Figure 12.12.

Due to heavy heat, there may be any fire breakout in the parking area. The system detects the fire at early stage; that is, it detects the smoke and alerts the user and management about the fire. When it detects the smoke, it sends a notification to the blynk app. The Figure 12.13 shows the notification sent to blynk app when smoke was detected.

FIGURE 12.9   Updation on Blynk app.

FIGURE 12.10 Unauthorized user entry.

FIGURE 12.11 Reservation through blynk app and conformation mail.

The blynk app allows users to reserve a parking spot. When the user reserves the slot, the confirmation email will be sent to their mail ID. Once conformed, the LCD near the parking entrance gate does not display the availability of the reserved slot. When all the slots are full, the LCD at the entrance shows the message as parking full.

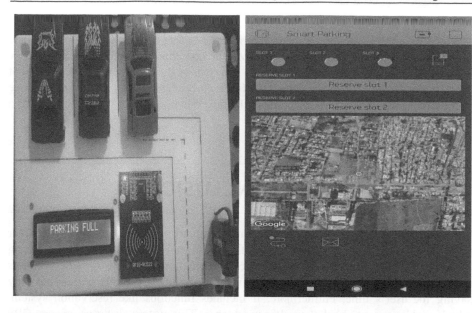

FIGURE 12.12   Parking full.

FIGURE 12.13   Smoke alert.

When all the slots are occupied, and if the user tries to enter into the parking area, the LCD display at the entrance shows the message No Space; it also does not open the gate of the parking area. Whether it is authorized or unauthorized user, it does not allow the user to enter into parking area. Due to heavy heat, there may be any fire breakout in the parking area. The system detects the fire at early stage; that is, it detects the smoke and alerts the user and management about the fire. When it detects the smoke, it sends a notification to the blynk app.

12.5 CONCLUSION

Safe and easy parking of vehicles is the aim of smart parking systems. This chapter presents a low-cost smart parking system that provides the best solution for a parking system. Information and a real-time process of parking slots are provided by this parking system. It increases the effectiveness of finding a suitable parking spot by saving the user's time. Furthermore, it includes functions like reservation system, which enables users to book their slots in advance. This system also uses sensors, GPS modules, wi-fi modules to update the users with accurate information about parking slots. Smart parking serves to alleviate issues like traffic congestion and air pollution, as well as improve people's lifestyles. The proposed system provides most of all the required facilities related to parking system. But the scope of IOT is enhanced day by day. For the future enhancement, payment gateway can be added and also a personalized mobile application and website can be created. Adding these features, the present implemented project can be made even more appealing.

REFERENCES

[1] Supriya Shinde, Ankita Patil, Sumedha Chavan, Sayali Deshmukh, and Subodh Ingleshwar, "IoT based Parking System using Google Maps," International Conference on I-SMAC (IoT in Social, Mobile, Analytics and Cloud), (2017).
[2] Krishna Yogi Borra, Sharan Sai G. N., and Jehova Honey Domma, "An IoT based Smart Parking System using LoRa," International Conference on Cyber-Enabled Distributed Computing and Knowledge Discovery, (2018).
[3] Omar Abdulkader, Alwi M. Bamhdi, Vijey Thayananthan, and Kamal Jambi, "A novel and Secure Smart Parking Management System (SPMS) based on Integration of WSN, RFID, and IoT"15th Learning and Technology Conference (L&T), (2018), pp. 102–106, 10.1109/LT.2018.8368492.
[4] Elakya R, Juhi Seth, Pola Ashritha, and R Namith, "Parking System using IoT," International Journal of Engineering and Advanced Technology (IJEAT), (2019).
[5] Madhur Dixit, Srimathi C, Robin Doss, Seng Loke, and M.A. Saleemdurai, "Smart Parking with Computer Vision and IoT Technology" (2020).
[6] Agustina Ampuni, Adi Fitrianto, Sopater Fonataba, and Gunawan Wang, "Smart Parking System with Automatic Cashier Machine Utilize the IoT Technology" (2019).

[7] Divya Pandey, and Seema Hanchate, "Navigation based-Intelligent Parking Management System using Queuing theory and IOT" (2018).

[8] Chandana M, Aniruddh M C, Anam Fathima, and Chandan G, "A Study on Smart Parking Solutions Using IoT," International Conference on Intelligent Sustainable Systems (ICISS), (2019).

[9] Saarika P S, Sandhya K, and Dr. Sudha T, "Smart Transportation System using IoT" (2017).

[10] Mahendra B M, Dr. Savita Sonali, Nagaraj Bhat, Raju, and Raghu T, "IoT Based Sensor Enabled Smart Car Parking for Advanced Driver Assistance System". (2019).

[11] Mohammad Saifullah Bin Mohd Salman, Assoc. Prof. Dr Mohd Noh bin Karsiti, and Noor Amin Shahriz Bin Rozly-Azni, "Dynamic Resource Allocation Strategy for Low-Cost Smart Parking System," 2nd International Conference on Smart Sensors and Application (ICSSA), (2018).

[12] Noah Sieck, Cameron Calpin, and Mohammad Almalag, "Machine Vision Smart Parking Using Internet of Things (IoTs) In A Smart University" (2020).

[13] Ihan Aydin, Mehmet Karakose, and Ebru Karakose, A Navigation and Reservation Based Smart Parking Platform Using Genetic Optimization for Smart Cities Computer Engineering Department, Firat University 2Civil Aviation School, Firat University, (June 2017).

[14] Marlia binti Morsin, Lim Hwei Hwa, Abdul Majeed Bin Zulkipli, and Tasiransurini Ab. Rahman, "Smart Parking Guidance System," Proceedings of EnCon2010 3rd Engineering Conference on Advancement in Mechanical and Manufacturing for Sustainable Environment, (2010).

[15] A. Chatzigiannakis, and A. Pyrgelis Vitaletti, "A Privacy-Preserving Smart Parking System using an IoT Elliptic Curve Based Security Platform," Computer Communications, vol. 89–90, pp. 165–177, (2016).

IoT Device Discovery Technique Based on Semantic Ontology

13

Raghu Nandan R[1] and Nalini N[2]

[1]*Department of Computer Science and Engineering, Navkis College of Engineering, Hassan, Karnataka, India*
[2]*Department of Computer Science and Engineering, Nitte Meenakshi Institute of Technology, Yelahanka, Karnataka, India*

Contents

DOI: 10.1201/9781003282990-13

13.1 INTRODUCTION

The Internet of Things (IoT) [1] is evolving exponentially by connecting almost every physical device to the internet. Well-organized device discovery and meaningful exchange of information is the need of the hour to enable IoT environment-based, customer-oriented products featuring value-added services to operate successfully. Varied business vendors have their own specific descriptions of the interaction techniques in IoT for their different emerged domains. These variability and limited proportions in IoT device, data, and service definition create conditions that are a major challenge to the success of IoT. Devices connected to the IoT should be defined in the same way. One of the paradigm changes is that the industry is adding semantics to IoT, as shown by Berners-Lee et al. in their landmark article on the semantic web [2,3], "development will bring significant new performance as machines become better able to process and understand data."

There is a need for each device to be uniquely identified so that it can be accessed easily though the internet. Adding semantics to the IoT devices will help in solving many problems. Devices should exchange messages embedding the raw data along with the semantics. Since the messages have the semantics that hold the meaning of raw data, IoT nodes do not need to know the node-specific information, and processing takes place in an identical manner. Because IoT devices are constrained devices in terms of memory, power consumption, and communication capabilities, there is a need for semantic technology to be adapted to this natural complexity of IoT devices. Advances in semantic technology will solve the complexities associated with the definition of IoT resources and services that provide information models, data access, and information exchange by producers and consumers and its seamless integration, discovery of devices, interoperability [3].

For effective resource discovery [4], it is necessary to provide a common format access, and there is a need to enrich the discovery protocols semantically. To semantically enable the protocols, it is necessary to find out the discriminating attributes of a device to embed them into the semantic layer. To make it a reality, semantic annotation of the IoT resources needs to be achieved. Semantic annotation of the IoT resource description helps in automatic extraction of resource capabilities. In semantic matching, machine understandable labels are mapped to the words from the description texts of the user request [5]. Automatic semantic annotation of the IoT resource is a challenging and growing area of research because of the large-scale integration of the heterogeneous devices into the network. There is a requirement of the efficient discovery and ranking of the retrieved resources with semantic labeling, which best suits the users' need based on the context and quality of services. Also the model needs to be self configuring in case of a fault or better service availability.

The semantic annotation [6] of the document involves searching for the text pieces of that file and inserting them into the ontology data. Annotation plays an important role in many semantic systems that include linked data generation, open source output, semantic search, and alignment of ontologies. Clearly, semantic search allows users to express their information needs on an informed basis. Semantic search can use semantic relationships in ontology to accomplish new tasks that include refining users' queries with broader or more specific definitions.

A semantic definition of a document involves finding similarities between the text fragments of a document and the situations or individuals in the ontology. Annotation plays an important role in a variety of semantic applications, such as the production of linked data, the extraction of open information, ontology alignment, and semantic search. Clearly, semantic search allows users to express their knowledge needs in terms of knowledge base. Unlike traditional keyword-based search, semantic search can use semantic relationships in ontology to accomplish new tasks, such as refining users' queries with broader or more specific meanings.

A semantic annotation of text involves tracing the text pieces of a document and mapping them in ontology cases. Annotation plays an important role in many semantic systems, including the production of linked data, the extraction of open information, semantic search, and alignment of ontologies. Clearly, semantic search allows users to express their knowledge needs in terms of knowledge base. Semantic search can use semantic relationships in ontology to accomplish new tasks that include refining users' queries with broader or more specific meanings.

The proposed approach is relied on gathering contextual semantic information from the vendor document description and mapping them to the concept of ontology.

In this paper, we propose a framework for automatic extraction of IoT device description from the vendor specifications of the IoT devices. These descriptions are mapped onto the IoT resource model. Developing the IoT device service capabilities is based on ontology-assisted semantic inference [5]. Reference device ontology [7,8] is applied on the device specification and maps the IoT devices to the IoT resources.

13.2 LITERATURE SURVEY

In this section, a brief overview of the various works carried in this research area is discussed. In paper [9,10], device profile and services are identified by training models based on training data on network traffic. But before installing the device in the environment, inferring the capabilities and services is desirable to make intelligent clustering of IoT diverse devices.

In [11], based on term frequency (TF) and inverse document frequency (IDF), is applied to identify important topics with respect to computer science ontology (CSO). Semantic similarity for a pair of words is measured assisted by ontology in [12], where similarity is determined by their common and different features of a particular word in ontology, as suggested by Tversky [13]. In [14], service-oriented entity annotation system is proposed, which performs annotation of the function, working state, and basic description of entities.

The study in most of the research is to provide semantic annotation to sensor data and make intelligent decisions on it. Depending on the service modelling and context, recommendation of the service is made.

An IoT resource R consists of set of sensors S, set of actuators A, set of computing entities. IoT resources exhibit several characteristics that need to be considered during the discovery process in ubiquitous environment.

1. An IoT resource may comprise of one/many physical devices and its related services. Hence, its important to identify them uniquely.
2. Device offers the service and the communication modules.
3. Many features like QOS parameters are temporal and spatial dependent and needs to be monitored.
4. IoT resources not only sense events but also can process them.

As per the proposed semantic resource component model [15], device entity refers to the physical entity, which can be sensor, actuator, computing unit embedded, or controlled by application entity. Service entity refers to the services and its quality attributes, which together form its capabilities. Telemetric entity refers to dynamic QOS attributes, space, location attributes, which are observed via device monitoring process.

The IoT resource specification contains the devices web pages, device specifications, and corresponding features documents, manufacturer documentation, NS technical specifications of the IoT devices. Developer documentation specifies the standard interfaces published by the product developer so that the applications can access them through the relevant web services. If the services or the capabilities of the IoT devices are available directly from the specification documents, then it is a simple static key-value word extraction. However, in real-world solutions, automatic service type extraction from the specifications is needed. As discussed in [12], TF-IDF may be adequate for word extraction from documents, given an extensive corpus. But to find IoT device service type from specifications, it may be misleading.

There is no standardization in industry for documenting the technical specifications of any IOT resources. Every IoT vendor follows their own template to describe the features and hardware parameters. The concise description makes its interpretation difficult. Also, the important indicative parameters may appear limited number of time. Also, the terminologies and taxonomies followed for describing IoT devices may be different from standard vocabularies. Hence, its important to include semantic knowledge during specification extraction and its inferring and mapping procedures.

The method that detects both IoT devices with public IP, as well as those behind NAT while preserving IoT users' privacy by extracting minimal information from IoT devices' traffic. Also, the method can be applied to flow-level traffic from a college campus and partial traffic from a IXP to detect real-world IoT devices [16]. The methods of classifying the IoT devices as to IoT or not based on the three different classifiers based on traffic features, DHCP and unified classifier. The unified classifier has the ability to classify both as traffic features and DHCP [17].

There are also one class clustering models [18], where each class trained independently and updated. The contributions are two fold: first, identification of IoT traffic attributes using real-time flow-level telemetry; Second, development of a classification scheme by device-specific clustering models augmented by refinement and filtering methods. An algorithm to classify the IoT devices into different classes along with an extra class of non-IoT devices [19]. The authors set up a test bed of 28 different IoT devices and collected communication data along with the network characteristics of the devices for about 6 months and used for the classification of this data by applying the multistage machine-learning classification algorithm and found the accuracy of above 99%.

The sensor ranking based on the active perception [20]. The techniques stated in the paper find the information generated by the sensors is correct or anomalous based on the content and context. The network characteristics of the devices are used to discover the IoT devices by a technique that determines type of an IoT by applying the hierarchical port scanning approach to perform optimal scanning by avoiding the unintended congestion in the network [20]. The authors found that it is enough to check for the port number for which the IoT devices are connected instead of scanning all available ports. The proposed technique identifies the devices with a short span and minimal number of port scans, but the port scan is limited to the TCP port alone, and it cannot be used for UDP ports.

Many algorithms have been proposed to identify the devices of IoT by taking the features such as time interval, traffic volume, protocol, and TLS features [20]. The classification of IoT and non IoT devices is made by the multi-task learning. The authors concentrate on semi supervised learning techniques in which there will be a few labeled data elements and the rest are unlabelled data which also includes data from non-IoT devices. The proposed techniques can differentiate different devices to the best possible extent. This technique is based on the convolutional neural network and multi-task learning, the technique achieved accuracy over 99% with only 5% labeled data.

A service discovery mechanism [21,22] based on the information available in the IoT environment. The earlier services search is based on the service information provided by the service provider, but in the novel technique provided by the authors, the user-centered service search environment construction through a search method using user IoT information did not consider in the available service search techniques. This new method provides the search of services that has the advantages of both provider-oriented service discovery and user-oriented service discovery. The inter-operability in network discovery from a thing-centric perspective by adopting symbolic processing on resource-constrained objects [23]. Instead of optimizing traditional protocols to work on limited devices, a novel symbolic algorithm is developed that can be executed by both resource-rich and resource-constrained IoT devices. The symbolic code of the protocol is included as network packet payload in the form of plain strings and is exchanged among different devices.

The service discovery of IoT devices by using semantic rules [24] for establishing relationship between the devices based on object profiling in SIoT environment for health application. The authors have evaluated the proposed work on different machine-learning approaches like naïve bayes, decision tree, KNN, ANN. It is observed that the decision tree and artificial neural network algorithms show accuracy of 100% compared to other algorithms.

Many authors have implemented a framework [25] for defining objects in IoT with services using web API notation and definition language. It also introduces a new two-step search approach that searches for entities with specific attributes served that match specific patterns of keywords and input types. In addition, flow constructs are also introduced, which determine the combination of different services at different stages to create new services that can perform complex tasks, leading to the development of new and practical structures in the IoT environment. [26] Ensures development of smart object discovery service based on new web standards (JSON and REST) discovery services provides the ability to integrate into various infrastructures due to its open structure. The advantage of the proposed search service is that it can be well suited for many scenarios. The proposed framework provides a mechanism for indexing, searching, and dynamically selecting smart objects based on functional characteristics (services provided) and non-functional characteristics (quality of service). A framework [27] for manufacturers to register devices and related services in this environment. Users are provided with the ability to retrieve services already registered with the framework using a specific query from the framework. Whenever the framework receives a request from a user, the underlying algorithm performs a semantic search on relevant data based on user-supplied input in the request, associates the device with that service, and returns that service to the requester service. The proposed method provides a platform for registering devices and services in one place.

An efficient approach to discover IoT semantic services [28] in dynamic context and semantic gateway layers. Within each gateway, an incremental clustering method is defined to create a group of similar services. Clusters thus created are refined over a period of time in terms of the number of clusters and the number of services in each cluster. The results of this approach show that the search cost is relatively low compared to the non-cluster approach. Service cost compliance is negligible compared to discovery cost. The relative proportion of generated updates sent to the parent of a semantic node in the hierarchy is very low.

Architecture provides an efficient infrastructure, which provides intelligent web services in IoT [29]. The architecture is a context collection that collects context information from various sources, a context knowledge base that stores the collected context information and is responsible for updating and managing the repository, and the context analyzer uses a dynamic Bayesian network to resolve conflicts context, and also responsible for getting context from a lower level to a higher level. The end users an architecture, which enables the composing of application to retrieve and process IoT data without either the knowledge of the source of data and its environment, nor do the end users know the implementations complexities of the algorithms [30]. The architecture also aims in embedding discovery and integrating services for autonomous composing at each layer such as device, data, and application layers. The model is closely aligned with the SOA cloud paradigm by re-using the notion of service registrars and service brokers.

A discovery service by name QoDisco [31,32] which is a semantic-based discovery service on IoT that operates on a set of repositories storing the resource descriptions and quality of context related information. QoDisco performs search based on large number of attributes, time series queries, varying interaction patterns, and QoC criteria. QoDisco holds an information model based on standard ontologies to semantically describe the resource and service. The common interface to discover IoT resources, a nomenclature information model, and a sophisticated semantic querying capability prove QoDisco possesses interesting features that is able to handle heterogeneity in the IoT. QoDisco also gives promising of the accurate resource discovery since the architecture provides distributed repositories and the search process is scalable and loosely coupled.

13.3 COMPARATIVE ANALYSIS OF THE SEARCH TECHNIQUES

REFERENCE NO	FINDINGS
[16]	It describes that the approach requires keen watching of the flow-level network traffic and knowledge of servers run by the vendors of the IoT devices.
[17]	The methods of classifying the IoT devices as to IoT or not based on the three different classifiers based on traffic features, DHCP, and unified classifier.
[18]	In this method a one-class clustering is employed where every device is classified into a single class of IoT devices, this technique requires training for all devices types.
[33,34]	They propose the device identification methods on the post scan of the IoT devices.
[23]	A lightweight network discovery algorithm is proposed, which helps in discovering the IoT network and thereby the IoT devices.
[35]	They propose a framework for categorizing IoT devices based on device finger-printing mechanism in the network traffic.
[22]	In this a general information on the web of things description, discovery and integration is proposed and the research avenues are specified in the paper.
[25]	They proposed a new approach which facilitates information interchange in the ecosystem leading to ubiquitous environment of IoT elements, a standard human to machine readable files, that can find one another and broadcast the IoT services using standard RESTful web APIs.
[28]	In this paper the authors propose the service discovery mechanisms in the dynamic environment, where the devices are tend to join into the network as well as the devices will go out of the network as well.
[36]	A general semantic search engine based on natural language processing is proposed and the advantages of natural language processing can be used efficiently to get the devices in the IoT network.
[37]	A brief introduction on the method of discourse analysis is proposed.

13.4 METHODOLOGY

Proposed system applies union of natural language processing technique and semantics of sentences over the filtered sentences to semantically extract the services offered by the devices.

Our model consists of the following steps:

4.1. Extracting information from the vendor specification.
4.2. Pre-processing of extracted information.
4.3. Keywords extraction.
4.4. Mining of discourse words.
4.5. Inference rules.

13.4.1 Extracting Information from the Vendor Specification

The varieties of devices are manufactured by the various vendors, and they give the description of their products in their own way that is not standardized. Since the description is not standard, the manufacturer will give information of their products as they wish, not following a common format. Hence, there is a requirement of extracting the information from the vendor specification and putting it in a standard form for further processing. The extraction of information from the vendor specification includes extraction of the features of the device and the services they offer. Then the extracted information is converted into a standard form that can be used for the higher analysis process; this means the information can be written suitable for the database management form, where specific queries can be applied to extract meaningful observations of the data gathered. One can also extract the relevant information about the IoT devices in web pages also. The gathered information from vendor specification, and the web pages will be fed for a series of processing such as preprocessing, normalization, suitably applying some natural language processing mechanism to identify the meaningful words that describe the names and services of the devices. Finally, a corpus of key value pair is created. This extracted information helps to build information base to do processing and to extract the relevant information (Figure 13.1).

13.4.2 Pre-processing of Extracted Information

During the pre-processing stage, the unstructured vendor specification for heterogeneous devices is cleaned, tokenized, normalized to key-value pair format and removal of noise. There are many steps in the text preprocessing, such as:

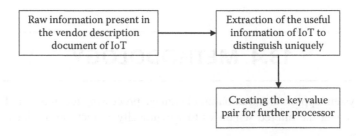

FIGURE 13.1 Extracting device identification form vendor specification.

- Removal of HTML tags

  Since we are extracting the vendor specifications, it is required to extract the specification from the web, so there is a possibility of the HTML text along with the extracted information; hence, it is required to remove the HTML tags.
- Removal of extra spaces.

  It is required to remove all extra whitespaces to make the document to be ready for the semantic extraction of the meaningful words.
- Conversion of accented characters to ASCII.

  If there are any accented characters it has to be converted to the ASCII form because it becomes difficult to assume the similarity between the accented characters and unaccented characters.
- Expanding contractions.

  Contractions are shorthand word forms such as we'll, I'm. Expanding such words to we will, I am helps to standardize text.
- Removal of special characters.

  Removal of special characters is the need because they don't have any special meaning in the text, so the special characters must be removed.
- Converting the entire text to lowercase.

  It is required to convert the entire text to the lowercase because the NLP module will treat the characters based on the ASCII value so the uppercase and lowercase letters are treated different, but for our context, the meaning of the words are same either they are represented in uppercase or the lowercase. Hence, the conversion is made.
- Removal of numbers.

  The number names are removed the numeric representation is used, so that the number will be treated as number and not as words, and they are not considered for semantic extraction.
- Removal of stop words.

  As the stops words are the words which are used most of the times, they do not hold any importance in the extraction of meaning words for our context. Hence, these words are removed to make the document ready for processing having comparatively less number of words for semantic extraction.
- Lemmatization

Lemmatization is the process of converting the words into their base form.

After the text preprocessing, corpus of keys and corpus of values is constructed. These corpuses are further utilized for annotation.

13.4.3 Keywords Extraction

Considering the unstructured specification, key labels, and its related content, the service type of the IoT device is discovered. There can be multiple service types associated with an IoT device. The keyword extraction [38] plays an important role in the device identification, as well as the services identification. Key words in the documents describe the devices, which helps in the device discovery. Similarly, the keywords present in

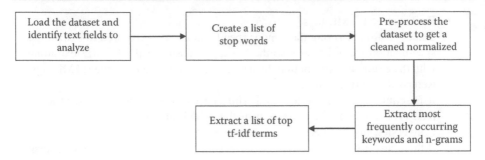

FIGURE 13.2   Keywords extraction from documents.

the user query helps in the matching of these keywords with the extracted keywords in the repository (Figure 13.2).

The above figure depicts the keyword extraction from the vendor specifications. The vendor, as part the device manual, provides basic information of the devices they manufacture, which includes the hardware characteristics and the functional characteristics of the devices that will be presented to the purchaser.

13.4.4 Mining of Discourse Words

Mining is an extraction of discourse words [37,39] system analyses unrestricted, real-world text. In opposition to information retrieval systems that return a reference to whole document, an information extraction system returns an ordered representation of just the information from within the text that is appropriate to a user's necessity, ignoring disappropriate content. Information extraction using discourse analysis is divided into two-steps: first is the discourse analysis, and second is content analysis. The former stage of discourse analysis [40] combines many references to the same objects to identify the logical relationship between the different sentence and spot the most important sentence part; it infers information that is not explicitly defined by the sentence analysis. In the latter, discourse sentence analysis has been carried out to make content selection identify the relevant object for the discourse identification and usually creates the case frame for representing referenced object (Figure 13.3).

13.4.5 Inference Rules

Considering any two syntactically processed text fragments, named text(t and hypothesis (h)), the objective of the inference system is to check whether t entails h. The prover attempts to obtain h from t by applying entailment rules that tries to transform t into h, iterating through a series of intermediate steps. If the proof is achieved, prover concludes the entailment holds good. Same as logic-based system, the inference framework consists of propositions and inference rules. The propositions include the t(assumption) and h(the goal), and intermediate premises inferred during the proof. The inference rules define the process of the generation new propositions from the previously established ones.

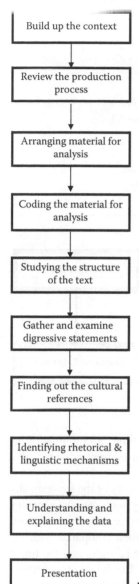

FIGURE 13.3   Discourse extraction form the processed documents.

Here inference rules play the important role of arriving at the conclusion of the semantically related extractions of the device specification and even if the devices and their services not directly holds good for the user query. The inference rules helps in identifying the correct services and the correct devices by applying the inference phenomenon such as the AND, OR, CONDITIONAL, EXCLUSIVE OR and the like to indirectly arrive at the related device identity (Table 13.1).

By applying the above stated rules for the services provided by different devices, we can arrive at new services that fulfill the needs of the requestor; thereby, if no

TABLE 13.1   Rules of inferences

INFERENCE RULES	
NAME OF THE RULE	*MATHEMATICAL REPRESENTATION OF THE RULES*
Modus Pones	$(A^\wedge(A{\rightarrow}B){\rightarrow}B$
Modus Tollens	$(\neg B^\wedge(A{\rightarrow}B)) \rightarrow \neg A$
Hypothetical syllogism	$((A{\rightarrow}B)^\wedge(B{\rightarrow}C)){\rightarrow}(A{\rightarrow}C)$
Disjunctive syllogism	$(\neg A^\wedge(A^\vee B){\rightarrow}B$
Addition	$A{\rightarrow}(A^\vee B)$
Exportation	$((A^\wedge B){\rightarrow}C){\rightarrow}(A{\rightarrow}(B{\rightarrow}C))$
Resolution	$((A^\vee B)^\wedge(\neg A^\vee C)){\rightarrow}B^\vee C$
Simplification	$A^\wedge B{\rightarrow}A$

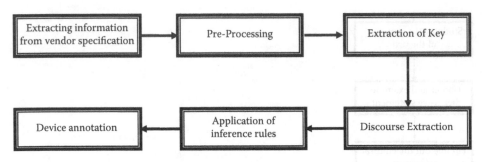

FIGURE 13.4   Device annotation flow diagram.

device is solely capable of providing services, then at that time, a combination of services provided by different devices could be integrated and used to provide required service to the service requester (Figure 13.4).

Once this annotation process is complete, we have the depository of the semantically annotated device specifications. Whenever the user queries the system, then the semantic extraction for the request is also done similar to the semantic device annotation process. The semantic meaning of the request is extracted, and it is then compared with the device-annotated repository; then the exact match of the device is found and the found device identity is given to the user as a result for interaction and fruitful communication.

The proposed approach relies on ontologies and on the extraction of contextual semantic information from vendor specifications and mapping them to the concepts in ontology.

13.5 CONCLUSION

In this work, we propose a method for device discovery using semantically annotated text documents from the vendor specifications. The semantically annotated documents are stored in a repository, the matching text from the user query is extracted, and the relevant device identification is sent to the requester. We have also proposed to match the devices based on their offered services. This method also finds the services offered by the devices by using the inference rules to get the matching service if the devices' offering services list does not contain the user's intended service. By making use of different inference rules, it is possible to trace the intended device, which offers the required service; thereby, the device identity is obtained, and it is sent to the intended user.

In the future, we plan to annotate device specifications based on the trajectory data of the devices.

REFERENCES

[1] Whitmore, A., Agarwal, A., and Da Xu, L., "The Internet of Things—A Survey of Topics and Trends", *Information Systems Frontiers* 2015, 17, 261–274.

[2] Datta, S. K. and Bonnet, C., "Describing Things in the Internet of Things: From CoRE Link Format to Semantic Based Descriptions", In *2016 IEEE International Conference on Consumer Electronics-Taiwan (ICCE-TW)*, 2016, pp. 1–2. 10.1109/ICCE-TW.2016. 7520965

[3] Hitzler, P. "A Review of Semantic Web Field", *Communications of the ACM*, February 2021, 64, 2, 76–83. 10.1145/3397512

[4] Vandana, C. P. and Chikkamannur, A. A., "Study of Resource Discovery Trends in Internet of Things", *International Journal of Advanced Networking and Applications* 2016, 08(03), 3084–3089, ISSN: 0975-0290.

[5] Thabet, S., "Ontology Development: A Comparing Study on Tools, Languages and Formalisms", *Indian Journal of Science and Technology* September 2015, 8(24). 10. 17485/ ijst/2015/v8i34/54249

[6] Pech, F., Martinez, A., Estrada, H., and Hernandez, Y., "Semantic Annotation of Unstructured Documents Using Concepts Similarity", *Hindawi Scientific Programming* 2017, 2017, Article ID 7831897, 10 pages.

[7] Vandana, C. P. and Chikkamannur, A. A., "S-COAP: Semantic Enrichment of COAP for Resource Discovery", *SN Computer Science* 2020, 1, 88.

[8] Rahman, H. and Hussain, M. I., "A Comprehensive Survey on Semantic Interoperability for Internet of Things: State-of-the-Art and Research Challenges", *Transactions on Emerging Telecommunications Technologies* 2020, 31, n. pag.

[9] Lopez-Martin, M., Carro, B., Sanchez-Esguevillas, A., and Lloret, J., "Network Traffic Classifier with Convolutional and Recurrent Neural Networks for Internet of Things", *IEEE Access* 2017, 5, 18042–18050.

[10] Marchal, S., Miettinen, M., Nguyen, T. D., Sadeghi, A., and Asokan, N., "AuDI: Toward Autonomous IoT Device-Type Identification Using Periodic Communication," *IEEE Journal on Selected Areas in Communications* 2019, 37(6), 1402–1412.

[11] Salatino, A., Osborne, F., Thanapalasingam, T., and Motta, E., "The CSO Classifier: Ontology-Driven Detection of Research Topics in Scholarly Articles," In *23rd International Conference on Theory and Practice of Digital Libraries, Lecture Notes in Computer Science*, 2019, Springer.

[12] Zhang, R., Xiong, S., and Chen, Z., "An Ontology-Based Approach for Measuring Semantic Similarity Between Words", *Advanced Intelligent Computing Theories and Applications*. ICIC 2015. Lecture Notes in Computer Science, vol. 9227. Springer, Cham.

[13] Tversky, A., "Features of Similarity", *Psychological Review* 1997, 84(4), 327–352.

[14] Jia, B., Liu, S., Guan, Y., Li, W., and Ren, W., "The Fusion Model of Multidomain Context Information for the Internet of Things," *Hindawi Wireless Communications and Mobile Computing* 2017, 2017, Article ID 6274824, 8 pages.

[15] Vandana, C. P. and Chikkamannur, A. A., "Semantic Ontology Based IoT-Resource Description", *International Journal of Advanced Networking and Applications* 2019, 11(6), 3022–3023.

[16] Guo, H. and Heidemann, J., "IP-Based IoT device detection", In *Proceedings of the 2018 Workshop on IoT Security and Privacy*, 2018, August, pp. 36–42.

[17] Bremler-Barr, A., Levy, H., and Yakhini, Z., "IoT or Not: Identifying IoT Devices in a Short Time Scale", In *NOMS 2020-2020 IEEE/IFIP Network Operations and Management Symposium*, 2020, April, pp. 1–9. IEEE.

[18] Sivanathan, A., Gharakheili, H. H., and Sivaraman, V., "Inferring IoT Device Types From Network Behavior Using Unsupervised Clustering", In *2019 IEEE 44th Conference on Local Computer Networks (LCN)*, 2019, October, pp. 230–233. IEEE.

[19] Sivanathan, A., Gharakheili, H. H., Loi, F., Radford, A., Wijenayake, C., Vishwanath, A., and Sivaraman, V., "Classifying IoT Devices in Smart Environments Using Network Traffic Characteristics", *IEEE Transactions on Mobile Computing* 2018, 18(8), 1745–1759.

[20] Costa, F. S., Nassar, S. M., and Dantas, M. A., "GoAT: A Sensor Ranking Approach for IoT Environments", In *CLOSER*, 2021, pp. 169–177.

[21] Sim, S. and Choi, H., "A Study on the Service Discovery Support Method in the IoT Environments", *The International Journal of Electrical Engineering & Education* 2020, 57(1), 85–96.

[22] Mathew, S. S., Atif, Y., Sheng, Q. Z., and Maamar, Z., "Web of Things: Description, Discovery and Integration", In *2011 International Conference on Internet of Things and 4th International Conference on Cyber, Physical and Social Computing, Dalian*, 2011, pp. 9–15. 10.1109/iThings/CPSCom.2011.165

[23] Gaglio, S., Re, G. L., Martorella, G., and Peri, D., "A Lightweight Network Discovery Algorithm for Resource-Constrained IoT Devices", In *2019 International Conference on Computing, Networking and Communications (ICNC)*, 2019, February, pp. 355–359. IEEE.

[24] Mohana, S. D., Prakash, S. S., and Krinkin, K., "Semantic Rules for Service Discovery in Social Internet of Things", In *2022 4th International Conference on Smart Systems and Inventive Technology (ICSSIT)*, 2022, January, pp. 119–124. IEEE.

[25] Khodadadi, F., Dastjerdi, A. V., and Buyya, R. "Simurgh: A Framework for Effective Discovery, Programming, and Integration of Services Exposed in IoT", In *International Conference on Recent Advances in Internet of Things (RioT)*, 2015, pp.1–6. IEEE.

[26] Fortino, G., Lackovic, M., Russo, W., and Trunfio, P., "A Discovery Service for Smart Objects over an Agent-Based Middleware", In Pathan, M., Wei, G., and Fortino, G. (eds.), *Internet and Distributed Computing Systems*. IDCS 2013. Lecture Notes in Computer Science, 2013, 8223. Springer, Berlin, Heidelberg. 10.1007/978-3-642-41428-2_23

[27] Akhileshwari, K. G. and Salian, S., "IoT Device and Service Discovery Framework", *International Journal of Recent Technology and Engineering (IJRTE)* ISSN: 2277-3878, July 2019, 8(2S6), 490–496.

[28] Fredj, S. B., Boussard, M., Kofman, D., and Noirie, L., "Efficient Semantic-Based IoT Service Discovery Mechanism for Dynamic Environments", In *IEEE 25th Annual International Symposium on Personal, Indoor, and Mobile Radio Communication (PIMRC)*, 2014, Sep 2014, Washington, United States, pp. 2088–2092. 10.1109/ PIMRC.2014.7136516. Hal-01171343

[29] Wei, Q. and Jin, Z., "Service Discovery for Internet of Things: A Context Awareness Perspective", In *Internetware '12: Proceedings of the Fourth Asia-Pacific Symposium on InternetwareOctober 2012 Article No.: 25*, 2012, pp. 1–6. 10.1145/2430475.2430500

[30] Georgakopoulos, D., Jayaraman, P. P., Zhang, M., and Ranjan, R., "Discovery-Driven Service Oriented IoT Architecture", In *2015 IEEE Conference on Collaboration and Internet Computing (CIC)*, Hangzhou, 2015, pp. 142–149. 10.1109/CIC.2015.34.

[31] Gomes, P., Cavalcante, E., Batista, T., Taconet, C., Conan, D., et al, "A Semantic Based Discovery Service for the Internet of Things", *Journal of Internet Services and Applications*, Springer, 2019, 10(1). 10.1186/s13174-019-0109-8ff.ffhal-02147177

[32] Khodadadi, F. and Sinnott, R. O., "A Semantic-aware Framework for Service Definition and Discovery in the Internet of Things Using CoAP", *Procedia Computer Science* 2017, 113, 146–153. 10.1016/j.procs.2017.08.334.

[33] Sivanathan, A., Gharakheili, H. H., and Sivaraman, V. "Can We Classify an IoT Device Using TCP Port Scan?" In *2018 IEEE International Conference on Information and Automation for Sustainability (ICIAfS)*, 2018, December, pp. 1–4. IEEE.

[34] Fan, L., Zhang, S., Wu, Y., Wang, Z., Duan, C., Li, J., and Yang, J., "An IoT Device Identification Method Based on Semi-Supervised Learning", In *2020 16th International Conference on Network and Service Management (CNSM)*, 2020, November, pp. 1–7. IEEE.

[35] Yadav, P., Feraudo, A., Arief, B., Shahandashti, S. F., and Vassilakis, V. G., "Position Paper: A Systematic Framework for Categorizing IoT Device Fingerprinting Mechanisms", In *Proceedings of the 2nd International Workshop on Challenges in Artificial Intelligence and Machine Learning for Internet of Things*, 2020, November, pp. 62–68.

[36] Pandiarajan, S., Yazhmozhi, V. M., and Praveen Kumar, P., "Semantic Search Engine Using Natural Language Processing." In *Advanced Computer and Communication Engineering Technology*. Lecture Notes in Electrical Engineering 2015, 315. Springer, Cham. 10.1007/978-3-319-07674-4_53.

[37] Powers, P. *The Methodology of Discourse Analysis (No. 14)*. Jones & Bartlett Learning, 2001.

[38] Rose, S., Engel, D., Cramer, N., and Cowley, W. "Automatic Keyword Extraction From Individual Documents", *Text Mining: Applications and Theory* 2010, 1, 1–20.

[39] Toussaint, Y., Orpailleur, L. É., Dargnat, M., and Discours, A. É., *Mining Texts at Discourse Level*, 2018.

[40] Shi, B. and Weninger, T., "Visualizing the Flow of Discourse with a Concept Ontology", In *Companion Proceedings of the Web Conference 2018*, 2018, April, pp. 89–90.

Women Safety and Monitoring System Using Geo-Fence

14

N Rajkumar[1], C Viji[2], R Jayavadivel[1],
B Prabhu Shankar[1], E Vetrimani[1], and
J Mary Stella[2]

[1]*Department of Computer Science and Engineering, School of Engineering, Presidency University, Bangalore, Karnataka, India*
[2]*Department of Computer Science and Engineering, HKBK College of Engineering, Bangalore, Karnataka, India*

Contents

DOI: 10.1201/9781003282990-14

14.1 INTRODUCTION

Women's safety can be a social issue and needs to be monitored and resolved as soon as possible. Almost 50% of girls are physically, emotionally, and socially abused. This abuse can affect the development and progress of the country. According to statistics, every day and every minute, women of all disciplines are harassed, hurt, and assaulted in different parts of our country. Areas such as streets, public squares, and transportation hubs are the territory of girl hunters. Female students studying at school or college and interacting with women need to protect themselves by taking self-defense classes, dressing tightly, and learning various techniques to protect themselves from criminals. Criminals are trying to kidnap children and women. Kidnapped children and women face problems such as psychological aggression, physical violence, stalking, rape, and other sexual violence. According to the statistics shown in Figure 14.1, children and women are exposed to different levels of physical violence.

In India, women are raped by criminals every 20 minutes, and women are afraid to go out alone. Women's safety is steadily declining. Men and women have equal rights, and the majority of members of parliament are women. Women are one step ahead of senior men. Women are involved in all cutting-edge science and technology. Women cannot be considered without generalization. Women's safety is of paramount importance to our country. Figure 14.1 clearly shows domestic violence against women.

According to the National Girl Child Safety Policy, the Department of Home Affairs has acquired a Women's Safety Unit to focus on the protection of girls in the country. The future generation purely depends on women. They are all eyes of our nation. Figure 14.2 shows the statistics of a national criminal record. The level of wrongdoing against women has increased over the years, especially in our nation.

Today, parents cannot control and keep track of their children's various activities. Girl children are often kidnapped on the roadside, resulting in crimes like child

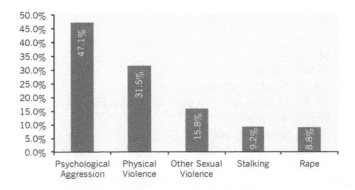

FIGURE 14.1 Domestic violence against women.

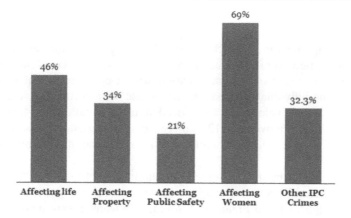

FIGURE 14.2 Decadal increase in IPC crimes.

trafficking, child work, sexual viciousness, etc. In the last 10 years, the recorded number of women and girls snatched is respectively 300,000 and 64,000. The total number of cases against females has increased by 11.73% per annum. Likewise, child abduction has increased by 23.2% annually, consistent with records provided by the independent government body, the National Crime Records Bureau (NCRB). Nearly 85% of all kidnapping cases occur everywhere in the country, consistent with records from the crime office. Figure 14.1 shows the steadiness of the impact on women's crime.

The National Crime Records Bureau report shows an increase in crime against females by 69% (10 years). The number of abductions and kidnappings of women and girls has increased to 163.8% since 2002. As per the National Crime Records Bureau's annual report, see Figure 14.3. The number of crimes against women increased in 2018 and 2019.

Cognizable Crime Reported

UNIT NAME	2017	2018	2019	2020	2021
Tirupathi Urban	4437	3272	3428	2357	3715
West Godavari	8833	9764	9190	9975	14171
Vishakhapatnam City	6976	7233	6452	5912	8041
Vijayawada City	7096	6519	6205	6350	8243
Guntur Urban	4566	4868	5194	4287	5318
Prakasham	6857	7270	7588	7630	9015
East Godavari	9065	9167	7367	8087	8491
Guntur	12491	10973	9447	8573	8486
Krishna	6915	6477	7957	7471	7334
Rajamahendravaram Urban	2386	2380	3660	3564	3496
YSR Kadapa	14564	15211	11129	6778	6456
Sri Potti Sri Ramulu Nellore	11413	12796	6756	7897	7513
Chittoor	3827	3957	5462	6365	5873
Vizianagaram	9743	5829	4325	4817	4197
Kurnool	8616	7137	8335	9866	8572
Anantapur	8143	6067	8145	11120	9363
Srikakulam	3263	4483	4176	6081	4743
Vishakhapatnam Rural	3030	3012	5854	5857	4100
Grand Total	132221	126415	120670	122987	127127

FIGURE 14.3 The National Crime Bureau's annual report.

To enhance women's safety, this work provides a technology-based tracking model using GPS-based mobile technology and geo-fencing. This model includes a location-based application to watch the situation of girls or children. The foremost commonly used method of constructing a geo-fence system. Geo-fencing may be a method of monitoring geographical location with a clear fence that will automatically detect an individual occupation or outside of a virtual fence method [1]. Mobile application development introduced a method called geo-fencing, which will track the object's movement. [2], emergency applications for disaster relief [3], monitoring of people with Alzheimer's [4], or maybe monitoring agricultural sites [5].

Women feel insecure in these situations, and they want to avoid certain situations in general. A harmful gender comparison between males and females is depicted in Figure 14.4. Table 14.1 and Figure 14.5 reveal that women were more affected than men in terms of physical threats.

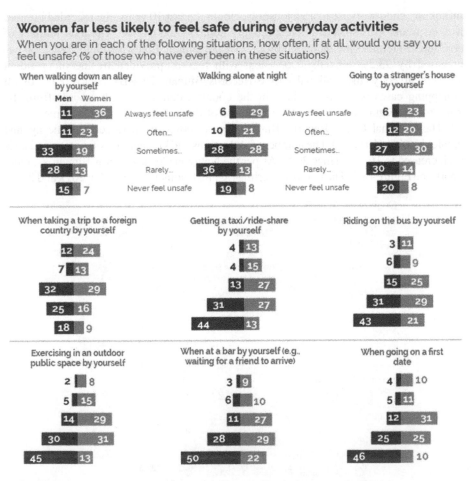

FIGURE 14.4 Gender-wise statistics feeling unsafe during everyday activity.

TABLE 14.1 Significantly fearing each circumstance by gender

	WOMEN	MEN
Sexual assault	53.7%	24.2%
Physical attack	50.0%	34.5%
Dying	49.8%	43.9%
Burglary or Vandalism	46.0%	34.6%
Mugging	43.9%	35.2%

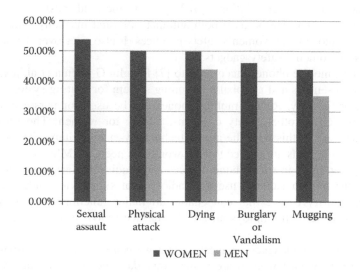

FIGURE 14.5 Comparision of significantly fearing each circumstance by gender.

In our proposed work, geo-fencing is employed to line women's workplaces. Parents put a label on places like schools, parks, friends' houses, nearby places, workplaces, etc. It includes their authorized and unauthorized areas. This application also supports motion detection and voice recording, and autonomously sends information to the servers and their parent's registered mobile. This work aims to supply technology-based security, which will facilitate parental monitoring. The utilization of the global positioning system (GPS) makes the proposed system send the current longitude-latitude information and record soundtracks from victims' mobile. The situation information and recorded voice are going to be sent to a highly secured centralized server and vary or registered on a mobile. Finally, this proposed system model of a technology-based secure tracking and monitoring system for young women and youngsters to deliver active and efficient monitoring and protection system.

14.2 RELATED WORKS

According to Ramachandiran et al., given the current circumstances, women's safety is a big concern in both urban and rural areas. Although changing the mindset of a whole culture is challenging, we can safeguard women by employing technology-enhanced safety equipment for women who are subjected to sexual harassment, acid assaults, harassment, and other forms of harassment. To improve women's safety and security, a variety of smart devices and mobile applications have been developed. The software repository contains a large number of apps. However, the majority of software solutions do not deliver better solutions. [6] Experts in the field must create a superior software solution that can be used both automatically and manually. This suggested project looks into several women's safety practices. It also goes over the benefits and drawbacks of women's safety gadgets.

The latest mobile phones, according to [7] Roselin G Leema et al.'s suggestion, are fitted with sensors and a global positioning system for routing systems that have been popular recently. Recent mobile phones can be used for personal safety and security, as well as other safety concerns, mostly for women. The Monolith for Women can achieve this with the use of technology-enabled items. The majority of software and programs are geared toward women in need. ARM controllers are most effectively employed in smartphone devices and require the least amount of power. To detect the hidden camera, use the radio repeat signal viewfinder. We've uncovered a security device that can enable all major functionalities with a single button press. Bluetooth employs an ARM interface to synchronize smartphones in this article.

R.A. Jain and colleagues' suggestion that women's safety is a serious concern. Rates of crimes against women are rising every day, therefore keeping women and girls safe at home, school, college, and the workplace is critical. Many steps have been taken to ensure women's safety and security. Even though various precautions have been put in place to protect women, there have been several crimes committed against women in recent years. In an emergency, smartphone applications allow users to reach emergency contact numbers in real-time. When users are in a risky scenario, mobile applications allow them to contact the appropriate authorities. The mobile application uses Map Box as the primary source to track the current exact location using the global positioning system and sends a message to the registered emergency numbers. This application was created using the Java database programming language and Firebase. When a victim approaches a possible attacker, this mobile application triggers the warning mechanism by shaking the smartphone repeatedly to inform the public. These kinds of features allow for day-to-day security and emergency response, making them the ideal choice for everyone. Victims can use this mobile application to not only warn others close to them about their situation but also to seek immediate support and action to avert undesirable situations [6].

Every day, women and children are becoming increasingly concerned about sexual harassment. Both developed and developing countries are facing dire circumstances.

As a result, women's empowerment and family expansion in the country face significant hurdles. They will continue to create IoT devices and mobile applications to make women's activities safer under this plan. By pressing the emergency button on their phone, women can receive immediate and comprehensive security assistance. The device can track the user's present location and relay location-related information to a local police station or volunteer in the event of an incident. Users can also use their phones to locate the closest safe zone [8–10]. This proposed system is unique in that it can operate in both online and offline modes. Even if their mobile phone does not have internet, users can utilize the gadget to contact the local police station or volunteer assistance. Arduino Nano, GPS, GSM, Bluetooth, and other components are included in this gadget. The combination of all of these features makes this device both inexpensive and simple to use.

Poonam Bhilare et al. discussed the importance of women's safety. They introduce the global positioning system enabled vehicle tracking and women employees that may track their situation. This can provide a mix of GPS devices and specialized software to trace women employees' vehicle locations, providing an emergency button that will provide additional security. By activating the emergency button, it will send an alert message to the concerned person. After they trigger the emergency button, it will send an alert SMS to the registered mobile numbers also [11–16].

Violence against women has been recognized as a worldwide problem that must be addressed in altogether countries. Maltreatment is additionally well-defined as a sort of social ill. There are four major categories of child abuse. Children are emotionally abused, physically abused, neglected, and sexually harassed [17,18]. Therefore, instant care and action must be taken from the independent governing bodies and caretakers. The kid protection commission is remitted to act as a central control for matters affecting women's protection by collecting information on sensitive problems, including family care. Women need more care and high protection in their working places, and children's rights must be strictly followed [19]. The government must introduce some autonomous bodies to require care of those sorts of issues. In our previous study [20], the government as a regulator and monitor must include the whole public, parents, children themselves, and neighbors. At home, parents must look out for their child, even when the child is near a workplace, a neighbor's home, or school. Additionally, to communicate, parents must actively participate in a program to stop maltreatment. Parents should monitor their working women's location-based activity.

However, this type of problem arises thanks to the unawareness of their parents like working, doing chores, etc. Recently, the technology boom will give attract additional importance. It helps us to make the interconnection of networks and share the knowledge effectively using the web anytime and anywhere as long as the needs are met [21]. By employing a Raspberry Pi, a monitoring system was developed that supports multimedia and mobility [22].

That system sequentially takes photographs, which are directly stored in Raspberry Pi, and it processes them and makes live video recordings. This system consists of a red box. The video recording and photos are stored in the centralized server through

Raspberry Pi. Receiving parental monitoring, this technique works as sort of a gadget working with an internet browser like Chrome, Edge, and Safari, which device must connect with the web. In another study [23–25], a mobile application is established to guard women and youngsters. That application uses motion detection using sensors and photo capturing using the interior camera [26–28]. If the smartphone gets moving, the appliance will send a notification to families or known relatives. The images are intended to prove abuse. Additionally, it'll store and forward those photographs and send the location-related information, which can help to rescue them.

The study of S. A. More [29] proposed a system that uses body temperature and pulse to detect the abnormal condition of the victim, sense the likelihood of an abnormality, and send notifications to the family members or relatives. They can monitor the current situation through the mobile application [30]. That system deals with digital image processing to spot any possible threat and suggests various possible solutions to guard women and youngsters. In [31], the authors have developed a tool that uses the PIC16F876A mini microcontroller, and therefore, the SIM808 module has some enhancement in the device. GSM, GPRS, and GPS support won't send notifications to their friends and family when victims press that emergency button within the developed system. In [1], a facial-based system is developed. It takes the facial reactions compared with the stored reactions. If the system found an abnormal facial reaction, then a report is submitted automatically to their parents or registered one.

For [2], we are building a highly secure device using GSM, GPRS, and GPS. The device communicates a message containing the target's body shape and height to the registered mobile number. [3] Android applications and arm devices are individually activated using a synchronized Bluetooth device connection. Audio and video tracks are sent to registered mobile numbers within the application and the site of the decision and alert message. In [4], a mobile application was developed that gives a location for a vulnerable woman by providing fake phone calls, video transfers, location, and care information. During this proposed method [5], vibrations, heartbeat rate, and blood heat are sensed using a temperature sensor, vibration sensor, and heartbeat sensor with the assistance of a uniform protected device that has a microcontroller with an Arduino Uno and some important sensors. During this system [32], three sensors are used: temperature, pulse, and accelerometer. These sensors are wont to detect an abnormal state, and therefore, the system will send a message and victim location-related information using GPS and GSM modules.

14.3 SYSTEM INFRASTRUCTURE

Our proposed application is beneficial for girl children's parents and dealing with women's parents, our system requires smartphones with GPS facilities that are used for location tracking. During this part, the infrastructure of the proposed system is engaging the utilization of recent technology like sensors, voice recorders, geo-fencing, and communication networks.

14.3.1 Geo-Fencing

Geofencing may be a location-based virtual fencing service where the developer uses wi-fi, GPS, or mobile internet to send/activate messages like email, SMS, or notifications or pre-defined actions where mobile devices enter, exit, or remain stationary during a particular fenced region. We will fix and mark the situation on a map and create a virtual fence around it. This 'fenced-in' area can now be monitored and communicated with mobile devices that violate its location. Geo-fence gives its developer the power to send email, SMS, or app-based notifications to mobile devices that enter, exit, or stay parked within the marked area (Figure 14.6).

14.3.1.1 How geo-fencing works

Geo-fencing is a method of creating a virtual boundary in a Google map. User can create their own trusted boundary in a simple map. That will help to monitor a person's location in the map if that person exits from the boundary region, the system will notify. These operations are performed with the help of the mobile application.

Geo-fencing is implemented with the help of mobile application code. Users need to choose the location service, and to do so, they must have a smart mobile phone with the geo-fencing application. This application is a smart solution for tracking a particular person within the fenced area. It will give a notification when the user enters/exit the fenced area. A geo-fenced application is the best, most flexible, and most efficient solution for individual tracking. It will notify the exact address or location

FIGURE 14.6   Sample geo-fencing.

when the user triggers the alert button. This is called the "if this, then that" command, where the application is programmed written to support this feature.

Geo-fencing is not a mobile application; it is a solution for creating virtual boundaries. Geo-fencing is implemented in our proposed system for women's or child live-location tracking. This system is useful for working women and school students for continuous monitoring of their location. This system makes them feel safe and secure. That will improve their self-confidence level. Geo-fencing has become a typical practice for several software and manufacturing industries. Geo-fencing is included different areas like marketing, social media, retail, hospital, and etc. Home delivery-related applications are also able to solve some delivery-related issues.

14.3.1.2 Common geo-fencing applications

- **Social networking:** Social media networking is one of the most identifiable user-related applications. It uses geo-fencing for notability, Snapchat, location-related filtering, stickers, and other location-related content sharing using geofencing. Location-related stories can be created for remembrance of happiness with the help of this virtual perimeter.
- **Marketing:** Geo-fencing is a popular way for a business to improve their sales to deliver in-store promotions. It alerts the customer who is entering into the shop boundaries and sending notifications related to offers and discounts. Geo-fencing is also useful to track their marketing executive and sales persons' present location and etc.
- **Audience engagement:** Geo-fencing is used to make open public interaction with a greater number of people in festivals, deals, events, contests, and more. For example, event location-related information may be shared with the help of geo-fencing.
- **Smart appliances:** Geo-fencing-enabled applications will be used to notify the shortage of groceries in your kitchen when you reach the boundary of the supermarket. For example, the system will notify you about the shortage of milk in your refrigerator.
- **Human resources:** Some industries use a geo-fencing to keep track of their employee location-related information. When the employee went for outsourcing, they need to keep track of their location, and they can some important location-related information.
- **Telematics:** Geofencing is also used in telematics. It allows the companies to draw virtual boundaries around their sites, work areas, and secure areas. When unauthorized trespassing happens in a secured area, that will send a notification to the security in charge.
- **Security:** Geo-fencing may sound invasive, and it may certainly have a desire to exaggerate how it is used. However, geo-fencing can also intentionally increase the security of mobile devices. For example, use a geo-fence to set your smartphone to unlock when you're at home, or alert you when someone goes in or out of your home.

14.3.2 Sensor Module

New smartphones have built-in sensors such as accelerometers and GPS technology. The proposed system uses these sensors. This proposed system includes geo-fencing technology for observing where children are using position sensors. Smartphones provide several ways to share current location information with latitude and longitude, such as global positioning system and internet-based location information. The proposed system uses GPS to identify the child/woman and their proximity to a particular location. A loved one describes these particular areas by specifying latitude, longitude, and radius. Position sensors continuously send current location information to determine if your child is in or out of the fenced area. Motion sensors are intended to detect the movement of mobile devices. This application uses a G-sensor to track the speed of your device. A G-sensor represents a flux sensor or accelerometer that detects the terrain, location, or height of your screen.

14.3.3 Voice Recording Module

The smartphone contains an audio recording that aims to record a sound near a lady or child during emergencies. Voice recording is taken into account because it can store evidence of abuse while the device is way away. Additionally, the voice recorder on smartphones doesn't require advanced data.

14.3.4 Communication Module

This module communicates the warning information to their relations using SMS, email, and notifications. The utilization of those will make sure that the message is going to be received by the family if relations haven't yet installed the application. Alternatively, the device sends location-related information to the server (Figure 14.7).

14.4 IMPLEMENTATION

The women's safety and tracking system is employed and tested in Android mobile phones. Figure 14.8 shows the flow of the women's safety and tracking management system application process. First, the relations will register who is going to be cared for. For every member, a registered loved one will erect a fence around a particular area. Fenced areas include areas that a loved one should monitor, like frequent visits or areas that a toddler shouldn't visit. The app will continuously monitor the situation. The GPS will send the location-related information continuously. The geo-fencing system is employed to watch user movements in fenced areas.

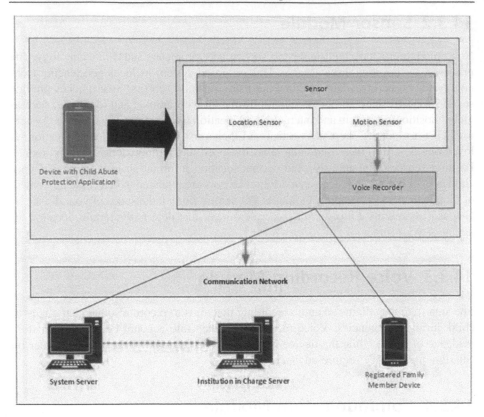

FIGURE 14.7   System model.

Now there could be two types of behavior segmentation here:

- Enter- Trigger sends a notification if the user enters the geo-fenced area.
- Exit sends a notification if anyone exits the geo-fence area.

Our proposed geo-fence-enabled system sends a notification to registered mobile phones. It also sends location-related information, such as someone entering into the fence or exiting the fenced area. This application continuously monitors the location-related information about the particular registered mobile. In an emergency, the user can move that device in some pattern. By monitoring the movement pattern, the system will detect that the user is in an emergency, and it will activate an alarm for their parent's and relatives' mobiles about possible maltreatment. Automatically, the sound and video recorder is activated. This recorded information is forwarded to the respective users. Voice messages are going to be communicated continuously for a particular period until the victim is safe (Figure 14.9 and Figure 14.10).

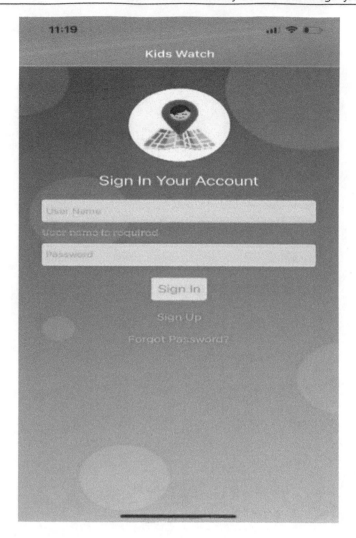

FIGURE 14.8 Login page.

14.5 WORKING

Our proposed work may be a mobile application that's used for women's safety and tracking management, which will ensure their safety and reassure their parent. It'll send notifications about the geographical location of their child. The workflow diagram of our proposed system is shown in Figure 14.11.

The toddler stepping out of the house is held with the GSM/GPS module with her, wedged in her pouch/backpack. The fence is then created within the toddler's

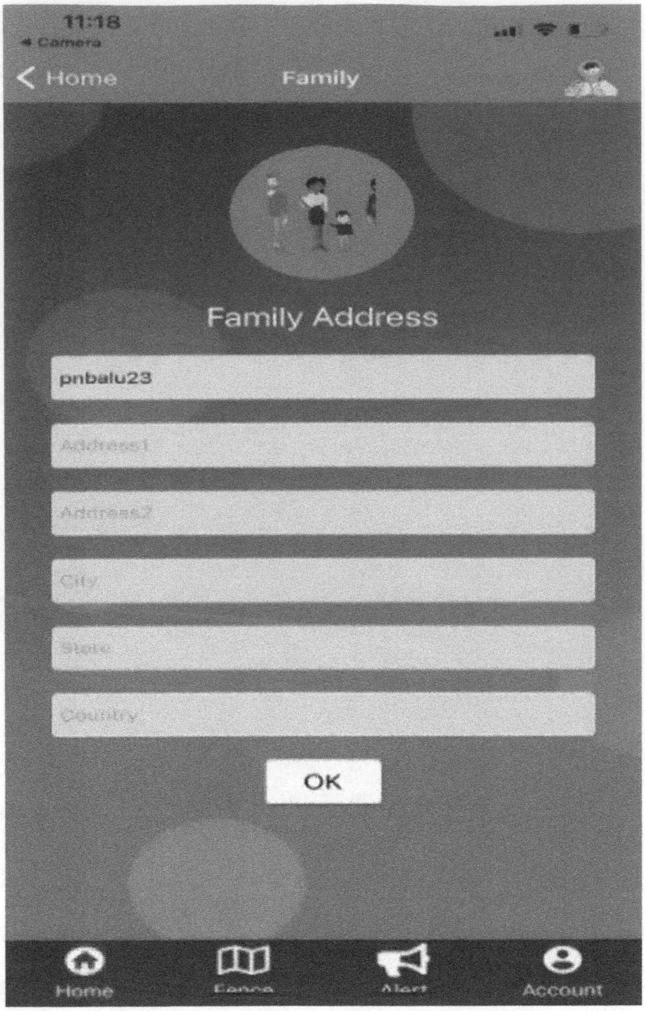

FIGURE 14.9 Registration.

boundary. The GSM module will continuously track the position of the toddler. When the toddler crosses the fencing area or encounters any troublesome situation, the tracker module consists of a push-button notification. The toddler can press the button during an emergency, sending a message to her parent. The notification will alert the parent to take necessary actions. This kind of geo-fencing logic is mostly applicable to school-going children.

The woman comes out of the house with a tracker module. Parents are ready to create virtual fences in a trusted area. Their location is monitored and tracked continuously using the global positioning system. The tracker module also ensures that the women or children don't leave the required phone without alerting the parent. The

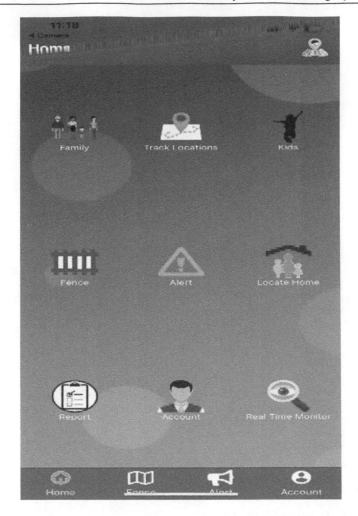

FIGURE 14.10   Add kids.

tracker module includes a push-button notification that will be used when they're in an unsafe situation.

14.6 CONCLUSION

Our proposed method is meant to trace kids and women. The answer represented during this work makes good use of smartphones that provide efficient features like Google maps, global positioning systems, short messaging systems, etc. Several simple jobs depend upon nonessential SMS-based tracking to urge an exact location. Our

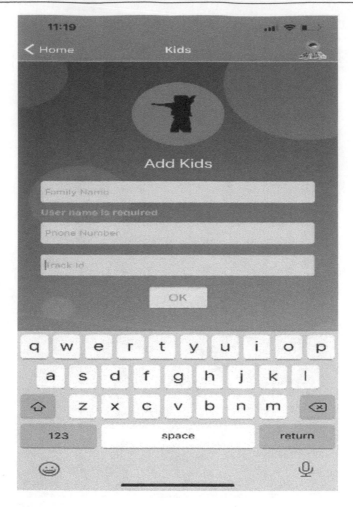

FIGURE 14.11   Proposed framework.

proposed system provided live monitoring and tracking system. Include more geofencing features, a panic alerting system, and emergency messaging services to enhance the protection. Other additional features like home access, location tracking, fence construction, warning, and reporting; to ensure the security of youngsters and extend their confidence, a security plan is proposed. Using the inspiration of this technology, the novel system is proposed to revamp existing systems by adding new features while making them safer. In the future, an equivalent solution could also be applied to smartwatches or small integrated devices. Child and women's safety and security are key issues in all. Our geo-fence-enabled system will help provide enhanced security and monitoring system for the working women and children by using geo-fencing for current location identification and a panic button to provide a sense of security. Previously proposed systems provide the technology-enhanced solution to track the women's vehicles. The victim tracking system includes additional features like alert messages and a panic button with our proposed model to overcome the problem of women's security. It can be implemented for children and working women in night shifts by the parents who are situated away from the working places. In the proposed method, the panic button is activated, and the alarm sends SMS to the relatives and a centralized server. The image capturing, sound recording, and video recording are done by connecting a hidden miniature device and sending this information when the victim triggers the panic button, providing a monitoring of their exact current location usng easily available geo-fence-enabled Google maps. All the images record voice, and video are stored in the centralized server. They provide security seamlessly at any time, but any functional or physical device failure interventions remain a future issue that needs to be resolved.

REFERENCES

[1] Remya George, Anjaly Cherian V, Annet Antony, Harsha Sebestian, Mishal Antony, Rosemary Babu T, "An Intelligent Security System for Violence against Women in Public Places", *International Journal of Engineering and Advanced Technology (IJEAT)* ISSN: 2249 – 8958, vol. 3 no. 4, April 2014.

[2] B. Vijaylashmi, Renuka S, Pooja Chennur, Sharangowda Patil, "Self[3] B.Vijaylashmi, Renuka.S, Pooja Chennur, Sharangowda.Patil" Self-defense System for Women Safety with Location Tracking and SMS alerting through GSM Network", *IJRET: International Journal of Research in Engineering and Technology*eISSN: 2319-1163 | pISSN:2321-7308., 2015.

[3] D.G. Monisha, M. Monisha, G. Pavithra, R. Subhashini, "Women Safety Device and Application-FEMME"*Indian Journal of Science and Technology*, vol. 9, no. 10, March 2016. 0.17485/ijst/2016/v9i10/88898

[4] Sridhar Mandapati, Sravya Pamidi, Sriharitha Ambati, "A Mobile-based Women Safety Application (I Safe App)"*IOSR Journal of Computer Engineering*, vol. 17, no. 1, Ver. I (Jan.– Feb. 2015).

[5] Deepak Sharma, Abhijit Paradkar, "All in One Intelligent Safety System for Women Security" *International Journal of Computer Applications*, vol. 130, no. 11, November 2015.

[6] Prof. R.A. Jain, Aditya Patil, Prasenjeet Nikam, Shubham More, Saurabh Totewar, "Women's Safety using IOT", *International Research Journal of Engineering and Technology(IRJET)*, vol. 04, no. 05 | May -2017.

[7] Roselin G. Leema, R. Rajesh, M. Rajeswari, V. Akshaya, D. Saravanan, N. Sangeetha, "Women Safety Android Application with Hardware Device", 2021 International Conference on System, Computation, Automation and Networking (ICSCAN), 06 September 2021.

[8] A.Z.M. Tahmidul Kabir, Al Mamun Mizan, Tasnuva Tasneem, "Safety Solution for Women using Smart Band and CWS App", 17th International Conference on Electrical Engineering/Electronics, Computer, Telecommunications and Information Technology (ECTI-CON), 04 August 2020.

[9] S. Pradeep, M. Kanikannan, A Anny Meedunganesh, Anny Leema, "Implementation of Women Safety System using Internet of Things", *International Journal of Trend in Scientific Research and Development (IJTSRD)*, vol. 4, no. 4, June 2020.

[10] Viji R, Vignesh K, Reshmashree, Ilamathi R, Rohini A, "Women's Safety Device and Health Monitoring", *International Journal of Latest Engineering and Management Research (IJLEMR)* vol. 4, no. 6, June 2019, pp. 120–124.

[11] Poonam Bhilare, Akshay Mohite, Dhanashri Kamble, Swapnil Makode, Rasika Kahane, "Women Employee Security System using GPS and GSM based vehicle tracking", *IJREST, Jamshed*.

[12] V.K. Raju, S. Srinivasa Rao, A.V. Prabu, T. Appa Rao, Dr. Y.V. Narayana, "GSM and GPS-based Vehicle Location and Tracking System - Baburao Kodavati", *International Journal of Engineering Research and Applications(IJERA)*, vol. 1, no. 3, pp. 616–625, ISSN: 2248-9622 www.ijera.com

[13] Velocity-based Tracking and Localization System using Smartphones with GPS and GPRS/3G Ibrahim AbdallahHag Eltoum, Mohammed Bouhorma Department of. Nicole, "Title of paper with the only first word capitalized," J. Name Stand. Abbrev., in press System and Telecommunication "LCST" FST, Abdelmalek Essaadi University, Tanger, Morocco.

[14] Positioning And Navigation System Using GPSJ. Parthasarathy International Archives of the photogrammetry, Remote Sensing and SpatialInformation Science, vol. XXXVI, Part 6, Tokyo Japan 2006.

[15] Francis Enejo Idachaba "Design of a GPS/GSM based tracker for the location of stolen items and kidnapped or missing persons in Nigeria" ARPN Journal of Engineering and Applied Sciences, vol. 6, no. 10 October 2011.

[16] R. Ramachandiran, L. Dhanya, M. Shalini, "A Survey on Women Safety Device Using IoT", IEEE International Conference on System, Computation, Automation, and Networking (ICSCAN) Published 2019.

[17] B. Corby, *Child Abuse: Towards a Knowledge Base*. Maidenhead: Open University Press, 2005.

[18] A.V. Scoyoc, J.S. Wilen, K. Daderko, S. Miyamoto, "Multiple Aspects of Maltreatment: Moving Toward a Holistic Framework," In D. Daro, A. Cohn Donnelly, L. Huang, B. Powell (Eds.), *Advances in Child Abuse Prevention Knowledge. Child Maltreatment (Contemporary Issues in Research and Policy)*. Springer.

[19] N. Boothby, L. Stark, "Data surveillance in child protection systems development: An Indonesian case study", *Child Abuse & Neglect*, vol. 35, no. 12, pp. 993–1001, 2011.

[20] "Child abuse and neglect by parents and other caregivers.", From World Report on Violence and Health, 57-86, 2002.Krug, E. G., Dahlberg, L. L (eds.),

[21] D. Lestarini, S.P. Rafflesia, K. Surendro, "A conceptual framework of engaged digital workplace diffusion," Proceeding 2015 9th International Conference on Computer, Information, and Telecommunication Systems TSSA, 2016.

[22] O. Permatasari, S.U. Masruroh, et al., "A Prototype of Child Monitoring System using Motion and Authentication with Raspberry Pi", Cyber and IT Service Management, International Conference, 2016, pp. 1–6.

[23] J.C. Chang et al., "IMace: Protecting Females from Sexual and Violent Offenders in a Community via Smartphones," Proceedings of the International Conference on Parallel Processing Workshops, 2011, pp. 71–74.

[24] J.P. Ehsani, F. O'Brien, B. Simons-Morton, "Comparing G-Force Measurement Between A Smartphone App and An In-Vehicle Accelerometer."Proceedings of Ninth International Driving Symposium on Human Factors in Driver Assessment, Training and Vehicle Design.

[25] G. Millete, A. Stroud, *Profesional Android Sensor Programming*. Indianapolis: John Wiley and Sons, Inc., 2012.

[26] M. Smitha, Pethana Dharshini, A. Priyatharsini, M. Sri Poorna Devi, M. Poorna devi. Women Safety Device using GPS Tracking and Alert. *International Journal of Recent Trends in Engineering & Research*. March 2019, pp. 492–495.

[27] Suma K. V, V. Simran Parveen, Sucheta, Kavya Jadav M, Gunjalla M, Women Security System using IoT. *International Journal of Recent Technology and Engineering*. ISSN: 2277-3878, vol. 8, no. 2S6, July 2019.

[28] R. Chougula, Smart Girls Security System", *International Journal of Application or Innovation in Engineering & Management*, vol. 3, no. 4, April 2014.

[29] S.A. More, R.D. Borate, S.T. Dardige, S.S. Salekar, Prof. D. S. Gogawale, "Smart Band for Women Security Based on Internet of Things (IoT)", *International Journal of Advance Research in Science and Engineering*, vol. 6, no. 11, November 2017.

[30] Mohamad Zikriya, Parmeshwar M G, Shanmukayya R. Math, Shraddha Tankasali, Dr. Jayashree D Mallapur, "Smart Gadget for Women Safety using IoT (Internet of Things)", *International Journal of Engineering Research & Technology (IJERT)*, ISSN: 2278-0181, NCESC – 2018 Conference Proceedings.

[31] Naeemul Islam, Md. Anisuzzaman, Sikder Sunbeam Islam, Mohammed Rabiul Hossain, Abu Jafar Mohammad Obaidullah, "Design and Implementation of Women Auspice System by Utilizing GPS and GSM", 2019 International Conference on Electrical, Computer and Communication Engineering (ECCE), 7–9, February 2019.

[32] Prof. R.A. Jain, Aditya Patil, Prasenjeet Nikam, Shubham More, Saurabh Totewar, "Women's safety using IOT", vol. 04, no. 05, |May-2017.

Machine-Learning Approach to Predict Air Quality – A Survey

15

Nimesh Mohanakrishnan, Tejaswini P R, Nashra Tanseer, Mohammed Saqlain, and Mohammed Hussam Khatib

Department of Computer Science and Engineering, Vidyavardhaka College of Engineering, Mysuru, Karnataka, India

Contents

15.1 INTRODUCTION

Air pollution is progressively increasing with the rapid growth of industries and human civilization. It affects the lives of living organisms on the planet. An estimation made by the World Health Organization ascertains that air pollution kills almost 7 million people every year. Polluted air is a primary concern for human beings because it elicits health factors such as lung cancer, stroke, heart disease, and many more. Moreover, it affects the environment on a large scale causing global warming, ozone layer depletion, and contaminating water and soil. Therefore, it is imperative to study and observe the air quality patterns caused by various pollutants.

Air pollutants in the earth's atmosphere result from anthropogenic processes caused by industries, factories, vehicles that run on fuel, and many more. They are classified based on origin, state of matter, and sources.

15.1.1 Depending on the Origin

Primary pollutants: These pollutants are a result of natural disasters and human activities. The primary pollutants include:

Carbon monoxide (CO): This pollutant is highly toxic and results from internal combustion engines, volcanoes, forest fires, and industries. It is also named a greenhouse gas. It produces carboxyhaemoglobin, which reduces oxygen capacity in the blood.

Carbon dioxide (CO_2): Carbon dioxide is heavier than air and results from volcanoes, fire, and many more. Humans too exhale CO_2. It is also a greenhouse gas. Inhaling high concentrations of CO_2 may cause dizziness and headache.

Chlorofluorocarbons (CFCs): Refrigerators, air conditioners, and aerosols use CFCs because of their physical structure and chemical nature. These are highly destructive to the ozone layer.

Nitrogen oxide (NOx): There are present in various forms of their oxides such as NO_2, NO_3, etc. They are responsible for smog, acid rain, and the greenhouse effect.

Sulphur dioxide (SO_2): They are pungent-smelling colourless gas mainly produced from industrial processes and volcanic activities. They affect humans by causing respiratory issues and premature deaths.

Benzene: They are found in petrochemicals and used as additive fuel.

Asbestos: They occur naturally as a fibrous silicate mineral. Prolonged exposure to this pollutant can cause fatal illnesses.

Secondary Pollutants: The formation of these pollutants is because of chemical reactions between atmospheric elements and primary pollutants. Examples of secondary pollutants are sulphuric acid and carbonic acid.

15.1.2 Depending on the State of Matter

Gaseous pollutants: These pollutants exist in gaseous forms. Examples include nitrogen oxide, sulphur dioxide, and carbon dioxide.

Particulate air pollutants: These are the suspended droplets or mixture of a few particles in the atmosphere.

15.1.3 Depending on the Sources

Natural sources: Although there are multiple sources the major contributors include volcanic eruptions. These eruptions release sulphur gases, which combine with water vapour to form sulfuric acid. Under extreme heat, natural flora can emit volatile organic chemicals like terpenes, which are one of the ozone precursor gases. Dust storms pick up fine grain particles that stay suspended in the subsurface airflow for a long time, adding to the air pollution; forest or wildfires add smoke and ashes to the air; sulfur springs, organic and inorganic decays, natural geysers, vegetative decays, cosmic dust, marsh gases, pollen grains of flowers, photochemical reactions, soil debris, and so on, are some more examples.

Man-made sources: Carbon dioxide, carbon monoxide, hydrocarbons, sulphur dioxide, nitrogen dioxides, and particulate matter (fine particles suspended in the air) are all released by power plants, companies, and automobiles. Man-made air pollution is largely caused by the burning of oil, coal, gasoline, and other fossil fuels. Many of the early nuclear tests were conducted in the atmosphere, causing radioactive contaminants to spread throughout the environment.

Air quality index (AQI) aids as a quotidian reporting measure of air quality. It works as a parameter to indicate how air pollution affects one's health over a defined period. The objective of AQI is to keep the individuals informed and aware about how local air quality can negative impact on their health. The Environmental Protection Agency (EPA) calculates AQI for five major air pollutants; this is calculated based on predefined national air quality guidelines aimed at protecting public health. The AQI number is directly proportional to contamination of air, thereby indicating an increased risk of human health. Many industrialised countries have adopted the application of AQI to make informed and responsible decisions over the past three decades. Air quality related information is easily acquired in real-time by the means of AQI.

To report air quality, various countries use different point systems. The United States, for example, employs a 500-point scale, with a score of 0 to 50 deemed satisfactory. A rating with values between 301 to 500 is considered dangerous. India uses this 500-point scale as well. Every day, sensors record the biggest contaminants' concentrations. EPA-developed standard equations are used to translate these raw combined values into a separate AQI value for individual pollutant (ground-level ozone, carbon monoxide, particle pollution, and sulphur dioxide). AQI value for that day is determined by the highest of these AQI readings.

The Table 15.1 below shows the remarks corresponding to the air quality index values for a 500-point scale measurement.

Various air pollutants contribute to air pollution. However, numerous research and studies show that particulate matter (PM2.5) impels majorly and severely for the poor quality of air. Therefore, it is imperative to study and forecast air quality more accurately to safeguard from numerous harmful effects. The conventional and orthodox methods include massive statistical and mathematical calculations to measure air quality. Nonetheless, machine learning, which is a segment of artificial intelligence (AI), proves to be better for predicting air quality. Since air quality prediction corresponds to time series prediction, choosing various machine-learning algorithms is optimal.

Various research focuses on the estimation of the air quality index using numerous machine-learning models. Many researchers have scrutinized machine-learning

TABLE 15.1 AQI and corresponding remarks

AQI	REMARKS
0–50	Excellent
51–100	Good
101–150	Lightly polluted
151–200	Moderately polluted
201–300	Heavily polluted
301+	Severely polluted

algorithms, such as decision trees, linear regression, random forest, support vector machines, and artificial neural networks. In section 15.2, we present a literature survey obtained by various researchers. In section 15.3, we examine the results of predicting air quality using different algorithms found by researchers. Lastly, in section 3, shows the results of numerous algorithms obtained by various researchers.

15.2 LITERATURE SURVEY

A lot of research is conducted to predict the air quality. Numerous authors have researched the prediction of air quality with differing pollutants and dataset, as follows:

1. Authors Wang Zhengua and Tian Zhihui have used an improved BP neural network by integrating the genetic algorithm to predict the AQI value. Their model has three layers. The input layer is 6 dimensions, and the output layer is 1 dimension. The hidden layer dimension is calculated by an empirical formula: ($\sqrt{n + m}$ + a) where n corresponds to input node number, and m is the output node number. a is a constant number between 1 to 10. However, the accuracy rate of prediction using the improved model was 80.44% only. The accuracy levels will have to be improved further.

2. In this paper, the authors examine and evaluate various air contaminants such as CO, SO2, PM2.5, PM10, NO2, and O3. They use three machine-learning algorithms: linear regression, decision tree, and random forest regression, and conclude by stating that the random forest algorithm gives a better prediction of air quality. Multitude of decision trees are constructed during the training time. It works as an meta estimator wherein it can either classify or predict results. The total number of functions at each node is split depending on the hyper parameter percentage. The drawback of this paper is that the prediction accuracy of various pollutants using random forest lies between 70% and 86% only. And other major pollutants, such as benzene, toluene, xylene, are not considered, as shown in Figure 15.1 and Figure 15.2.

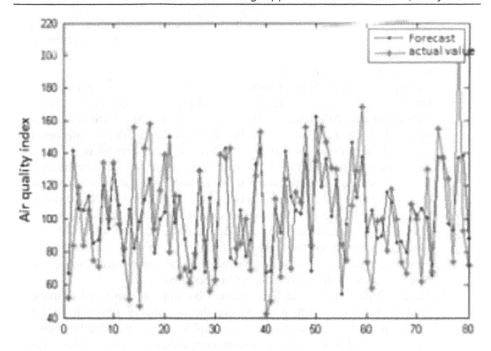

FIGURE 15.1   Output before optimization.

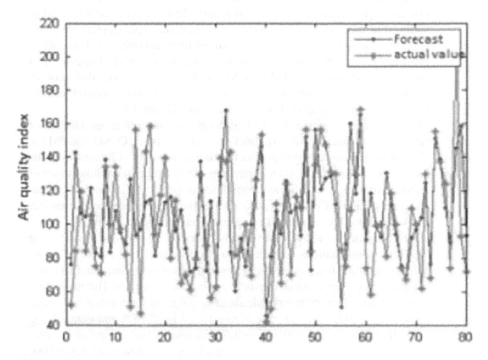

FIGURE 15.2   Output after optimization.

3. Kostandina and Angel have examined the accuracy differences between neural networks, K-nearest neighbors, decision trees, and support vector machinea. They have considered the unsupervised neural network where the output value is unknown. The neural network constructed by them contains 6 input attributes, 1 hidden layer with 10 neurons, and the output layer outputs 3 classes: high, medium, and low. When the total dataset is partitioned into 70% training, 10% validation, and 20% testing, the data attains the highest accuracy of 92.3%. The neural network performs better than other algorithms for daily predictions and not hourly basis.

4. Arwa Shawabkeh et al. (2018), in their study, estimated the concentration levels of benzene in correlation with CO using a support vector machine (SVM) and artificial neural networks (ANN). They found ANN to result in fewer errors. They used 5 hidden layers in their proposed methodology and Levenberg-Marquardt algorithm: an algorithm designed to work with loss functions specifically that take the form of a sum of squared errors. However, with an increase in data samples, the mean square value and mean absolute value of errors in SVM decreased.

5. Yuelai Su has utilized the light gradient boosting machine and eXtreme gradient boosting machine to predict the air quality (through PM2.5 measurements) and used 50,000 data samples. They concluded by stating that light GBM works more optimally compared to eXtreme. While segmenting data points, the light GBM does not use a pre-sorting algorithm: an algorithm that pre-sorts all features by values and uses cost to find optimal segmentation points of each feature. Instead, they use a method of sorting buckets, such as histogram algorithm that splits eigenvalues according to the intervals. This mechanism ensures that only small amount of precision is lost, and massive computing memory is saved. However, with increasing data samples, light GBM would reduce the running time of machine learning. And hence, short-term prediction becomes almost impossible; see Figure 15.3, Figure 15.4, and Figure 15.5.

6. Lidia Contreras Ochando et al. (2015) developed an application, Airvlc, that employs a regression model to predict real-time levels of CO, NO, and PM2.5. They built datasets aimed to predict the concentration of pollutants from the intensity of traffic and weather parameters. They extract the following set of features from the data collected from different sources • Climatological features: temperature (Celsius degrees), relative humidity (percentage), pressure, wind speed (km/h), rain (mm/h) • calendar features: year, month, day in the month, day in the week, hour • traffic intensity features: traffic level in the surrounding stations (vehicles/hour), traffic level 1, 2, 3 and 24 hours before • pollution features: pollution level in the target station 3 and 24 hours before. They use mean squared error as performance measure. The application also provides information to people about air pollutant concentrations through sensors, as shown in Figure 15.6, Figure 15.7, Figure 15.8, and Figure 15.9.

7. Soubhik Mahanta et al. (2019) predicted air quality and compared the efficiency using linear regression, lasso regression, neural network regression, decision forest, elasticNet regression, extra trees, XGBoost, boosted decision

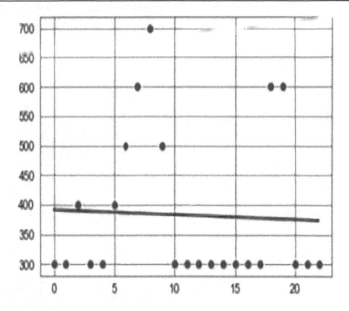

FIGURE 15.3   Linear regression fitted curve for CO.

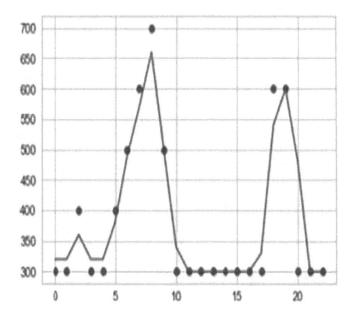

FIGURE 15.4   Random forest fitted curve for CO.

tree, KNN, and ridge regression. In their research, they found that the performance of the extra tree regression model was better and resulted in an accuracy of 85%. The reason is that the arrangement of features was in decreasing order.

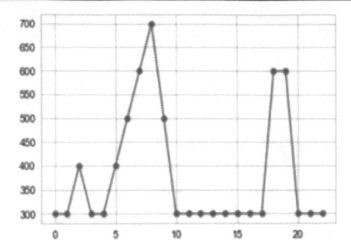

FIGURE 15.5 Decision tree fitted curve for CO.

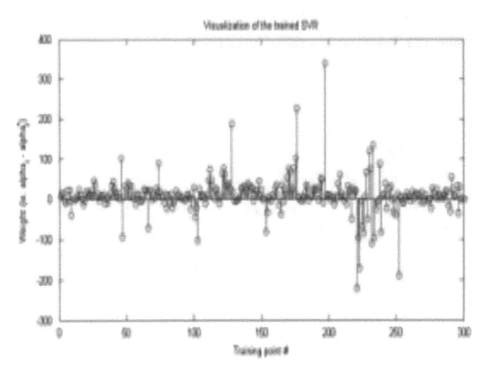

FIGURE 15.6 Trained SVR on 10-days dataset length.

8. The authors, in the quest to predict air quality, have used the CERL hybrid ensemble model to exploit the working of recurrent neural networks as well as the working of forwarding neural networks. The pollutants used for measuring and predicting air quality are CO, PM2.5, NO2, SO2 and O3.

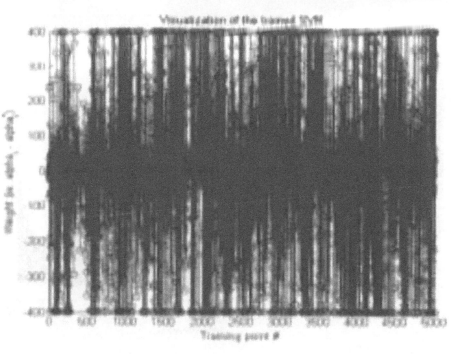

FIGURE 15.7   Trained SVR on 30-weeks dataset length.

They have also used AQI values while predicting the air quality. CERL improves prediction performance using recurrent neural networks. Furthermore, the predictions work better for the hour level. Hybrid CERL model is formed by combining forward neural networks with recurrent neural network. Here, the prediction results are grouped together. These groupings occur as the features of training and test sets to build the hybrid model. They evaluation methodology metrics used are mean absolute deviation (MAE), mean absolute percentage error (MAPE), root mean square error (RMSE), and correlation coefficients(R). However, the accuracy for long-term prediction is low. The authors have also suggested future work to be explored using a convolutional neural network for air quality prediction as shown in Figure 15.10.

$$MAE = \left(\frac{1}{n}\right) \sum_{i=0}^{n} |xi - x'|$$

$$RMSE = \sqrt{\left(\frac{1}{n}\right) \sum_{i=0}^{n} x^2 - x'^2 - 2x^2x'^2}$$

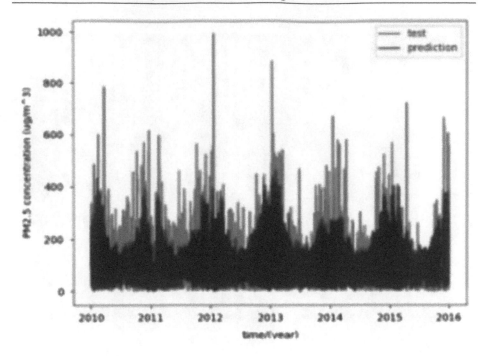

FIGURE 15.8   XGBoost prediction result.

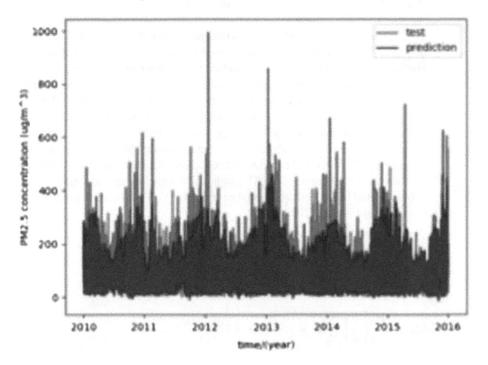

FIGURE 15.9   Light GBM prediction result.

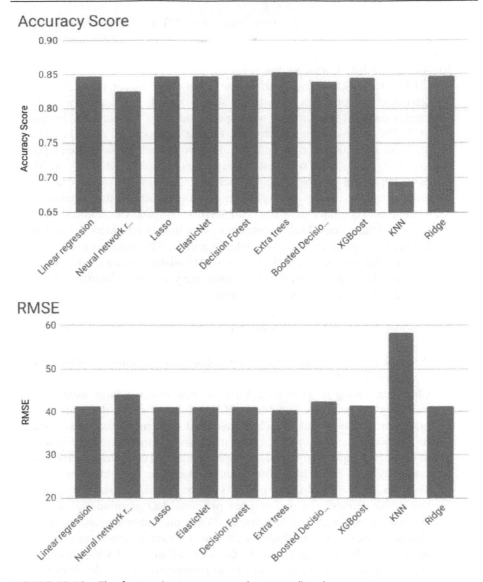

FIGURE 15.10 The feature importance graphs as predicted.

Where xi and x' represent the actual and predicted values and n represents the number of test samples.

9. The authors considered five different machine-learning algorithms: random forest, k-nearest neighbors (KNN), support vector machine (SVM), naive Bayesian, and neural network. Their results show that neural networks with integrated sensors give the highest accuracy of detecting air pollutants. They have compared the working of the neural network by varying the number of hidden layers weight decays. When the number of hidden layers is 5 and weight decay is 1×10^{-4}, the neural network yields higher accuracy.

For prototyping purposes, they have used DTH 11 Arduino sensors. However, the response time increases with increase of data the dataset, and it is incapable to work with deficient and partial data set.

10. Author Burhan Baran, in his research, used extreme learning machine (ELM) to predict the air quality. They also made use of three different activation functions for estimation: sine, sigmoid, and hard limit. The dataset included temperature, wind speed, humidity, pressure, PM10, and SO2. The hard-limit function had the highest test accuracy of 74.17 and a test period of 0,0004156 seconds for 50 neuron counts in the hidden layer.

11. Limei Ma et al. (2020) state that it is very effective to predict the air quality using dependent variables than independent variables. They also state that multivariate regression is significantly more practical than univariate regression. They have used PM2.5, PM10, SO2, NO2, CO, and 03 values to predict the values. Multivariate regression mainly considers correlation between a dependent and independent variable. The equation consists of x values that correspond to the independent variables, and a random error. The only drawback is that they have used one year's data. Insufficient data may lead to incorrect prediction results.

$$\gamma = \beta 0 + \beta 1x1 + \beta 2x2 + \ldots + \beta pxp + \in$$

Where x represents independent variables, xp represents cut off, and $\in$ representers random error.

12. Chuanting Zhang & Dongfeng Yuan in their research have used spark technology to parallelly distribute real-time meteorological data values for prediction of the air quality. They have used the random forest algorithm for predicting the air quality. In their methodology, they have used spark's in-memory computation model to overcome massive computation problems caused by trees. Spark has master node, worker node, and cluster manager. The cluster manager allocates resources and communicates between masters and worker nodes. The master node performs data partition and worker nodes are used for execution purposes. While implementing random forest algorithm, they eliminate features that do not have meteorological information and the missing values in the data set are filled with attribute's average value. Their methods allow faster prediction of the results. However, the accuracy rate is only 79.25%.

1) Accuracy:

$$accuracy = \frac{TP+TN}{P+N}$$

2) Recall:

$$recall = \frac{TP}{P}$$

3) Precision:

$$Precision = \frac{TP}{TP+FP}$$

Where P represents positive tuples, N represents negative tuples, TP represents true positives, TN represents true negatives; FP represents false positive.

13. Liying et al. (2019) have utilized Amazon S3, MongoDB, and Apache Spark as means for distributed computing model. They have used random forest and reported an accuracy of 81%. They have also showed that a standalone system is not very sufficient in processing real-time air quality data for better prediction results (Figures 15.11 and 15.12).

14. Krittakom Srijiranon & Narissara Eiamkanitchat proposed a neuro-fuzzy model that includes 14 input features. These features are further divided into meteorological and air pollution data. They have used ensemble neural network with neighborhood component analysis, which gives highest accuracy of 79.79%.

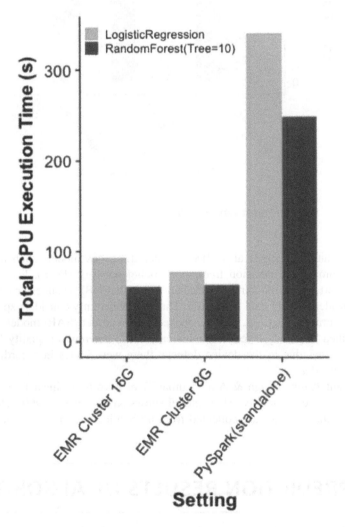

FIGURE 15.11   Comparison of model training time.

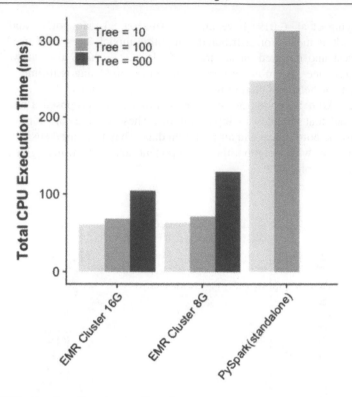

FIGURE 15.12   Random Forest execution time.

15. The author Kang et al. (2018) compared various models such as ANN, random forest, decision trees, deep belief network (DBF), least squares support vector machine model, and found that DBF is superior because it considers hourly data prediction. The DBF inherently considers spatial and temporal correlations. Also, a stacked auto-recorder (SAE) model which is trained in greedy layer-wise manner extracts inherent air quality features. However, due to the device defects, there were issues in recording high quality data.

16. Jayant Kumar Singh & Amit Kumar Goel have used linear regression to predict the air quality. Their model shows an accuracy of 96%. However, the data attributes are collected from a specific zone of Delhi only.

15.3 PREDICTION RESULTS OF ALGORITHMS

The Table 15.2 below shows the results of numerous algorithms obtained by various researchers.

TABLE 15.2 Algorithms and corresponding results

REFERENCE NO.	ALGORITHM	PREDICTION RESULT
[1]	BP Neural Network	Accuracy: 80.44%
[2]	Random Forest	Accuracy: 70–86%
[3]	Neural Network	Accuracy: 92.3%
[4]	Artificial Neural Network	MRE: −0.16
[5]	Light GBM	MSE: 3762.021
[6]	Random Forest	MSE: 0.153(CO Concentration), 29.517(NO Concentration), 3.214(PM2.5 Concentration)
[7]	Extra trees	Accuracy: 85.3%
[8]	CERT	AQI accuracy: 0.9792
[9]	Neural Network	Accuracy: 99.86%
[10]	Extreme Learning Machine	Accuracy: 74.17%
[11]	SPSS Algorithm	Standard Deviation: 0.997 Error rate: 10%
[12]	Random Forest Algorithm	Accuracy: 79.25%
[13]	Random Forest Algorithm	Accuracy: 81%
[14]	Ensemble Neural Network with Neuro-Fuzzy Logic	Accuracy: 79.79%
[15]	Linear Regression	Accuracy: 96%
[16,17]	Deep Belief Neural Network	Error rate: 1.6%(PM2.5)

REFERENCES

[1] Wang Zhenghua, and Tian Zhihui, Prediction of Air Quality Index based on Improved Neural Network, 2017 International Conference on Computer Systems, Electronics and Control (ICCSEC).

[2] Venkat Rao Pasupuleti, Uhasri, Pavan Kalyan, Srikanth, and Hari Kiran Reddy, Air Quality Prediction of Data Log by Machine Learning, 2020 6th International Conference on Advanced Computing & Communication Systems (ICACCS).

[3] Kostandina Veljanovska, and Angel Dimoski, Air Quality Index Prediction Using Simple Machine Learning Algorithms, 2018, International Journal of Emerging Trends & Technology in Computer Science (IJETTCS).

[4] Arwa Shawabkeh, Feda Al-Beqain, Ali Rodan, and Maher Salem, Benzene Air Pollution Monitoring Model using ANN and SVM, 2018, The Fifth HCT Information Technology Trends (ITT 2018), Dubai, UAE, Nov., 28 - 29 2018.

[5] Yuelai Su, Prediction of Air Quality based on Gradient Boosting Machine Method, 2020 International Conference on Big Data and Informatization Education (ICBDIE).

[6] Lidia Contreras Ochando, Cristina I. Font Julian, Francisco Contreras Ochando, and Cesar Ferri, Airvlc: An Application for Real-Time Forecasting Urban Air Pollution, 2015 Proceedings of the 2nd International Workshop on Mining Urban Data, Lille, France.

[7] Soubhik Mahanta, T. Ramakrishnudu, Rajat Raj Jha, and Niraj Tailor, *Urban Air Quality Prediction Using Regression Analysis*, 2019, IEEE.

[8] Zhili Zhao, Jian Qin, Zhaoshuang He, Huan Li, Yi Yang, and Ruisheng Zhang, Combining Forward with Recurrent Neural Networks for Hourly Air Quality Prediction in Northwest of China, *Environmental Science and Pollution Research*, 2020.

[9] Timothy M. Amado, and Jennifer C. Dela Cruz, *Development of Machine Learning-based Predictive Models for Air Quality Monitoring and Characterization*, 2018, IEEE.

[10] Burhan Baran, *Prediction of Air Quality Index by Extreme Learning Machines*, 2019, IEEE.

[11] Limei Ma, Yijun Gao, and Chen Zhao, Research on Machine Learning Prediction of Air Quality Index Based on SPSS, International Conference on Computer Network, Electronic and Automation (ICCNEA), Shijiazhuang, China, 2020, IEEE.

[12] Chuanting Zhang, and Dongfeng Yuan, *Fast Fine-Grained Air Quality Index Level Prediction Using Random Forest Algorithm on Cluster Computing of Spark, UIC-ATC-ScalCom-CBDCom-IoP*, 2015, IEEE.

[13] Liying Li, Zhi Li, Lara G. Reichmann, and Diane Myung-kyung Woodbridge, *A Scalable and Reliable Model for Real-time Air Quality Prediction, SmartWorld, Ubiquitous Intelligence & Computing, Advanced & Trusted Computing, Scalable Computing & Communications, Cloud & Big Data Computing, Internet of People and Smart City Innovation*, 2019, IEEE.

[14] Krittakom Srijiranon, and Narissara Eiamkanitchat, Neuro-Fuzzy Model with Neighborhood Component Analysis for Air Quality Prediction, 2021 7th International Conference on Engineering, Applied Sciences and Technology (ICEAST), 2021, IEEE.

[15] Gaganjot Kaur Kang, Jerry Zeyu Gao, Sen Chiao, Shengqiang Lu, and Gang Xie, Air Quality Prediction: Big Data and Machine Learning Approaches, 2018, International Journal of Environmental Science and Development.

[16] Jayant Kumar Singh, and Amit Kumar Goel, Prediction of Air Pollution by using Machine Learning Algorithm, 2021 7th International Conference on Advanced Computing & Communication Systems (ICACCS), 2021, IEEE.

[17] NAAQS Table. (2015). [Online]. Available: https://www.epa.gov/criteria-air-pollutants/naaqs-table

Air Canvas – Air-Writing Recognition Model for Environmental and Socioeconomic Issues

16

Meghana R, Pallavi K J, Aditi S, and
Asha S Manek

*Department of Computer Science and Engineering, RV
Institute of Technology and Management, Bangalore, India*

Contents

DOI: 10.1201/9781003282990-16

16.1 INTRODUCTION

Advancement in technology has given birth to virtual reality and novel techniques for human-computer interaction. Pen-based interaction is one among them and is becoming extremely important in current scenarios. There are two ways of pen-based interactions i.e., contact pen interaction and contactless pen interaction. The pen is used to write on a solid plane surface just like an electronic pen used to write on the electronic whiteboard in contact pen interaction method. In contactless pen interaction, the pen is operated in three-dimensional (3D) air space without making touch with any solid flat surface [1].

Contactless pen interaction i.e., Air-writing word recognition enables natural user-computer interaction without physically connected gadgets. Air-writing is a procedure of composing something in a 3D space by utilizing characters, signals or trajectory data. Basically, air-writing is writing with the pen in the air. Air writing comprises of three steps:

Firstly, detecting the green tipped object, secondly tracking its movement from frame to frame and lastly recognizing and displaying what is written or drawn. In this paper, a model is proposed where a green-tipped pen is held pointing towards the camera to write a word in air. A laptop camera was utilized to trace the movement of the pen of a particular colour (here we use green tip) and once this data is collected, it is stored as an image which is then given as input to the handwritten text recognition model.

Dyslexia is a Greek phrase that combines the terms "dys" and "lexis" to indicate "difficulty with words." Specific developmental dyslexia is another name for dyslexia. Dyslexia is a learning disability caused by a neurological problem [2]. It is characterised by reading, spelling, word decoding, and writing impairments. People with dyslexia typically read at a much lower level than is expected. Many explanations about dyslexia have been proposed by many experts; however, the exact aetiology is unknown. Dyslexia is most commonly found in young children. Children with dyslexia typically have trouble concentrating and find it difficult to follow directions. They'll have a lot of messy work, with a lot of student cancellations, letter reversals, uneven spelling of the same word, and letter confusion (e.g., b to d) [3].

Dysgraphia is a disorder that is related to dyslexia. The key distinction is that people with dysgraphia have a hard time producing written words and characters (letters and numbers) [4]. Other signs and symptoms that these people will experience include difficulty understanding the relationship between spoken words, sounds, and written letters. Learning disability characterized by problems with writing is known as dysgraphia. Dysgraphia is a neurological disorder that can affect children or adults. In addition to writing words that are difficult to read, people with dysgraphia tend to use the wrong word for what they're trying to communicate. The cause of dysgraphia isn't always known, though in adults it sometimes follows a traumatic event.

Air writing can help to some extent to overcome the difficulties faced by school students suffering from dysgraphia [5]. Some common characteristics of dysgraphia are incorrect spelling and capitalization, mix of cursive and print letters, inappropriate sizing and spacing of letters, difficulty copying words, slow or laboured writing, difficulty visualizing words before writing them, unusual body or hand position when writing, tight hold on pen or pencil resulting in hand cramps, watching your hand while you write, saying words aloud while writing, omitting letters and words from sentences, etc. Students with dysgraphia may also be accused of being sloppy or lazy because their handwriting isn't neat. This situation can affect self-esteem and lead to anxiety, a lack of confidence, and negative attitudes toward school.

Researchers are still learning the reasons why some children have learning disabilities, such as dysgraphia or hyperlexia. Learning disabilities often run in families or are related to prenatal development, such as being born prematurely. One can find a hyperlexic child writing letters and/or complete words in the air as if they are writing them down on paper. They are usually writing something specific, not randomly scribbling or drawing. Air writing can help children and adults to form letters and sentences recognised by the proposed model. Air writing can be used to help with self-regulation. That means that writing letters and words in the air can be calming and soothing for the hyperlexic child. It's essentially a built-in coping strategy they can use when they are feeling overwhelmed or anxious. The hyperlexic or dysgraphia child might also be using air writing to help them remember things and visualize the words they hear. With hyperlexia, if it isn't written down, it might not exist. In that sense, air writing can be used as a tool to help them "write it down" and see the words they are hearing, improving recall and comprehension. It's easy to see that air writing is beneficial for hyperlexic and dysgraphia child [6].

In the proposed model, a deep learning-based algorithm, convolutional recurrent neural network (CRNN) was developed; it is a composite of convolutional neural network (CNN) and recurrent neural network (RNN) to predict the words in the image drawn in air. IAM handwritten dataset was used to test the accuracy and showed an accuracy of about 85%.

The organization of the rest of the paper is: Section II describes the related work; Section III and Section IV provide the motivation and problem statement to develop proposed model. Section V provides methods and techniques, and Section VI describes proposed model. Section VII shows experiment and evaluation of proposed work. Performance analysis of the model as compared to the models in the papers referred is explained in Section VIII, and Section IX explains the significance. Section X concludes the paper.

16.2 RELATED WORK

Alam M.S. et al. [7] projected a character-recognition technique that used trajectory-based air writing. The CNN classifier gave an accuracy of 97.29% on a manually developed dataset of 10 participants of 8 males and 2 females aged between 23 and 30 graduate students. Though the accuracy was high, the recognition rate of some characters was low. Bastas et al. [8] compared TCN, CNN, LSTM, and BLSTM models for air-writing recognition on few collected data. They concluded that LSTM gives the best accuracy of 99.5%.

Chen Y. H. et al. [9] proposed a mask R-CNN and a three-layer CNN model for air-writing in smart glasses through fingertip detection. The model used Google API to recognize the written characters. Rahman et al. [10] proposed a system for air-writing recognition that used RNN-LSTM networks. This enabled the elimination of noise and recognized digits. The accuracies obtained for single digit and multidigit English numerals using the MNIST dataset were 98.75% and 85.27%.

Roy et al. [11] proposed a technique that used a convolution neural network (CNN). A marker of fixed colour was used to perform gestures in front of a camera. For this, colour-based segmentation was done to identify the marker tip and its trajectory. Three different datasets were used in different languages; each dataset was collected from 20 different individuals. This method does not involve depth or motion sensors. Accuracy rates were 97.7%, 95.4%, and 93.7%

Alam et al. [12] used a fusion of convolution neural network with long short-term memory (CNN-LSTM). Datasets used were RTD and RTC, which contained 20,000 digits and 30,000 characters, respectively. It consisted of two CNN with consecutive pooling, two LSTM, and two dense layers; an Intel Core i5 processor with Windows 10, a 64-bit operating system, was employed to train the network. ReLU was employed as an activation function.

Zhang et al. [13], used a fingertip detection algorithm along with compact modified quadratic discriminant function to detect the trajectory. A dual-mode switching algorithm was proposed in which all expected hand poses are covered. The projected system was tested on a PC with an Intel Core i5–2400 CPU running at 3.10 GHz and 4 GB of RAM at 20 frames per second.

A model is developed by Chen et al. [14] for detecting and recognizing characters written in air without delimitation. It uses a dataset, which is a combination of writing and non-writing finger motions. The finger is tracked using LEAP from leap motions. This provides marker-free and glove-free finger tracking. The air-written characters are detected and extracted using a window-based approach. A segment error of 9.84% for letter recognition and 1.15% for word recognition is obtained.

Huang et al. [15] employed Unity 3D to build a synthetic dataset. Mask R-CNN method is proposed for detecting a finger based on the region, using CNN classifier. A three-layer CNN technique is proposed for fingertip location. ResNet-based CNN technique recognises characters from the fingertip trajectories.

In [16], an off-the-shelf smart-band worn by the user captures text by analysing motion signals. There are two air-writing recognition methods employed by Yanay et al. The first method is a user-dependent method that is based on K Nearest-Neighbours with dynamic-time warping as the distance measure. Another method is a user-independent method that is based on a convolutional-neural network.

An air-writing method based on a network made of millimetre wave radars is proposed by Arsalan et al. [17]. An approach consisting of a two-stage process for detection and extraction of handwritten gestures is proposed. The first approach is to extract and detect the character drawn using LSTM, BLSTM, and ConvLSTM with CTC loss function. The second approach is to reconstruct the image of the character drawn and to use a DCNN for the classification of the characters drawn by the user.

16.3 MOTIVATION

One of the applications of text recognition is OCR (optical character recognition), which is a solution for automating data extraction from printed or written text from a scanned document or image file and then converting the text into a machine-readable form to be used for data processing, like editing or searching [18]. It improves information accessibility for users. Due to the simple writing style, it has a great advantage over the gesture-based system. However, it is a challenging task because of the non-uniform characters and different writing styles. This serves a great purpose in helping especially disabled persons to communicate easily [19]. Also, this technology can be incorporated into IoT devices.

Another application of this technique is in biometric system verification where the user's authentication can be done in the air itself preventing the user to touch the surface, which could be a huge help current in situations like COVID [20]. This technology can even be improved by providing the gestures symbols used by people who are hearing or sight impaired, which helps them to communicate with the people.

16.4 PROBLEM DEFINITION

The proposal focuses primarily on resolving several critical socioeconomic issues.

1. People's auditory perception impairment: Despite the fact that we take hearing and prying for granted, they communicate or communicate using sign languages. Without a translator, the bulk of the world would be unaware of their feelings and emotions.
2. Overutilization of smart-devices: Smart device overuse causes accidents, depression, diversions, and more maladies that we as living beings have yet to uncover. Although its versatility and convenience of use are highly praised, the drawbacks include life-threatening situations.

3. Applications to help patients with dyslexia or dysgraphia: There are no or few such applications available to help patients with dyslexia, dysgraphia, and hearing and sight impairment. And the ones that are available aren't really engaging, and they all have a lot of flaws. Also, no application has been developed to assist people with either of these conditions in receiving therapy. Deep-learning models trained on available dataset is used in the proposed application to train and practise patients in reading a set of words and character writing.

4. Paper wastage is not scary news: We squander a lot of paper in scribbling, writing, drawing, and other activities. Some simple facts include: one A4 dimension paper requires 5 litres of water on average, 93% of scribbling comes from trees, 50% of occupation waste is paper, 25% of dumping ground is paper, and the list goes on. Paper waste is bad for the environment since it wastes water and forests and produces a lot of garbage.

These issues can be solved quickly by writing in air. It will serve as a communication tool for persons who are sight or hearing impaired. AR can be used to exhibit the air-written text, or it can be turned to speech. You can rapidly sketch in the air and get back to work without being interrupted. Furthermore, there is no need for paper when writing in the air. Everything is stored electronically to manufacture one A4 size paper, 93% of writing comes from trees, 50% of business trash is paper, 25% of land fill waste is paper, and so on. Paper waste pollutes the environment by wasting water and forests, as well as producing loads of garbage. These problems can be swiftly resolved by using air writing. It will serve as a communication tool for persons who are deaf or hard of hearing. Their handwritten text can be augmented reality (AR) exhibited or transformed to speech. You can write in the air fast and get back to work without being distracted. Furthermore, writing in the air does not necessitate the use of paper. Everything is kept on a computer [21].

16.5 METHODS AND TECHNIQUES

16.5.1 Fingertip Detection

The air-written text is captured using OpenCV [22] and the laptop's webcam. A pen having a specific-coloured tip is used to write in the air. The colour (here, green) is detected with the help of NumPy library functions, and its movement is traced from frame to frame. Using the functions of OpenCV, the text written is displayed on a black screen. It allows the user to write in four different colours: green, red, violet, and yellow. We have enabled writing on the screen along with pressing the spacebar on the keyboard to prevent pen up and pen down motion. So, only when the user clicks the spacebar, the green-tipped object is tracked and displayed. It also enables clearing of the whole canvas by pointing at a location on the top left corner, which has a clear button. The keyboard key c can also be used to clear the screen. A screenshot can be taken and saved into the user's laptop using imwrite () function of OpenCV. The user must click on the letter *s* on the keyboard twice to take a screenshot.

16.5.2 CRNN

CRNN is a combination of convolutional neural network (CNN) [23] and recurrent neural network (RNN) [24]. It is one of the most common methods used for text recognition, after OCR (optical character recognition). In CRNN, the output of convolutional layers is converted into a series of feature vectors and given to a bidirectional RNN model. Connectionist temporal classification (CTC) loss is mainly used to deal with outputs of CRNN models as for each target input it gives multiple sequences of probabilities. CTC loss helps in tackling sequence problems where time varies. The matrix of CTC loss calculates the loss and is used to train the neural network. The output of the CRNN model can also be decoded using the CTC loss matrix [25]. Epochs, hidden layers, the nodes in each hidden layer and the activation function are the hyper parameters used in model proposed in this paper.

16.5.2.1 Hyper Parameters

The hyper parameters [26] used are:

1. Epochs: When a whole dataset is only transported forward and backward through the neural network once, it is called an epoch. This shows the number of passes of the entire training dataset the machine-learning algorithm has completed. We used 40 epochs with a batch size of 128 in our experiment.
2. Number of hidden layers: Convolutional layers, pooling layers, fully connected layers, and normalising layers are common hidden layers in CNNs. It simply means that convolution and pooling functions are utilised as activation functions instead of the regular activation functions stated above. In CNN, we have used three hidden layers.
3. Activation function: The activation function is a node that is placed at the end or in the middle of a neural network. They play a role in determining whether or not a neuron will fire. The nonlinear transformation we perform on the input signal is called the activation function. The output is then processed and provided as input to the next layer of neurons. ReLU is used as an activation function in this research.
4. Nodes in each hidden layer: A single layer of weights connects each node in the single layer to an input variable and contributes to an output variable. Because the outputs do not interact, a network with N outputs can be divided into N single-output networks. There are 32 nodes in the first hidden layer, 64 nodes in the second hidden layer, and 128 nodes in the third hidden layer are used.

In the proposed model, the CRNN model takes the image of air writing as an input, extracts the features, and gives the recognized text as output. Some 40 epochs with a batch size of 128 were used. Convolution function and pooling functions are used for activation, with three hidden layers in CNN. A total of 32, 64 and 128 nodes are used in the first, second, and third hidden layers, respectively. The modified output is fed to the next layer of neurons as input. In the proposed model, ReLU is used as an activation function.

16.5.3 Dataset Description

16.5.3.1

The dataset used to train this model is the IAM handwriting dataset. It is a collection of handwritten passages by several writers, as shown in Figure 16.1, which is represented in the form of both images and .csv files. 657 writers contributed samples of their handwriting in the IAM handwriting dataset. It consists of 115320 isolated and labelled words or 5685 isolated and labelled sentences in 1539 pages of scanned text. A few sample images are shown in Figure 16.2. The dataset was downloaded from Kaggle [27] and split into train, test, and validation in the ratio of 8:1:1. Around 3, 00,000 images were used for training the CRNN model. As the number of images used to train was high, the accuracy obtained was also high.

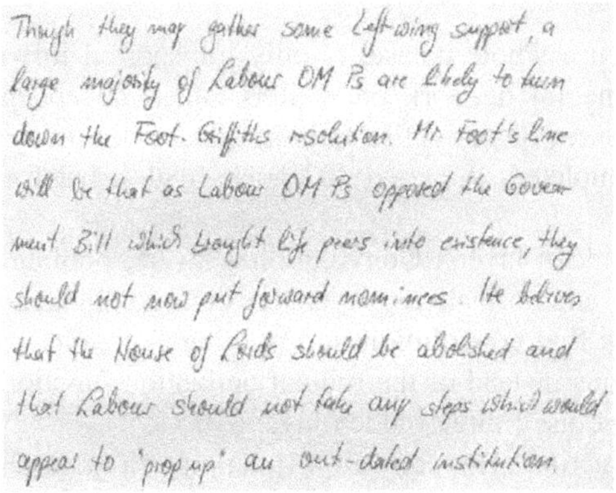

FIGURE 16.1　Sample of handwritten passage from IAM handwriting dataset.

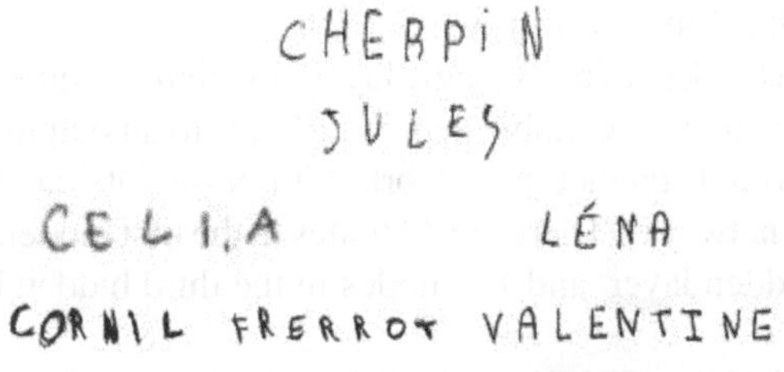

FIGURE 16.2　Sample images from IAM handwriting dataset.

16.6 PROPOSED WORK

The proposed system focuses on text recognition of handwritten text which is the input given to the model. The project developed on proposed system is divided into two parts. The first part focuses on displaying the characters or words drawn in air and storing it as an image. So, a camera has to be used so that it can capture the object which we use to write in air. The word written in air is then given as input to the model which recognizes the word written and that is the final output of the proposed system.

Laptop camera is used to detect the object movement using OpenCV. In proposed system, we have used a green object to be detected such as a green pen and the camera is made to detect it using RGB colour values. Once detection is done, using spacebar key, whatever we write is displayed on the laptop screen and then it can be saved as an image using the *s* key.

In the second part, the image saved during the first part of the procedure is the input given to the model for recognizing the handwritten words. The predicted output is displayed on the screen. The model proposed is CRNN, i.e., convolutional recurrent neural network, which is a combination of RNN (recurrent neural network) and CNN (convolutional neural network). Libraries such as NumPy, pandas, and matplotlib were used for this purpose. Keras and TensorFlow were used to build the text recognition model.

The dataset used here is the IAM handwritten dataset, which is downloaded from Kaggle. The dataset has been split into test, train, and validation with around 3lakhs test images. The dataset has both CSV files and image files in a large collection. The editor used for prototyping is Jupyter, and the system is Nvidia TitanX GP102 GPU as using GPU for running the model helps to reduce time to run each epoch which helps to fasten the overall process.

The entire process consists of several steps. The initial step is to import datasets used, which refers to importing IAM dataset from Kaggle in this case. The downloaded dataset is split into three parts: the test, train, and validation. This has been used as it is in the program: to test, train, and validate the CRNN model being developed. The CSV files in the dataset were used for the same purpose.

The next step is to pre-process the dataset. In this process, several modifications on the dataset were made so that it will apt to use it for the model. Firstly, null or blank images were dropped. Secondly, the unreadable images were removed as it was not recognizable, and it would definitely be meaningless to use it. The third modification done was to crop the images. It was cropped to size (64,256) and rotated to make it appropriate.

The next modification done was to convert the images to binary. This is because the program would recognize text written in binary format. The block diagram of the proposed system is as shown in Figure 16.3.

The block diagram represents the entire flow of process starting from the air-canvas part and its output being fed to the model before, which it has been pre-processed and trained. Three layers were used in the model starting with the input layer, followed by convolution layers with conv2D as the parameter indicating the number of output filters. Batch normalization introduces a new layer to perform operations on outputs from the previous layer of CRNN. The summary of CRNN model is tabulated in Table 16.1. Here

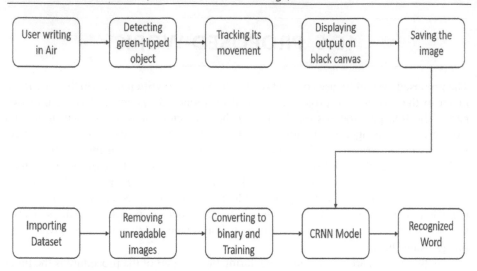

FIGURE 16.3   Block diagram of proposed model.

TABLE 16.1   CRNN model summary

LAYER (INPUT)	OUTPUT SHAPE	NUMBER OF PARAMS
Input (InputLayer)	[(None, 256, 64, 1)]	0
Conv1 (Conv2D)	(None, 256, 64, 32)	320
Batch_normalization (BatchNo)	(None, 256, 64, 32)	128
Activation (Activation)	(None, 256, 64, 32)	0
max1 (MaxPooling2D)	(None, 128, 32, 32)	0
conv2 (Conv2D)	(None, 128, 32, 64)	18496
batch_normalization_1 (Batch	(None, 128, 32, 64)	256
activation_1 (Activation)	(None, 128, 32, 64)	0
max2 (MaxPooling2D)	(None, 64, 16, 64)	0
dropout (Dropout)	(None, 64, 16, 64)	0
conv3 (Conv2D)	(None, 64, 16, 128)	73856
batch_normalization_2(Batch	(None, 64, 16, 128)	512
activation_2 (Activation)	(None, 64, 16, 128)	0
max3 (MaxPooling2D)	(None, 64, 16, 128)	0
dropout_1 (Dropout)	(None, 64, 16, 128)	0
reshape (Reshape)	(None, 64, 1024)	0
dense1 (Dense)	(None, 64, 64)	65600
lstm1 (Bidirectional)	(None, 64, 512)	657408
lstm2 (Bidirectional)	(None, 64, 512)	1574912
dense2 (Dense)	(None, 64, 30)	15390
SoftMax (Activation)	(None, 64, 30)	0
Total params:2,406,878 Trainable-params:2,406,430 Non-trainable params:448		

the activation function used is ReLU or rectified linear activation function. One of the advantages of this function is that it is easier to train and also gives better performance, which is also the reason it is used in many neural networks. The basic functionality of ReLU is to give the input as output if it is positive and zero otherwise.

This is followed by max pooling layer, which calculates maximum value, meaning the feature which has the greatest number of occurrences. The dropout layer is used to remove or ignore some neurons in the network, which means ignoring some features temporarily. Many neural networks accept a specific size of images reason being the design of that particular neural network. So, images are reshaped to the desired value.

Long short-term memory (LSTM) is a type of neural network that is recurrent or sequential and allows information to remain for a long time. The vanishing gradient problem faced by RNN can be handled by LSTM. Its architecture consists of three parts known as gates. It is mainly used for classifying, processing, and making predictions. Usually the in the last layer, SoftMax function is applied. This helps in normalizing the neural network so that the output fits between certain values.

16.6.1 Pseudocode for the Proposed Model

The pseudocode of the proposed model is as below:

1. Begin by reading the frames.
2. Convert the captured frames to HSV colour space.
3. Prepare the canvas frame and attach the appropriate ink button.
4. To find the coloured marker mask, adjust the track bar values.
5. Pre-process the mask with morphological operations (erotion and dilation).
6. Detect contours, locate the largest contour's centre coordinates, and then store them in an array for subsequent frames (arrays for drawing points on canvas).
7. Finally, on the frames and canvas, draw the points recorded in the array.

16.7 EXPERIMENT AND EVALUATION

The IAM dataset is split into three sets namely, test, train and validation set. These three sets are divided in the ratio of 8:1:1. Only 10% of the training and validation datasets are being used for the proposed model. The experiment was conducted using a laptop with an inbuilt webcam. Python programming language was used for building and training the model. The proposed model was implemented using modules such as Keras, TensorFlow, and cv2. The Keras module is used for constructing layers for the convolutional neural network by specifying the number of nodes in each layer and the filter size for the output of the image from each layer, which will be passed on as input to the next layer. This module also helps in setting the activation function. The proposed model makes use of this module for building RNN, bidirectional LSTM (long short-term memory), which is used in the last two layers of the model.

A CRNN model is used for recognizing the text written in air canvas by the user. This model consists of a convolutional neural network (CNN), which extracts the features from the handwritten text image and predicts the handwritten word based on the extracted feature. The handwritten text written on the air canvas is collected from the user as an image that is later saved and given as input to the CRNN model for prediction.

We used the 12GB NVIDIA Tesla K80 GPU provided by Google Colab. This GPU can be used continuously for about 12 hours. The GUI displays the information about the trajectory and the different colours available to the user. The text is recognized by tracking a green object that the user uses to write in the air.

When the program is run, the camera is activated to track the green object. On pressing the spacebar, the user can start writing in the air with an object (pen) that has a green tip so its trajectory can be tracked. The frame displays different options: clear all (to clear the screen) and blue, violet, green, red, yellow colours. When the pen is taken in front of the option, it gets selected, which is shown in Figure 16.4. When the user is finished with writing, the text can be saved as an image by pressing the letter *s* twice on the keyboard. An example of the image saved is shown in Figure 16.5. The image is later cropped and converted to black and white, as shown in Figure 16.6, and then converted to binary, as shown in Figure 16.7.

FIGURE 16.4   Air writing.

FIGURE 16.5   Text recognition and displayed on the canvas.

FIGURE 16.6   Cropped black and white image.

FIGURE 16.7   Binary image.

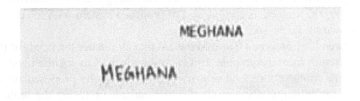

FIGURE 16.8   Output of CRNN model.

The binary image is taken as an input by the model for handwritten text prediction, and the predicted word is displayed on the screen, as shown in Figure 16.8. The first line shows the predicted text; the image input is displayed below.

We performed the experiment using the CRNN model, which was trained using the IAM dataset. The input given was the air-writing screenshots taken. It was observed that the CRNN model achieved an accuracy of 84% for word prediction, and the validation loss incurred was 2.1181.

16.8 PERFORMANCE ANALYSIS

Some digits and characters have a higher error rate, according to the models proposed in the papers referred. The user must know many movements to execute and write what is on his/her mind. This is a problem encountered while trying to develop a real-time system. Absence of pen up-down motion is also a major drawback, as analysed from the related work. The image will be absurd and will not be recognized by the model in

TABLE 16.2   Comparison of work [15] with the proposed system

RESEARCH WORK	LANGUAGE USED	DATASET AND NUMBER OF IMAGES
Work [15]	Chinese language	EgoFinger dataset, containing 12,974 images
Proposed Work	Indian language	Kaggle IAM handwriting dataset, containing 3,00,000 images

TABLE 16.3   Comparison of work [28] with the proposed system

RESEARCH WORK	METHODOLOGY USED	ACCURACY
Work [28]	EEG scanning and the flexion and extension of the fist	75%
Proposed Work	CRNN model with computer vision techniques	85%

this case. We have tried to overcome this problem by using a few keys of the keyboard to help the user to write efficiently.

To compare the proposed scheme with existing methods, we have used same methodology on the Indian-language dataset, i.e., Kaggle IAM handwriting dataset, containing 3,00,000 images. A comparison of proposed system with the research work [15] is as shown in Table 16.2.

The research [28] proposes a movement aid that eliminates the need for therapy for the people suffering from dysgraphia. EEG scanning is used to acquire hand movement signals from the motor cortex and sensory brain areas in the proposed methodology. These signals are subsequently converted into commands utilising the brain computer interface (BCI2000), which includes features selection, extraction, and translational algorithms. The hand movement gadget is then controlled using these commands. To conduct various hand movements, the hand movement device employs the FES, which is attached to the forearm. The flexion and extension of the fist are the topic of this research.

The system's overall efficiency has been estimated to be around 75%. Increasing the number of electrodes over the motor cortex and sensory brain can improve efficiency. This research paper is confined to solely fist extension and flexion. A proposed model uses CRNN for recognizing the text written in air canvas by extracting optimal features by the user. Comparison of proposed system with the research work [28] is as shown in Table 16.3.

16.9 SIGNIFICANCE

An important area where text recognition can be applied is OCR (optical character recognition). In this technique, the words which are handwritten are scanned first, after which they are converted to machine-encoded texts. For this, the text written has to be recognized, which is where the text recognition comes. This technique is then used in data processing like editing or searching.

Some of the OCR-processed digital files include receipts, contracts, and invoices and so on. This helps in easy accessibility along with saving time and resources for business organizations. Some of the other uses are: to eliminate manual entry, reduce errors, improve productivity, and save resources. Also, by using this technology, any business will be able to reduce costs, accelerate the process, and secure data.

If scanned documents have to be updated, text recognition can be used where the data can be converted to desired formats such as Word. Also, helps in searching and improves customer service by providing the information required. Leads to higher productivity in any business.

This system also improves accessibility for users since it will allow users to write in a touchless system and also solves the problem of gesture-based interaction, including augmented and virtual reality. One of the major advantages is that this system helps disabled persons to communicate easily.

Now we have seen a pandemic, COVID-19, where the virus spreads through contact, usefulness of text recognition comes into this too. In user-authentication systems, verification can be done in air only preventing the user to touch any surface, which is a major help during pandemics. This technology can be further improved to help people who are sight or hearing impaired by providing symbols that help them to communicate.

We can extend this system to control IoT devices and as a software for smart wearables. This system can aid senior citizens and also people who are not comfortable with keyboards. Primarily, this system helps people communicate easily.

Dysgraphia is a written-language disorder in which the ability to write mechanically is impaired. Because it manifests itself in poor writing skills, this condition has an especially obvious impact on school-aged children. These children have an average IQ and no apparent neurological abnormalities or perceptual-motor impairments. It may still be tough for them to participate in school activities without difficulties. Writing notes, recipes, prescriptions, messages, checks, and applications all require the individual's correct writing talents; therefore, assistance is required [29].

Although using a keyboard can help children with dysgraphia with their handwriting, a virtual pen can also help children with dysgraphia in other ways. E-pens and specific apps can have a significant impact on the life of a dysgraphic youngster, not only by addressing his/her needs but also by improving his/her condition over time. This virtual pen aids pupils in overcoming many of the frustrations they experience when writing. Writing becomes less frightening and more approachable with the opportunity to quickly erase any errors, and dysgraphic students might benefit from tasks designed just for them.

Our proposed air pen is incredibly light and portable, making it easier for kids to complete their homework at school and at home. A tool like this can make a significant impact in the learning experience of anyone who has a learning handicap.

16.10 CONCLUSION

Through this study, we have proposed a CRNN-based text-recognition model involving two phases. The first step was air-writing, in which the camera was programmed to recognise a green object, in this case, a pen. Once air writing is done, whatever text written is saved in the form of a.jpeg or.png image; both of the processes are done with the help of keyboard keys.

The image is then given to the model, which recognizes the word or text written and prints the output to the user. The model was trained on IAM handwritten dataset downloaded from Kaggle consisting of very large number of train and test images; this was very useful and important to train the model which results in a higher accuracy.

OpenCV was used for the air-writing part since images are used for training the model. Some of the libraries used in the model are Keras and TensorFlow. The tool used to develop the model is Jupyter, and the model had three layers with ReLU as the activation function. The accuracy obtained was 85%.

The text-recognition system involves something that is not traditional; by traditional, we mean writing or making notes in mobile. This eliminates the very need to carry mobile phones with us wherever we go since air-writing does not need any physical instrument or device to write any message. Through air writing, people can communicate in a much easier and a faster way.

Any project or technology developed will definitely have further improvements and modifications to be done, which results in a better version than before and helps in its growth and development. This system can be further improved to include more features and to improve the accuracy obtained. Also, it can be experimented with different algorithms and datasets along with different specific methods.

The EMNIST dataset isn't a proper air-character dataset. The accuracy and speed of fingertip recognition can be improved with upcoming object-detection techniques like YOLO v3. Advances in artificial intelligence will improve the efficiency of air-writing in the future.

REFERENCES

[1] Yan, Xuezhi and Sun, Xuedi, (Student Member, IEEE), and Haiyun Wang *"Research on conscious interactive angle of pen in 3D contactless air-drawing and writing"*. Sept 2020, IEEE, vol. 8, pp. 162683–162691.
[2] Koebele, Jennifer, *"Dyslexia statistics, facts and figures"*. [Online]. Available: http://www.dyslexia-reading-well.com/dyslexia-statistics.html. [Accessed: 13-May-2018].
[3] Kelly, Kate, *"The difference between dysgraphia and dyslexia"*. [Online]. Available: https://www.understood.org/en/learning-attention-issues/child-learning-disabilities/dysgraphia/the-difference-between-dysgraphia-and-dyslexia. [Accessed: 18-May-2018].
[4] *"What is Dysgraphia?"* dsf. [Online]. Available: https://dsf.net.au/what-is-dysgraphia/. [Accessed: 25-Mar-2018].
[5] Kurniawan, D.A. and Sihwi, S.W., 2017, November, *"An expert system for diagnosing dysgraphia"*. In 2017 2nd International Conference on Information Technology, Information Systems and Electrical Engineering (ICITISEE) (pp. 468–472). IEEE.
[6] Berninger, V.W., 2001. *"Understanding the 'lexia'in dyslexia: A multidisciplinary team approach to learning disabilities"*. Annals of Dyslexia, 51(1), pp. 21–48.

[7] Alam, M.S., Kwon, K.C., and Kim N. 2019 September. *"Trajectory Based air writing character recognition using convolutional neural network"*. In *2019 4th International Conference on Control, Robotics and Cybernetics* (CRC) (pp. 86–90). IEEE.

[8] Bastas, G., Kritsis, K., and Katsouros, V., 2020, September. *"Air-writing recognition using deep convolutional and recurrent neural network architectures"*. In 2020 17th International Conference on Frontiers in Handwriting Recognition (ICFHR) (pp. 7–12). IEEE.

[9] Chen, Y.H., Su, P.C., and Chien, F.T., 2019, October. *"Air-writing for smart glasses by effective fingertip detection"*. In 2019 IEEE 8th Global Conference on Consumer Electronics (GCCE) (pp. 381–382). IEEE.

[10] Rahman, A., Roy, P., and Pal, U., 2021. *"Air writing: Recognizing multi-digit numeral string traced in air using RNN-LSTM architecture"*. SN Computer Science, 2(1), pp. 1–13.

[11] Roy, P., Ghosh, S., and Pal, U., 2018, August. *"A CNN based framework for unistroke numeral recognition in air-writing"*. In 2018 16th International Conference on Frontiers in Handwriting Recognition (ICFHR) (pp. 404–409). IEEE.

[12] Alam, M.S., Kwon, K.C., Imtiaz, S.M., Hossain, M.B., Rupali, S. and Hyun, J., *"AIR-writing recognition using a fusion CNN-LSTM neural network"*.

[13] Zhang, X., Ye, Z., Jin, L., Feng, Z., and Xu, S., 2013. *"A new writing experience: Finger writing in the air using a Kinect sensor"*. IEEE Multimedia, 20(4), pp. 85–93.

[14] Chen, M., AlRegib, G., and Juang, B.H., 2016. *"Air-writing recognition—Part II: Detection and recognition of writing activity in continuous stream of motion data"*. IEEE Transactions on Human-Machine Systems, 46, 436–444.

[15] Chen, Y.H., Huang, C.H., Syu, S.W., Kuo, T.Y., and Su, P.C., 2021. *"Egocentric-view fingertip detection for air writing based on convolutional neural networks"*. Sensors, 21(13), p. 4382.

[16] Yanay, Tomer and Shmueli, Erez, 2020. *"Air-writing recognition using smart-bands"*. Pervasive and Mobile Computing, 66, p. 101183.

[17] Arsalan, M. and Santra, A., 1 Oct.1, 2019. *"Character recognition in air-writing based on network of radars for human-machine interface"*. IEEE Sensors Journal, 19(19), pp. 8855–8864, 10.1109/JSEN.2019.2922395.

[18] Manwatkar, P.M. and Yadav, S.H., 2015, March. *"Text recognition from images"*. In 2015 International Conference on Innovations in Information, Embedded and Communication Systems (ICIIECS) (pp. 1–6). IEEE.

[19] Gentile, A., Santangelo, A., Sorce, S., and Vitabile, S., 2011. *"Human-to-human interfaces: Emerging trends and challenges"*. International Journal of Space-Based and Situated Computing, 1(1), pp. 3–17.

[20] Elshenaway, A.R. and Guirguis, S.K., 2021. *"On-air hand-drawn doodles for IoT devices authentication during COVID-19"*. IEEE Access, 9, pp. 161723–161744.

[21] Khan, W., Nisar, Q.A., Sohail, S., and Shehzadi, S., 2021. *"The role of digital innovation in e-learning system for higher education during COVID 19: A new insight from pedagogical digital competence"*. In Innovative Education Technologies for 21st Century Teaching and Learning (pp. 75–100). CRC Press.

[22] https://opencv.org/

[23] Hassaballah, M. and Awad, A.I. eds., 2020. *"Deep Learning in Computer Vision: Principles and Applications"*. CRC Press.

[24] Julie, E.G., Robinson, Y.H., and Jaisakthi, S.M. eds., 2021. *"Handbook of Deep Learning in Biomedical Engineering and Health Informatics"*. CRC Press.

[25] Scheidl, H., Fiel, S., and Sablatnig, R., 2018, August. *"Word beam search: A connectionist temporal classification decoding algorithm"*. In 2018 16th International Conference on Frontiers in Handwriting Recognition (ICFHR) (pp. 253–258). IEEE.

[26] Kim, J.Y. and Cho, S.B., 2019, June. *"Evolutionary optimization of hyperparameters in deep learning models"*. In 2019 IEEE Congress on Evolutionary Computation (CEC) (pp. 831–837). IEEE.

[27] https://www.kaggle.com/landlord/handwriting-recognition

[28] Ahmed, W., Hasan, S.-U., Shoaib, S., Houlden, N., and Nestiurkina, M., 2020. *"A writing aid for dysgraphia affected people"*. In 2020 IEEE Conference of Russian Young Researchers in Electrical and Electronic Engineering (EIConRus), pp. 2456–2459, 10.1109/EIConRus49466.2020.9039211

[29] Kamal, N., Sharma, P., Das, R., Goyal, V., and Gupta, R., 2022. *"Virtual technical aids to help people with dysgraphia"*. In Approaches and Applications of Deep Learning in Virtual Medical Care (pp. 222–235). IGI Global.

Index